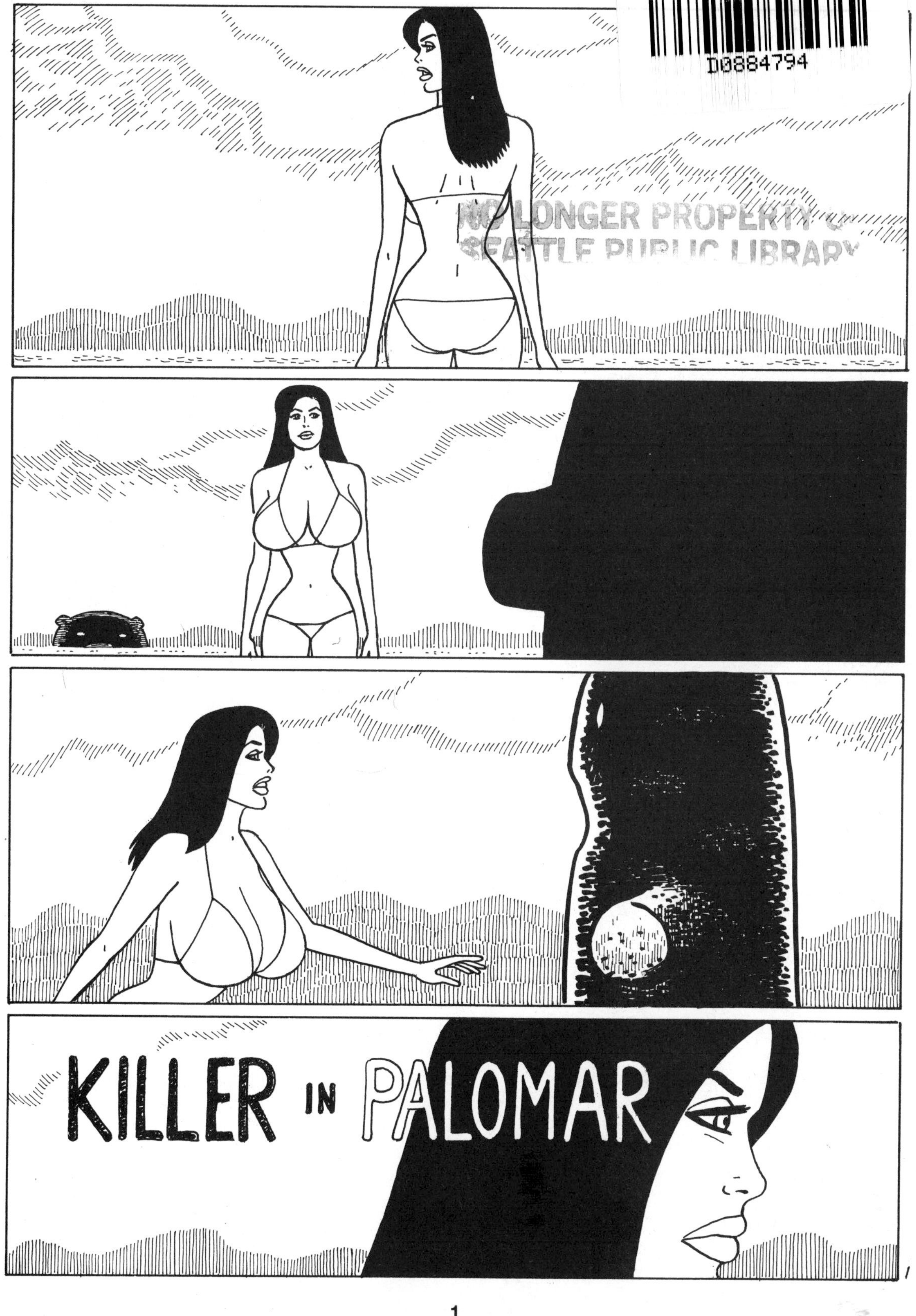
KILLER IN PALOMAR

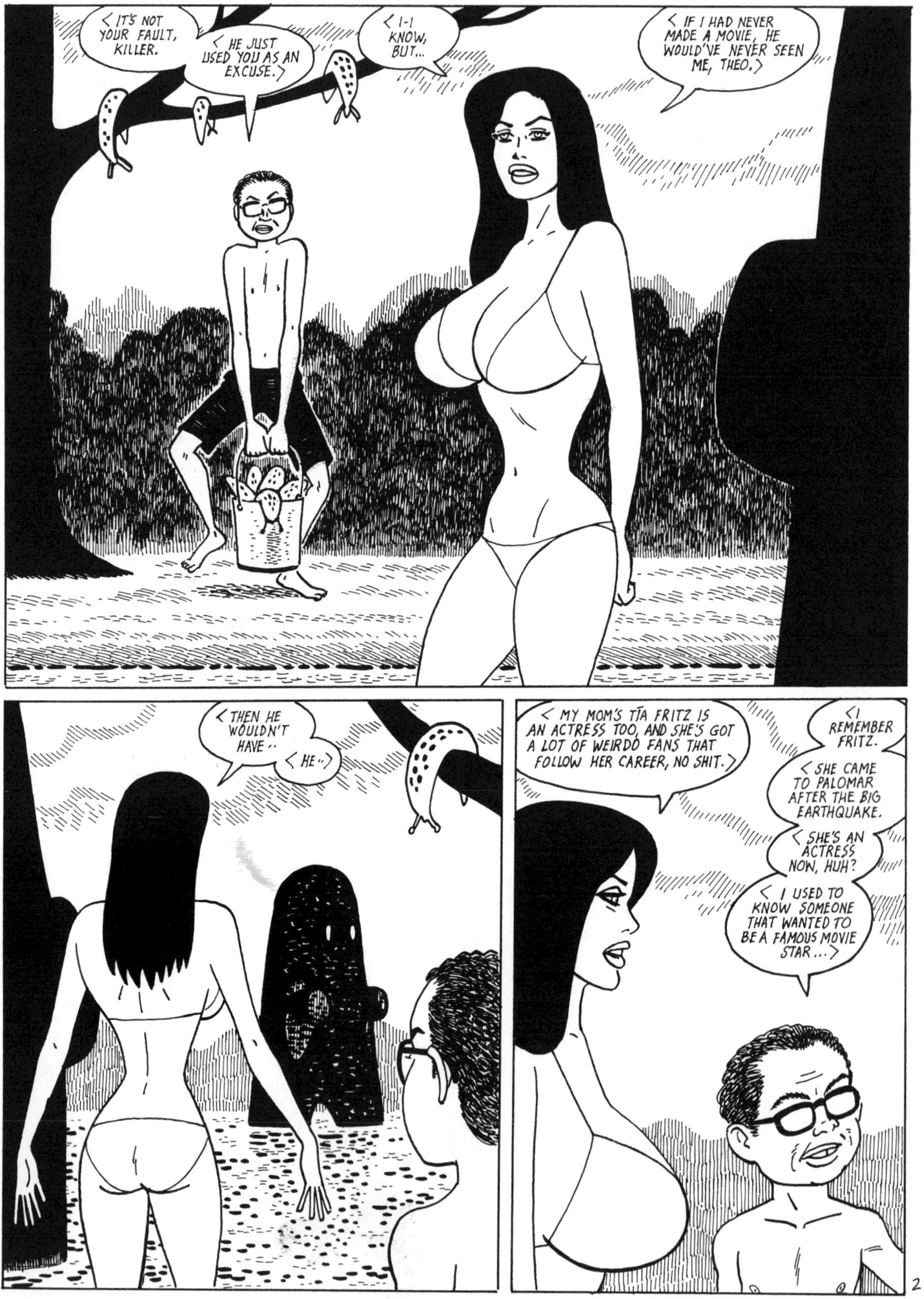
< IT'S NOT YOUR FAULT, KILLER.
< HE JUST USED YOU AS AN EXCUSE.>
< I-I KNOW, BUT...
< IF I HAD NEVER MADE A MOVIE, HE WOULD'VE NEVER SEEN ME, THEO.>
< THEN HE WOULDN'T HAVE ..
< HE ..>
< MY MOM'S TÍA FRITZ IS AN ACTRESS TOO, AND SHE'S GOT A LOT OF WEIRDO FANS THAT FOLLOW HER CAREER, NO SHIT.>
< I REMEMBER FRITZ.
< SHE CAME TO PALOMAR AFTER THE BIG EARTHQUAKE.
< SHE'S AN ACTRESS NOW, HUH?
< I USED TO KNOW SOMEONE THAT WANTED TO BE A FAMOUS MOVIE STAR ...>
2

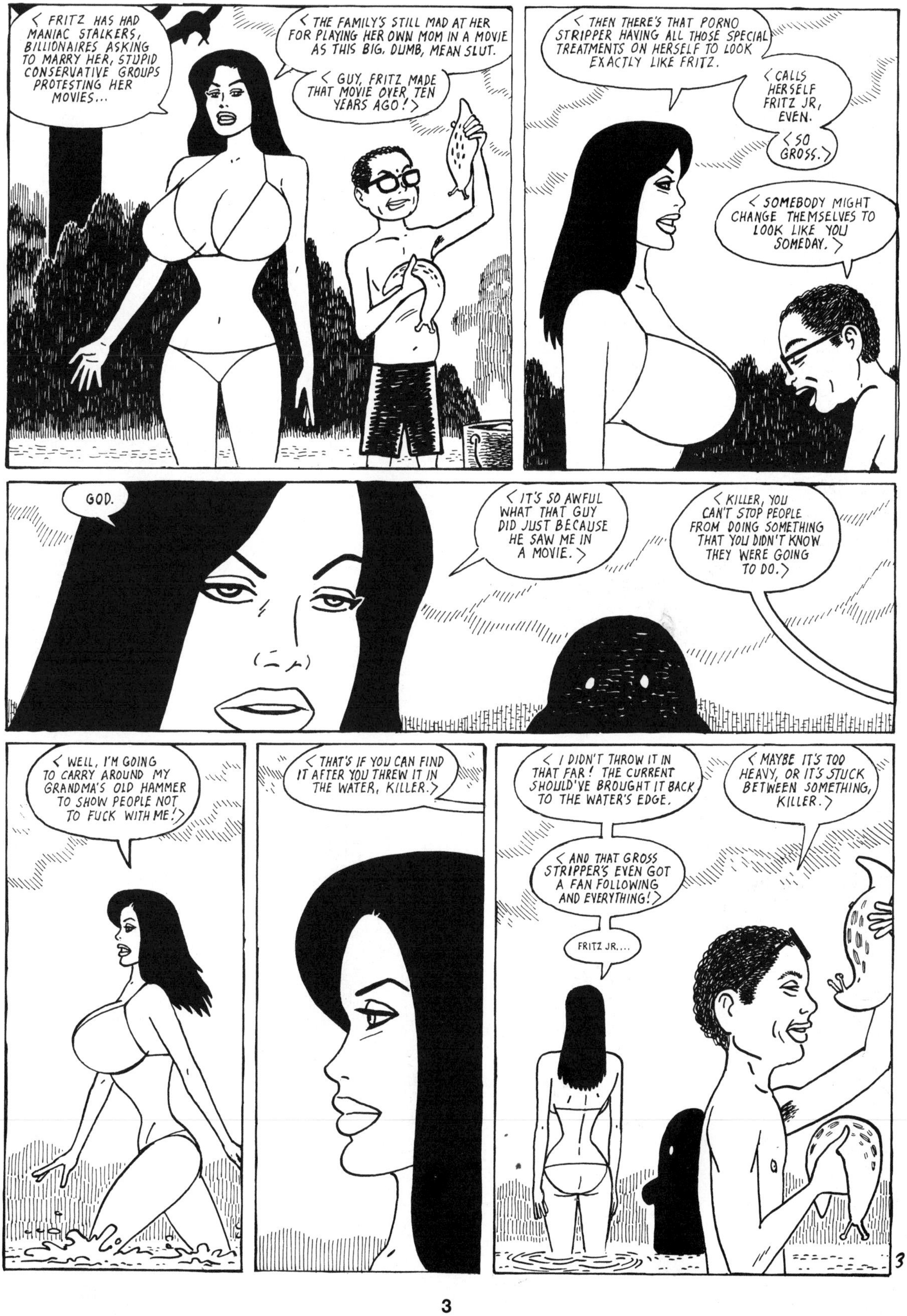
< FRITZ HAS HAD MANIAC STALKERS, BILLIONAIRES ASKING TO MARRY HER, STUPID CONSERVATIVE GROUPS PROTESTING HER MOVIES...
< THE FAMILY'S STILL MAD AT HER FOR PLAYING HER OWN MOM IN A MOVIE AS THIS BIG, DUMB, MEAN SLUT.
< GUY, FRITZ MADE THAT MOVIE OVER TEN YEARS AGO! >
< THEN THERE'S THAT PORNO STRIPPER HAVING ALL THOSE SPECIAL TREATMENTS ON HERSELF TO LOOK EXACTLY LIKE FRITZ.
< CALLS HERSELF FRITZ JR, EVEN.
< SO GROSS. >
< SOMEBODY MIGHT CHANGE THEMSELVES TO LOOK LIKE YOU SOMEDAY. >
GOD.
< IT'S SO AWFUL WHAT THAT GUY DID JUST BECAUSE HE SAW ME IN A MOVIE. >
< KILLER, YOU CAN'T STOP PEOPLE FROM DOING SOMETHING THAT YOU DIDN'T KNOW THEY WERE GOING TO DO. >
< WELL, I'M GOING TO CARRY AROUND MY GRANDMA'S OLD HAMMER TO SHOW PEOPLE NOT TO FUCK WITH ME! >
< THAT'S IF YOU CAN FIND IT AFTER YOU THREW IT IN THE WATER, KILLER. >
< I DIDN'T THROW IT IN THAT FAR! THE CURRENT SHOULD'VE BROUGHT IT BACK TO THE WATER'S EDGE.
< AND THAT GROSS STRIPPER'S EVEN GOT A FAN FOLLOWING AND EVERYTHING! >
FRITZ JR....
< MAYBE IT'S TOO HEAVY, OR IT'S STUCK BETWEEN SOMETHING, KILLER. >
3

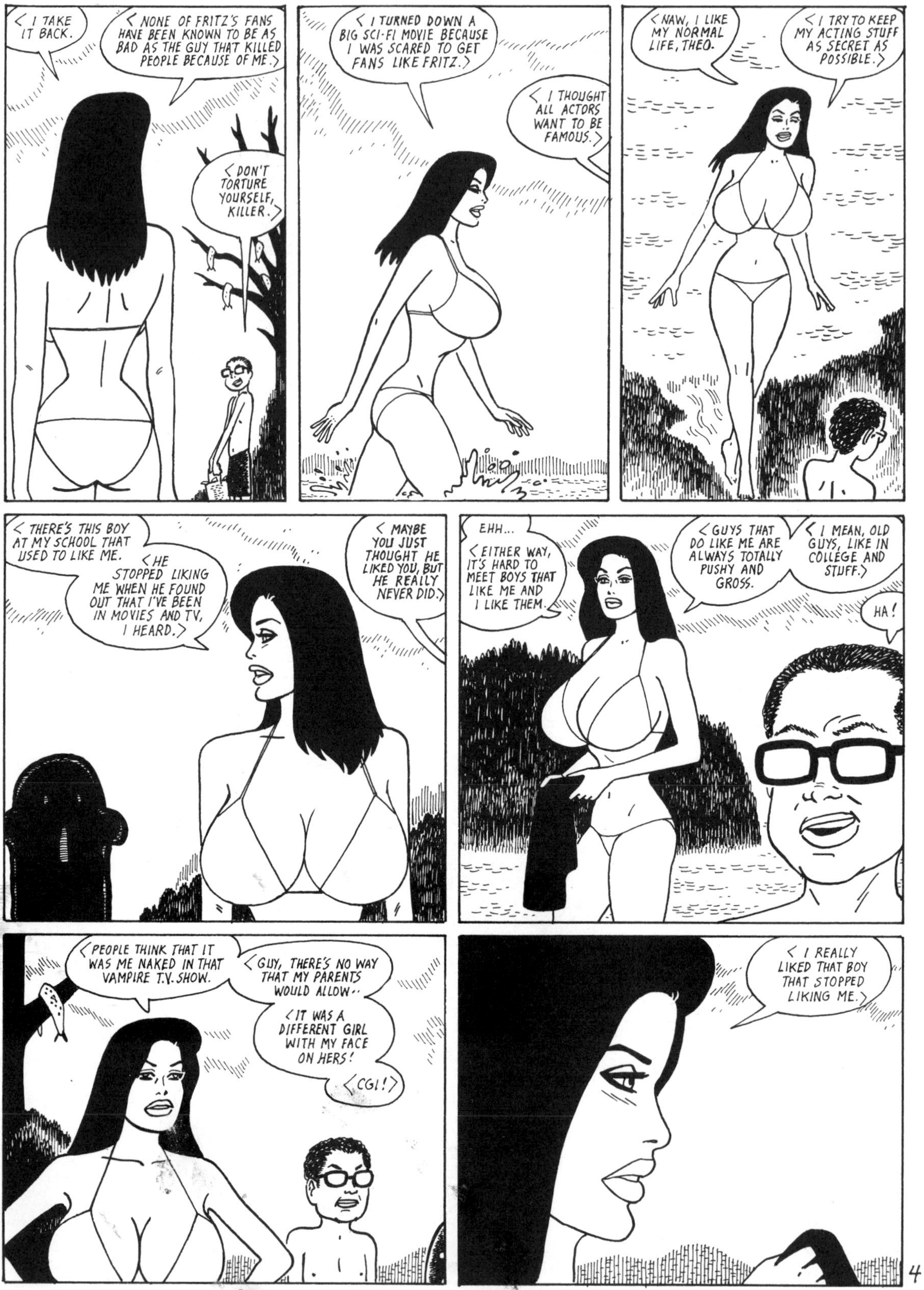

< I TAKE IT BACK.
< NONE OF FRITZ'S FANS HAVE BEEN KNOWN TO BE AS BAD AS THE GUY THAT KILLED PEOPLE BECAUSE OF ME.>
< DON'T TORTURE YOURSELF, KILLER.>
< I TURNED DOWN A BIG SCI-FI MOVIE BECAUSE I WAS SCARED TO GET FANS LIKE FRITZ.>
< I THOUGHT ALL ACTORS WANT TO BE FAMOUS.>
< NAW, I LIKE MY NORMAL LIFE, THEO.
< I TRY TO KEEP MY ACTING STUFF AS SECRET AS POSSIBLE.>
< THERE'S THIS BOY AT MY SCHOOL THAT USED TO LIKE ME.
< HE STOPPED LIKING ME WHEN HE FOUND OUT THAT I'VE BEEN IN MOVIES AND TV, I HEARD.>
< MAYBE YOU JUST THOUGHT HE LIKED YOU, BUT HE REALLY NEVER DID.>
EHH...
< EITHER WAY, IT'S HARD TO MEET BOYS THAT LIKE ME AND I LIKE THEM.
< GUYS THAT DO LIKE ME ARE ALWAYS TOTALLY PUSHY AND GROSS.
< I MEAN, OLD GUYS, LIKE IN COLLEGE AND STUFF.>
HA!
< PEOPLE THINK THAT IT WAS ME NAKED IN THAT VAMPIRE T.V. SHOW.
< GUY, THERE'S NO WAY THAT MY PARENTS WOULD ALLOW..
< IT WAS A DIFFERENT GIRL WITH MY FACE ON HERS!
< CGI!>
< I REALLY LIKED THAT BOY THAT STOPPED LIKING ME.>
4

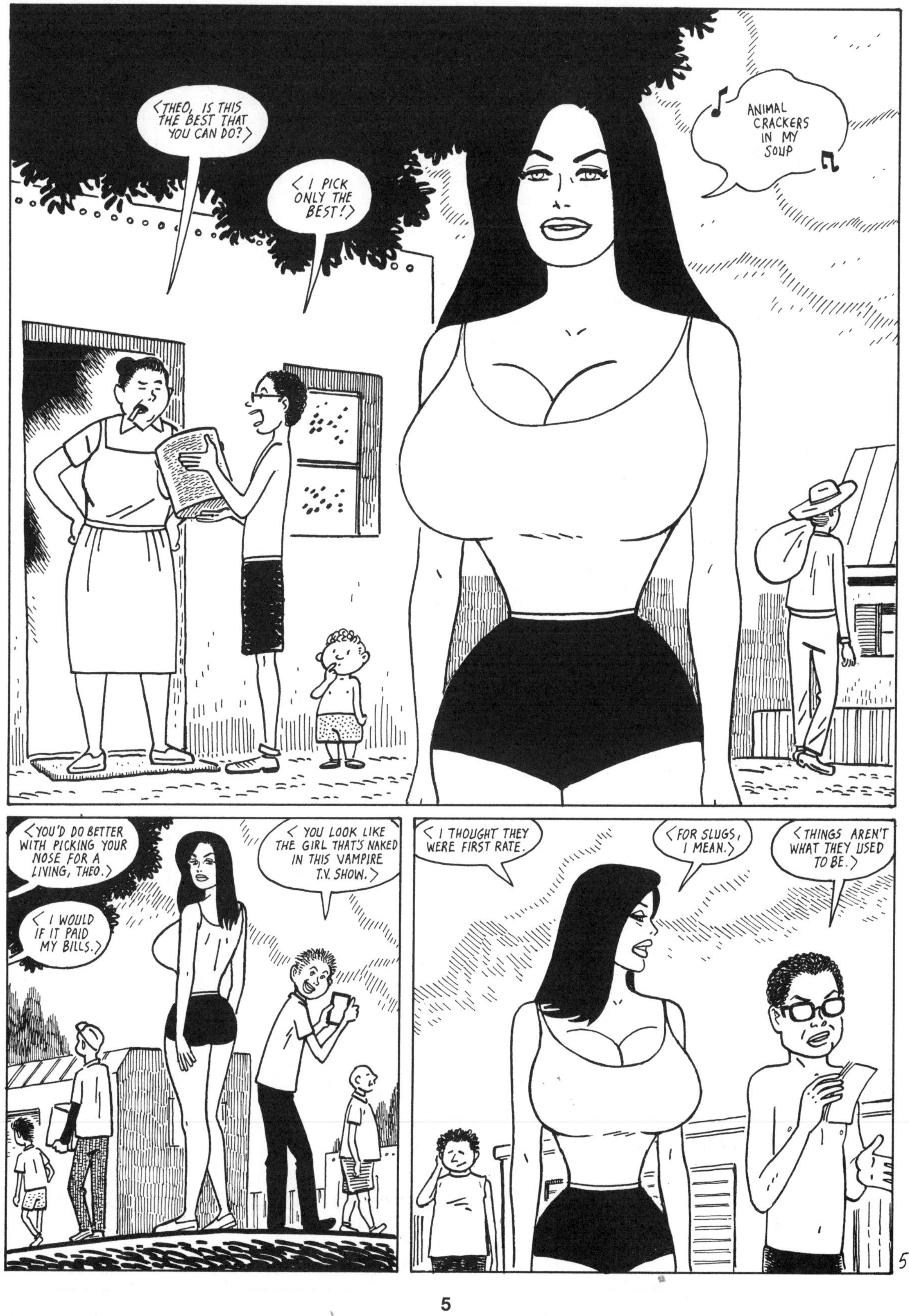
<THEO, IS THIS THE BEST THAT YOU CAN DO?>
<I PICK ONLY THE BEST!>
ANIMAL CRACKERS IN MY SOUP
<YOU'D DO BETTER WITH PICKING YOUR NOSE FOR A LIVING, THEO.>
<I WOULD IF IT PAID MY BILLS.>
<YOU LOOK LIKE THE GIRL THAT'S NAKED IN THIS VAMPIRE T.V. SHOW.>
<I THOUGHT THEY WERE FIRST RATE.
<FOR SLUGS, I MEAN.>
<THINGS AREN'T WHAT THEY USED TO BE.>
5

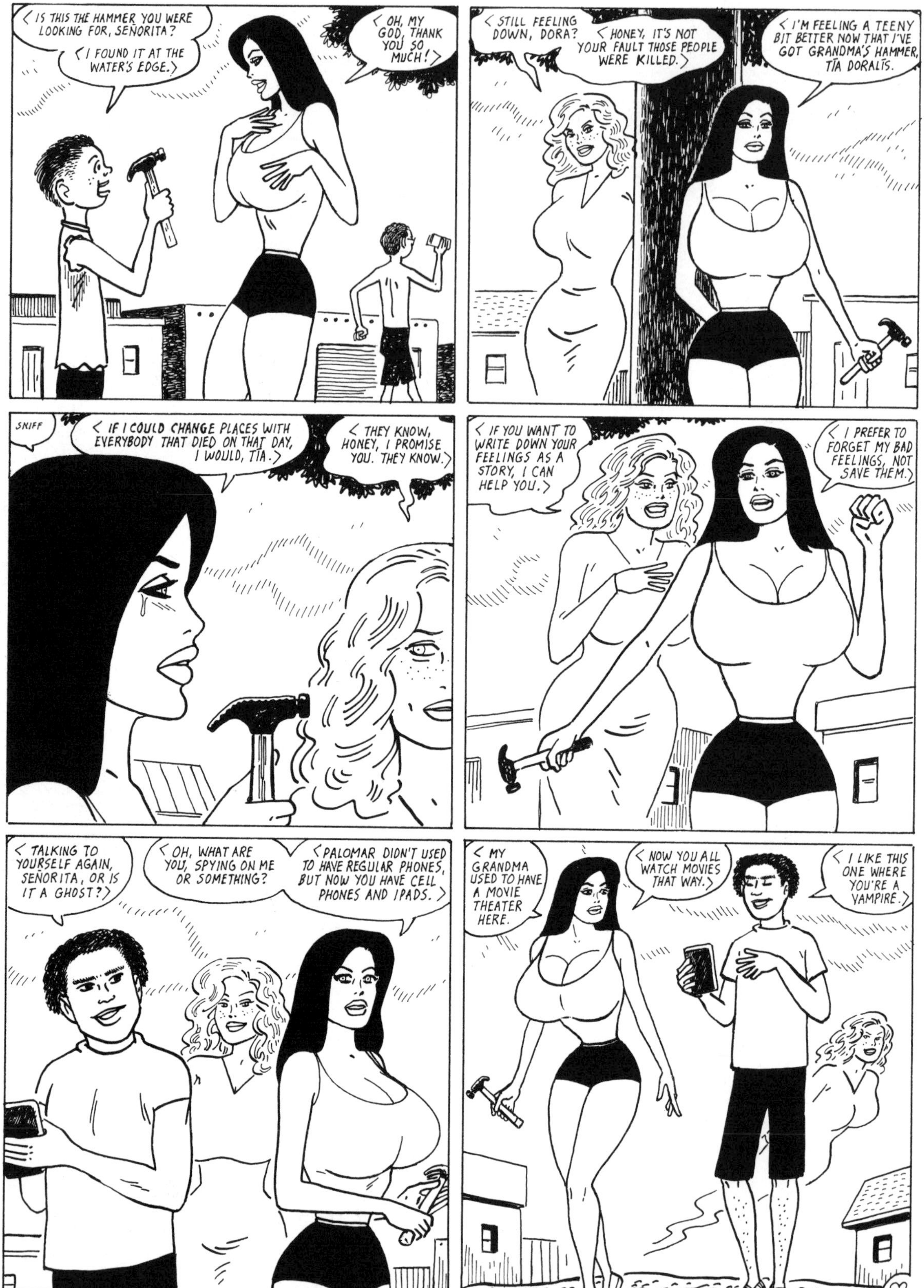
< IS THIS THE HAMMER YOU WERE LOOKING FOR, SEÑORITA?
< I FOUND IT AT THE WATER'S EDGE. >
< OH, MY GOD, THANK YOU SO MUCH! >
< STILL FEELING DOWN, DORA?
< HONEY, IT'S NOT YOUR FAULT THOSE PEOPLE WERE KILLED. >
< I'M FEELING A TEENY BIT BETTER NOW THAT I'VE GOT GRANDMA'S HAMMER, TÍA DORALÍS.
SNIFF
< IF I COULD CHANGE PLACES WITH EVERYBODY THAT DIED ON THAT DAY, I WOULD, TÍA. >
< THEY KNOW, HONEY, I PROMISE YOU. THEY KNOW. >
< IF YOU WANT TO WRITE DOWN YOUR FEELINGS AS A STORY, I CAN HELP YOU. >
< I PREFER TO FORGET MY BAD FEELINGS, NOT SAVE THEM. >
< TALKING TO YOURSELF AGAIN, SEÑORITA, OR IS IT A GHOST? >
< OH, WHAT ARE YOU, SPYING ON ME OR SOMETHING?
< PALOMAR DIDN'T USED TO HAVE REGULAR PHONES, BUT NOW YOU HAVE CELL PHONES AND IPADS. >
< MY GRANDMA USED TO HAVE A MOVIE THEATER HERE.
< NOW YOU ALL WATCH MOVIES THAT WAY. >
< I LIKE THIS ONE WHERE YOU'RE A VAMPIRE. >

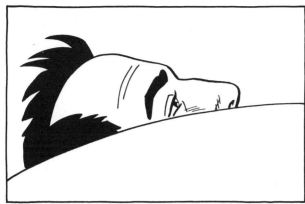

WHAT?

I SAID, WHAT ARE YOU GOING TO DO WHILE I'M GONE?

OH, STARE LONGINGLY OUT THE WINDOW... CRY IN MY SUGAR POPS...

I'LL ONLY BE GONE TWO NIGHTS.

... DROWN MYSELF IN THE BATHTUB...

MANNY MOTA

ARE YOU SURE YOU CAN'T DRIVE ME TO THE TRAIN STATION?

I TOLD YOU, I GOT THAT STUPID INTERVIEW.

OH, RIGHT! WOULD YOU RATHER I NOT GO?! SHOULD I...?

NO! GO! HAVE FUN! GET DRUNK! SHOOT UP! HUERTA! HOPPERS! ¡AJUA!

YOU'RE NOT PLANNING TO VISIT YOUR MOM OR YOUR HOMIES...

IS THERE A LAW THAT STATES YOU AND I CAN'T BE IN THE SAME TOWN NOT HANGING OUT TOGETHER?

ALL RIGHT THEN, GO TO HUERTA, IF YOU WANNA BE STINKY ABOUT IT!

I... ... WOULDN'T DREAM OF SPOILING YOUR SECRET PUNK REUNION.

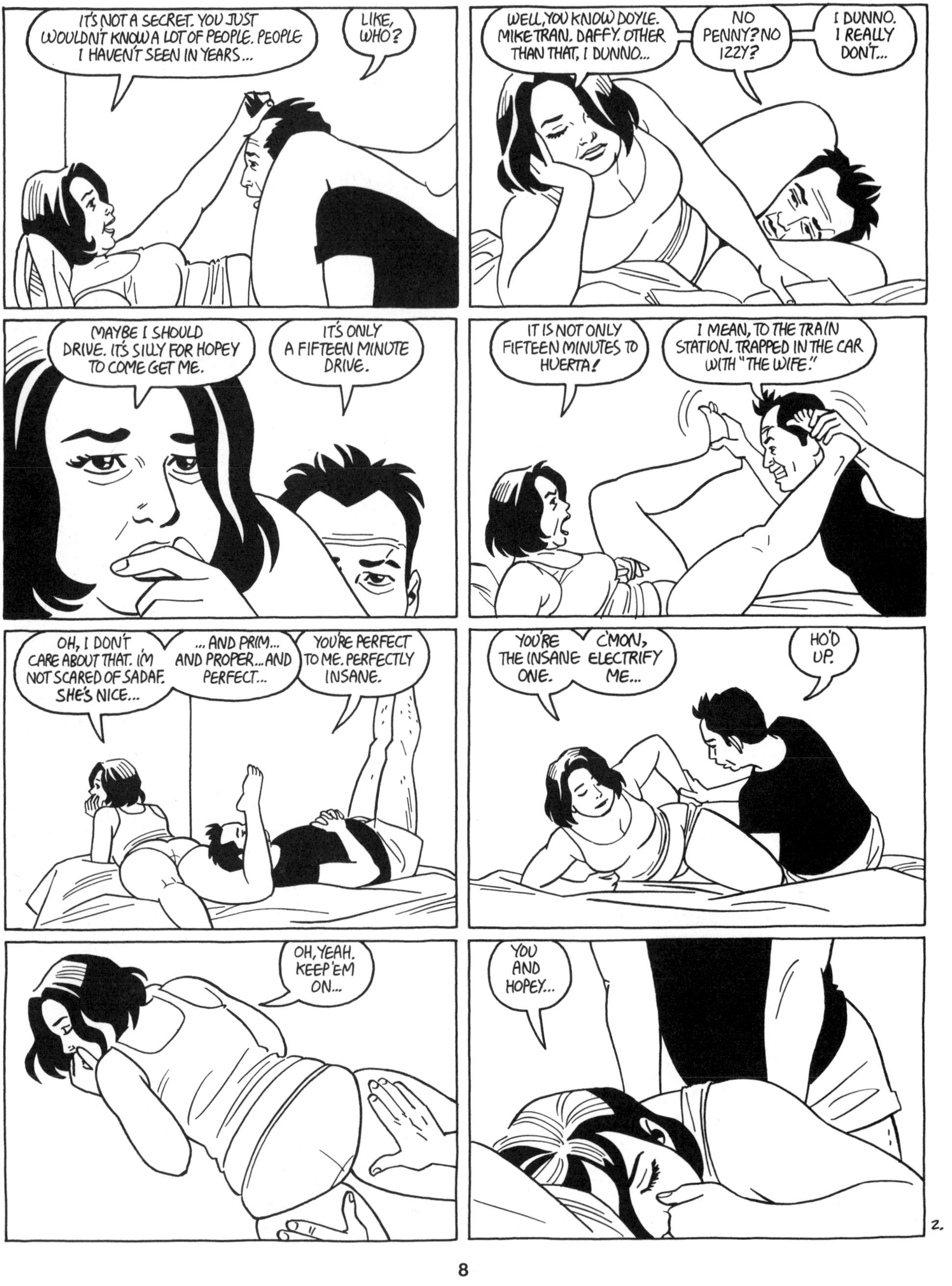
IT'S NOT A SECRET. YOU JUST WOULDN'T KNOW A LOT OF PEOPLE. PEOPLE I HAVEN'T SEEN IN YEARS...
LIKE, WHO?
WELL, YOU KNOW DOYLE. MIKE TRAN. DAFFY. OTHER THAN THAT, I DUNNO...
NO PENNY? NO IZZY?
I DUNNO. I REALLY DON'T...
MAYBE I SHOULD DRIVE. IT'S SILLY FOR HOPEY TO COME GET ME.
IT'S ONLY A FIFTEEN MINUTE DRIVE.
IT IS NOT ONLY FIFTEEN MINUTES TO HUERTA!
I MEAN, TO THE TRAIN STATION. TRAPPED IN THE CAR WITH "THE WIFE."
OH, I DON'T CARE ABOUT THAT. I'M NOT SCARED OF SADAF. SHE'S NICE...
...AND PRIM... AND PROPER... AND PERFECT...
YOU'RE PERFECT TO ME. PERFECTLY INSANE.
YOU'RE THE INSANE ONE.
C'MON, ELECTRIFY ME...
HO'D UP.
OH, YEAH. KEEP 'EM ON...
YOU AND HOPEY...
2.

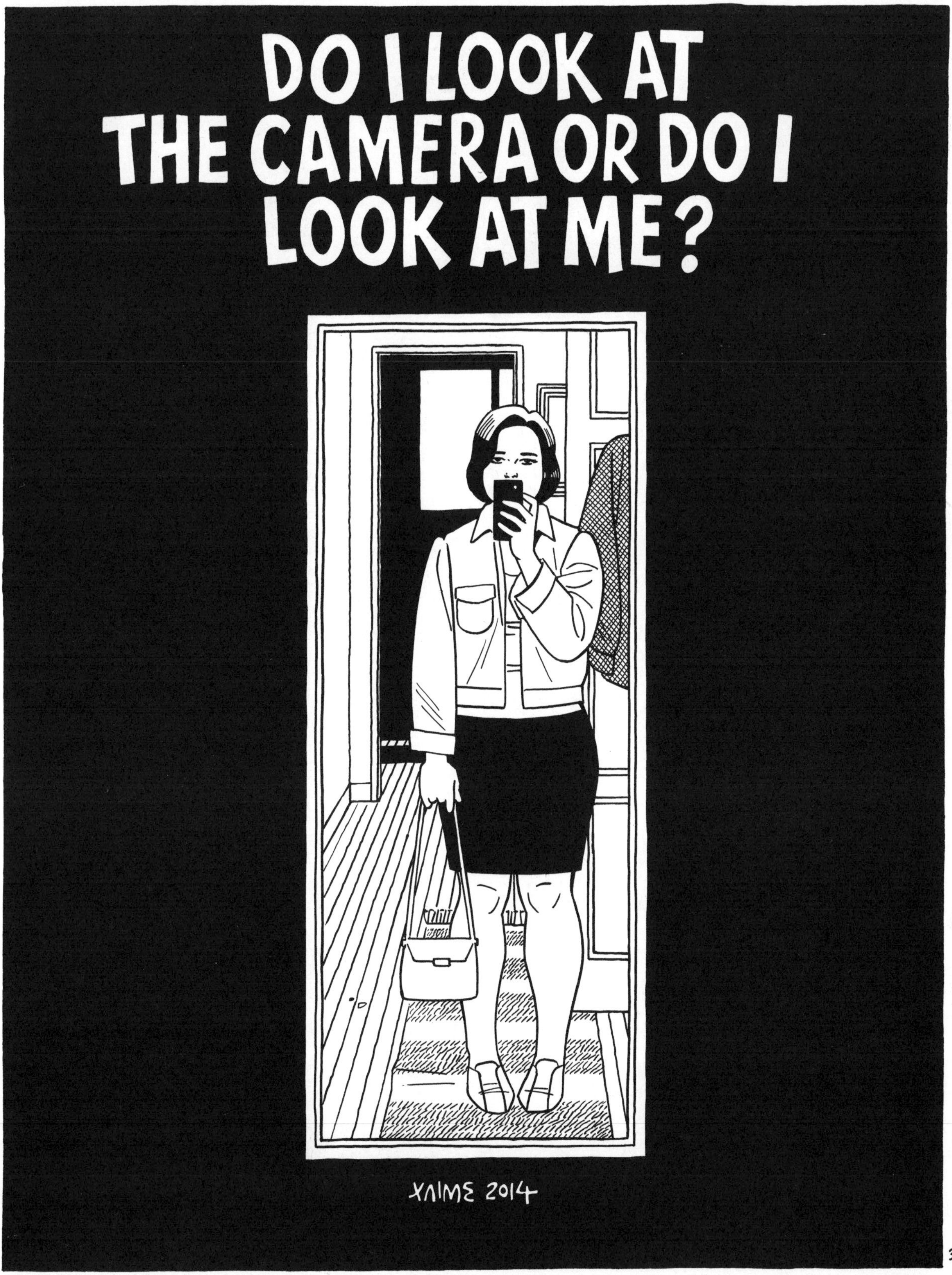
DO I LOOK AT THE CAMERA OR DO I LOOK AT ME?
XAIME 2014

3.

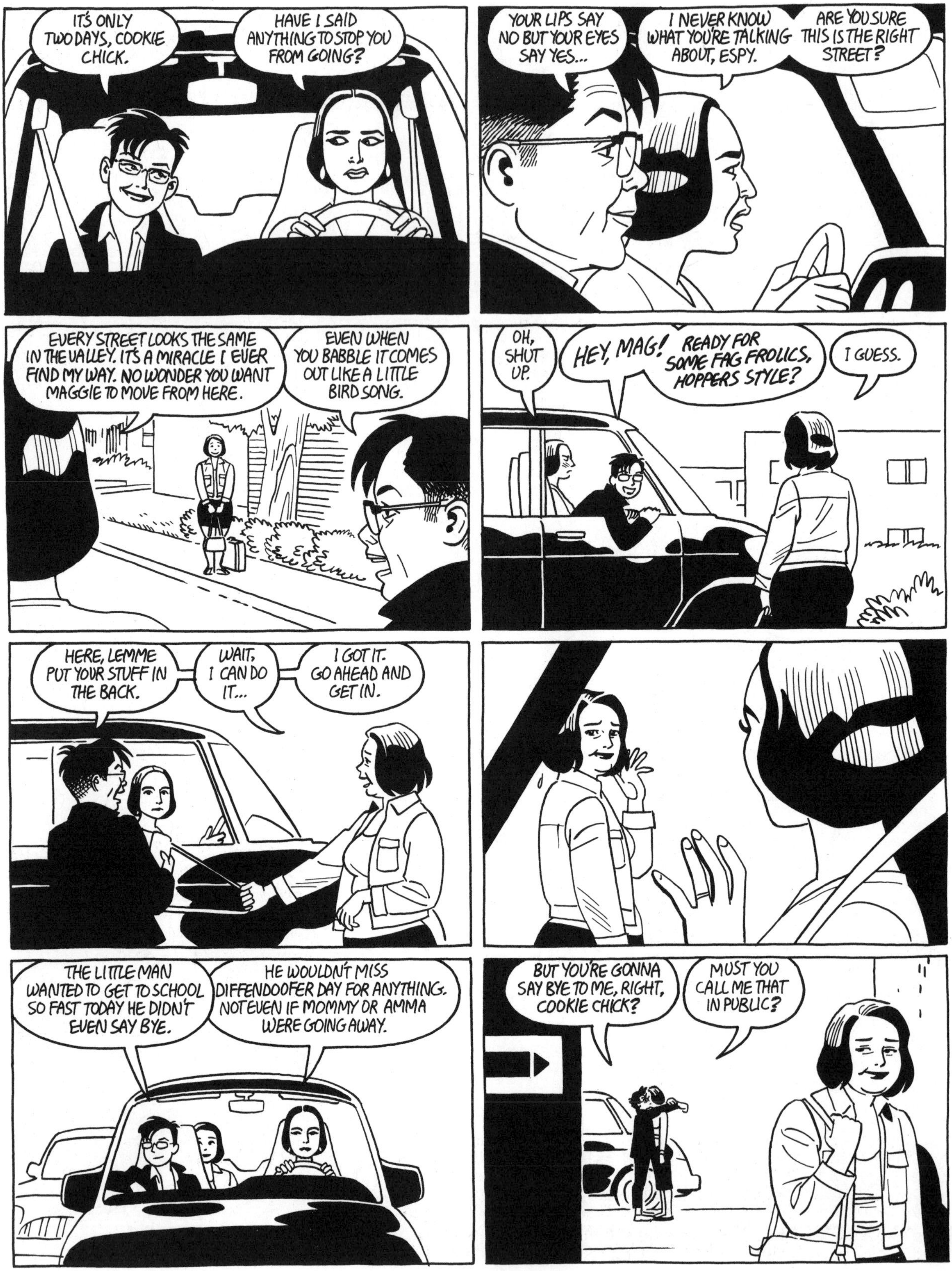
IT'S ONLY TWO DAYS, COOKIE CHICK.
HAVE I SAID ANYTHING TO STOP YOU FROM GOING?
YOUR LIPS SAY NO BUT YOUR EYES SAY YES...
I NEVER KNOW WHAT YOU'RE TALKING ABOUT, ESPY.
ARE YOU SURE THIS IS THE RIGHT STREET?
EVERY STREET LOOKS THE SAME IN THE VALLEY. IT'S A MIRACLE I EVER FIND MY WAY. NO WONDER YOU WANT MAGGIE TO MOVE FROM HERE.
EVEN WHEN YOU BABBLE IT COMES OUT LIKE A LITTLE BIRD SONG.
OH, SHUT UP.
HEY, MAG!
READY FOR SOME FAG FROLICS, HOPPERS STYLE?
I GUESS.
HERE, LEMME PUT YOUR STUFF IN THE BACK.
WAIT, I CAN DO IT...
I GOT IT. GO AHEAD AND GET IN.
THE LITTLE MAN WANTED TO GET TO SCHOOL SO FAST TODAY HE DIDN'T EVEN SAY BYE.
HE WOULDN'T MISS DIFFENDOOFER DAY FOR ANYTHING. NOT EVEN IF MOMMY OR AMMA WERE GOING AWAY.
BUT YOU'RE GONNA SAY BYE TO ME, RIGHT, COOKIE CHICK?
MUST YOU CALL ME THAT IN PUBLIC?
4.

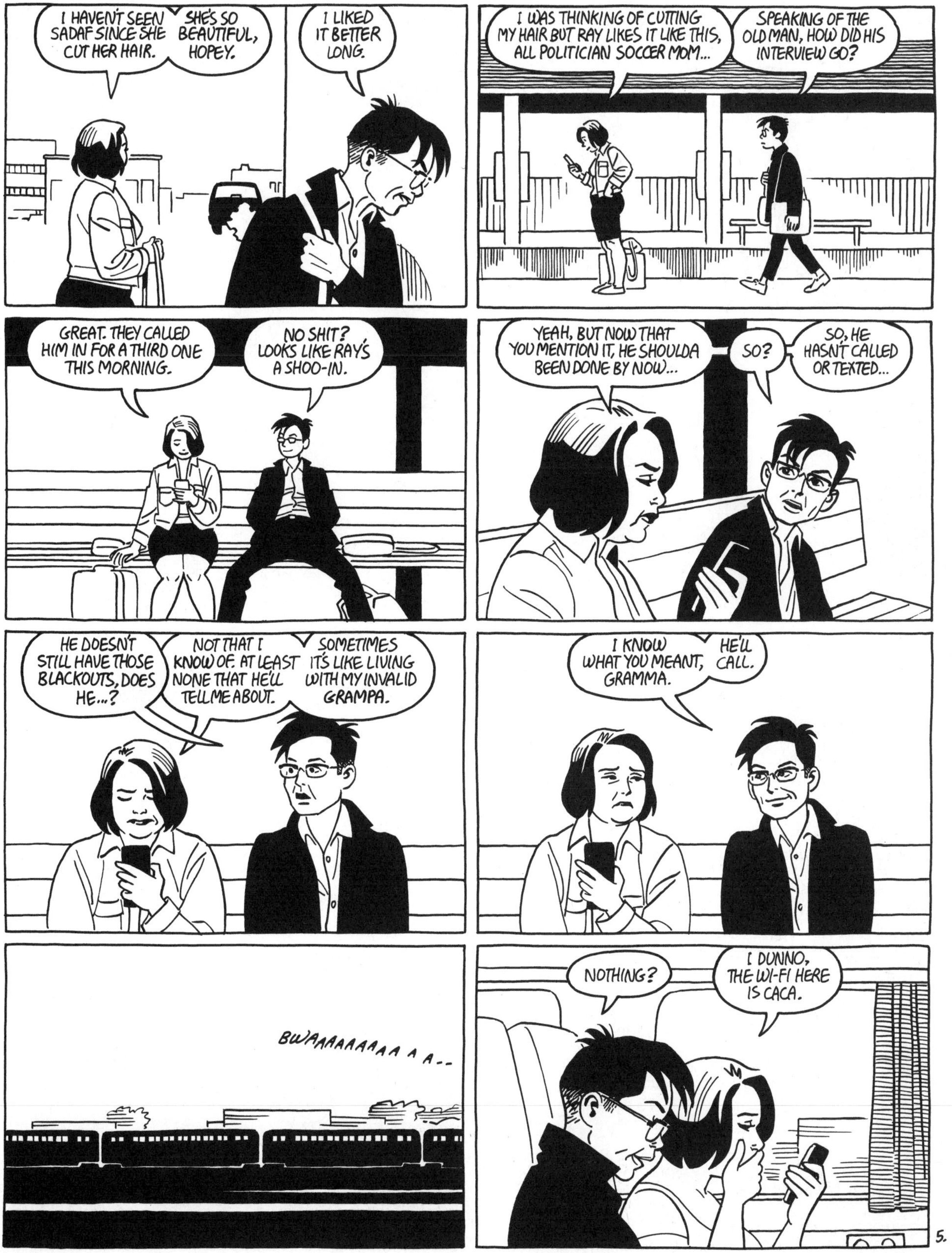
I HAVEN'T SEEN SADAF SINCE SHE CUT HER HAIR.
SHE'S SO BEAUTIFUL, HOPEY.
I LIKED IT BETTER LONG.
I WAS THINKING OF CUTTING MY HAIR BUT RAY LIKES IT LIKE THIS, ALL POLITICIAN SOCCER MOM...
SPEAKING OF THE OLD MAN, HOW DID HIS INTERVIEW GO?
GREAT. THEY CALLED HIM IN FOR A THIRD ONE THIS MORNING.
NO SHIT? LOOKS LIKE RAY'S A SHOO-IN.
YEAH, BUT NOW THAT YOU MENTION IT, HE SHOULDA BEEN DONE BY NOW...
SO?
SO, HE HASN'T CALLED OR TEXTED...
HE DOESN'T STILL HAVE THOSE BLACKOUTS, DOES HE...?
NOT THAT I KNOW OF. AT LEAST NONE THAT HE'LL TELL ME ABOUT.
SOMETIMES IT'S LIKE LIVING WITH MY INVALID GRAMPA.
I KNOW WHAT YOU MEANT, GRAMMA.
HE'LL CALL.
BWAAAAAAAAA A A A...
NOTHING?
I DUNNO, THE WI-FI HERE IS CACA.
5.

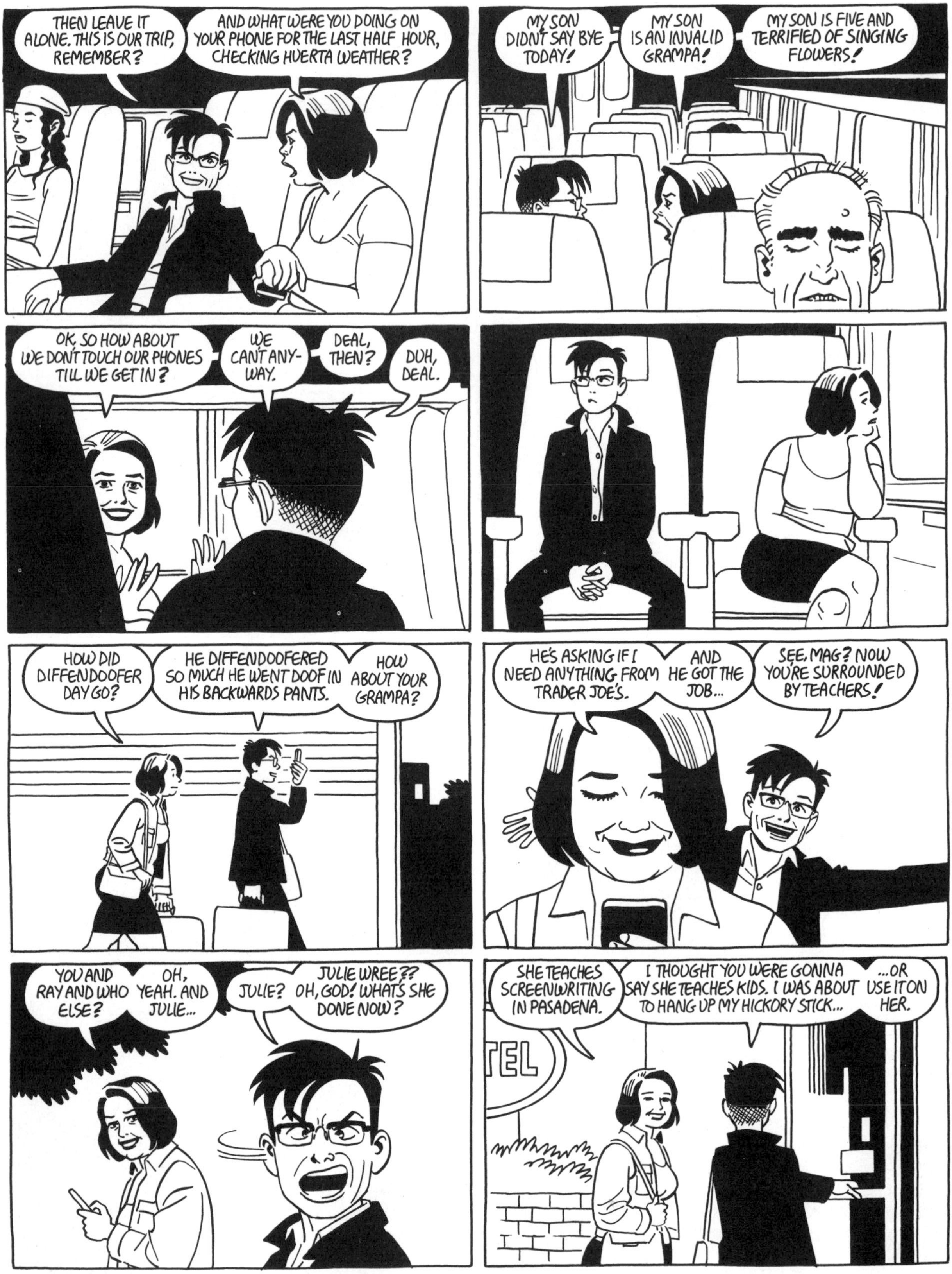

THEN LEAVE IT ALONE. THIS IS OUR TRIP, REMEMBER?
AND WHAT WERE YOU DOING ON YOUR PHONE FOR THE LAST HALF HOUR, CHECKING HUERTA WEATHER?
MY SON DIDN'T SAY BYE TODAY!
MY SON IS AN INVALID GRAMPA!
MY SON IS FIVE AND TERRIFIED OF SINGING FLOWERS!
OK, SO HOW ABOUT WE DON'T TOUCH OUR PHONES TILL WE GET IN?
WE CAN'T ANY-WAY.
DEAL, THEN?
DUH, DEAL.
HOW DID DIFFENDOOFER DAY GO?
HE DIFFENDOOFERED SO MUCH HE WENT DOOF IN HIS BACKWARDS PANTS.
HOW ABOUT YOUR GRAMPA?
HE'S ASKING IF I NEED ANYTHING FROM TRADER JOE'S.
AND HE GOT THE JOB...
SEE, MAG? NOW YOU'RE SURROUNDED BY TEACHERS!
YOU AND RAY AND WHO ELSE?
OH, YEAH. AND JULIE...
JULIE?
JULIE WREE?? OH, GOD! WHAT'S SHE DONE NOW?
SHE TEACHES SCREENWRITING IN PASADENA.
I THOUGHT YOU WERE GONNA SAY SHE TEACHES KIDS. I WAS ABOUT TO HANG UP MY HICKORY STICK...
...OR USE IT ON HER.
TEL

6.

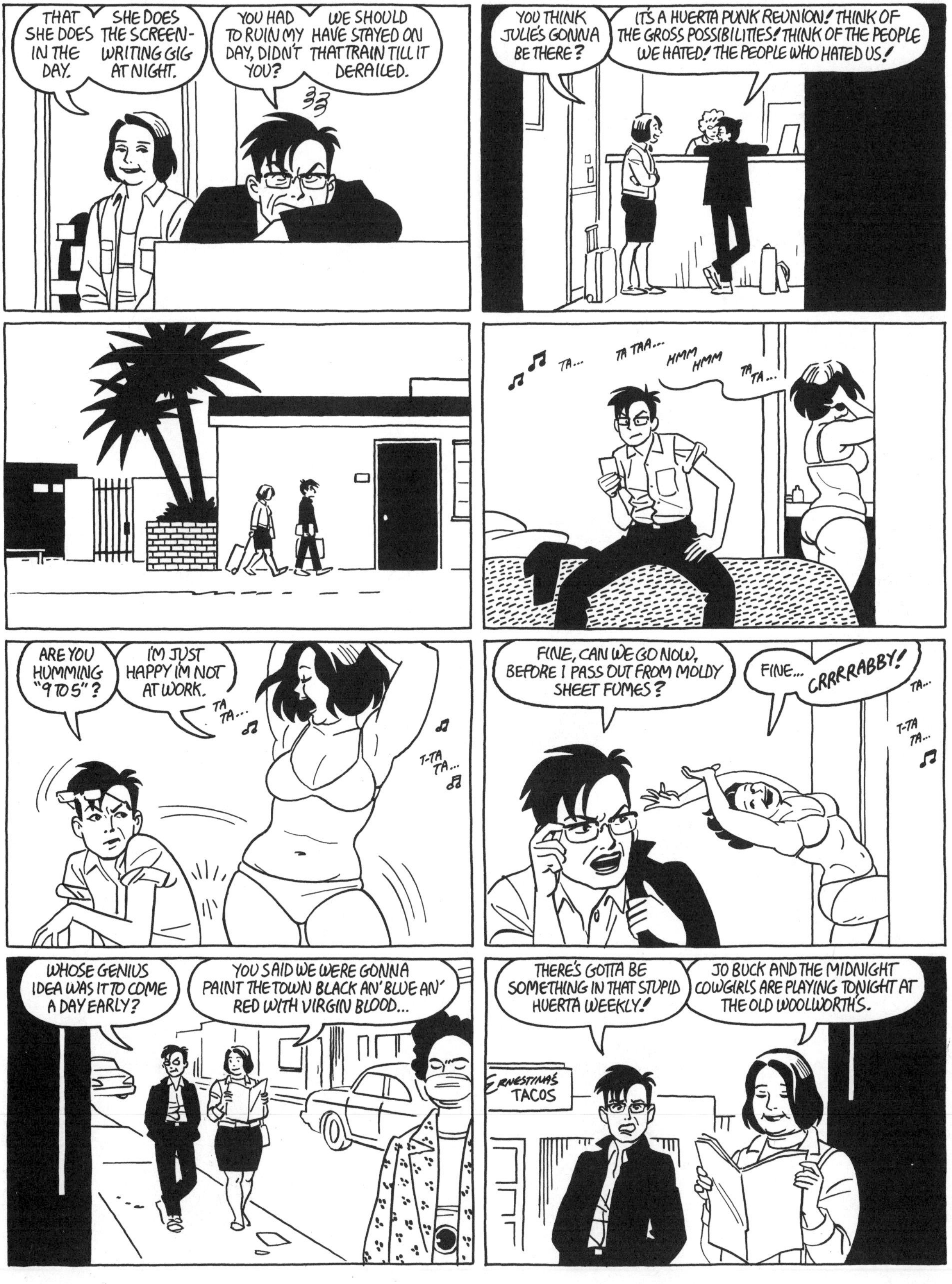
THAT SHE DOES IN THE DAY.
SHE DOES THE SCREEN-WRITING GIG AT NIGHT.
YOU HAD TO RUIN MY DAY, DIDN'T YOU?
WE SHOULD HAVE STAYED ON THAT TRAIN TILL IT DERAILED.
YOU THINK JULIE'S GONNA BE THERE?
IT'S A HUERTA PUNK REUNION! THINK OF THE GROSS POSSIBILITIES! THINK OF THE PEOPLE WE HATED! THE PEOPLE WHO HATED US!
TA... TA TAA... HMM HMM TA TA...
ARE YOU HUMMING "9 TO 5"?
I'M JUST HAPPY I'M NOT AT WORK.
TA TA...
T-TA TA...
FINE, CAN WE GO NOW, BEFORE I PASS OUT FROM MOLDY SHEET FUMES?
FINE... CRRRRABBY!
TA...
T-TA TA...
WHOSE GENIUS IDEA WAS IT TO COME A DAY EARLY?
YOU SAID WE WERE GONNA PAINT THE TOWN BLACK AN' BLUE AN' RED WITH VIRGIN BLOOD...
THERE'S GOTTA BE SOMETHING IN THAT STUPID HUERTA WEEKLY!
JO BUCK AND THE MIDNIGHT COWGIRLS ARE PLAYING TONIGHT AT THE OLD WOOLWORTH'S.
ERNESTINA'S TACOS

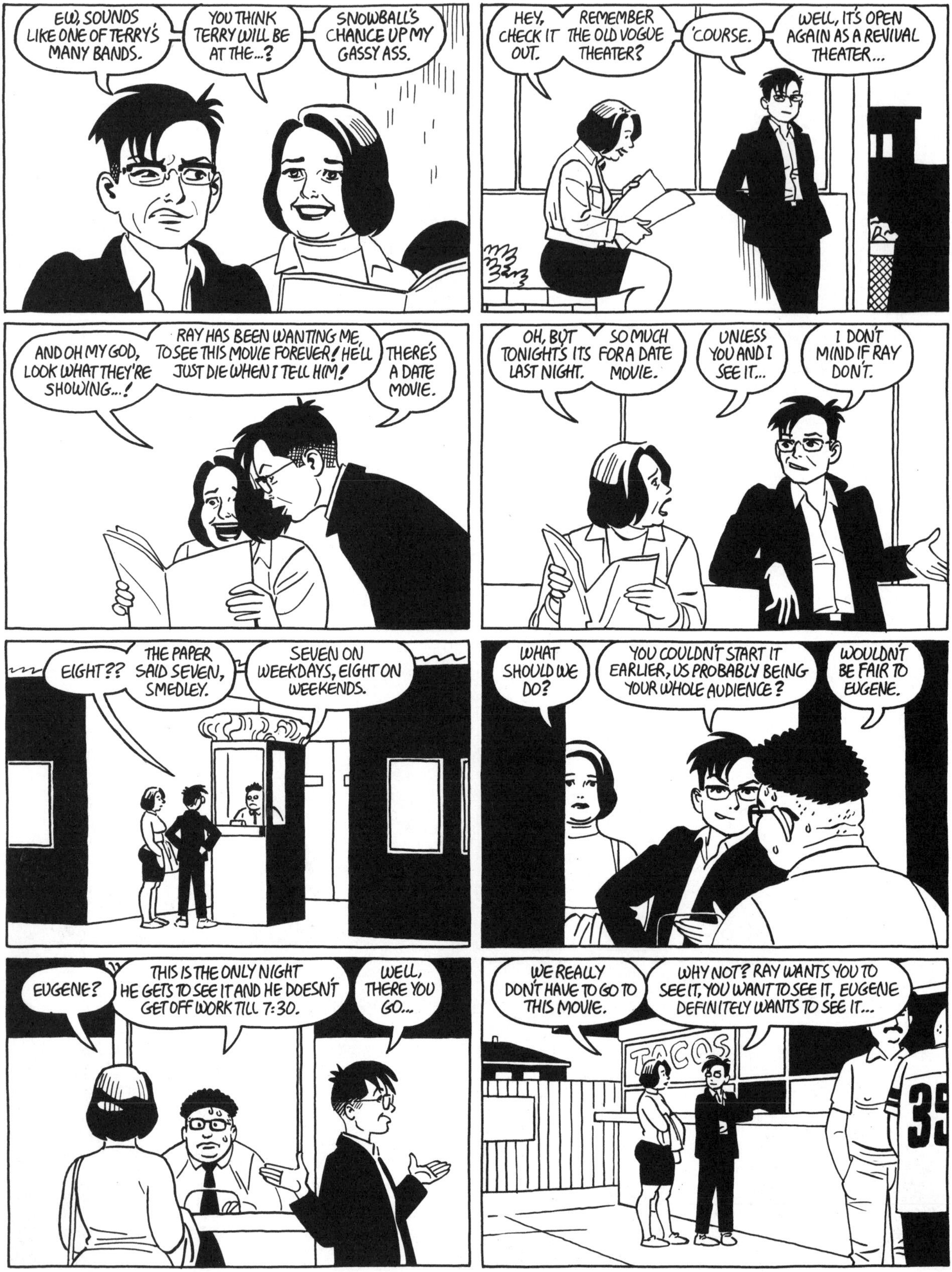
EW, SOUNDS LIKE ONE OF TERRY'S MANY BANDS.
YOU THINK TERRY WILL BE AT THE...?
SNOWBALL'S CHANCE UP MY GASSY ASS.
HEY, CHECK IT OUT.
REMEMBER THE OLD VOGUE THEATER?
'COURSE.
WELL, IT'S OPEN AGAIN AS A REVIVAL THEATER...
AND OH MY GOD, LOOK WHAT THEY'RE SHOWING...!
RAY HAS BEEN WANTING ME, TO SEE THIS MOVIE FOREVER! HE'LL JUST DIE WHEN I TELL HIM!
THERE'S A DATE MOVIE.
OH, BUT TONIGHT'S ITS LAST NIGHT.
SO MUCH FOR A DATE MOVIE.
UNLESS YOU AND I SEE IT...
I DON'T MIND IF RAY DON'T.
EIGHT??
THE PAPER SAID SEVEN, SMEDLEY.
SEVEN ON WEEKDAYS, EIGHT ON WEEKENDS.
WHAT SHOULD WE DO?
YOU COULDN'T START IT EARLIER, US PROBABLY BEING YOUR WHOLE AUDIENCE?
WOULDN'T BE FAIR TO EUGENE.
EUGENE?
THIS IS THE ONLY NIGHT HE GETS TO SEE IT AND HE DOESN'T GET OFF WORK TILL 7:30.
WELL, THERE YOU GO...
WE REALLY DON'T HAVE TO GO TO THIS MOVIE.
WHY NOT? RAY WANTS YOU TO SEE IT, YOU WANT TO SEE IT, EUGENE DEFINITELY WANTS TO SEE IT...
TACOS
35
8.

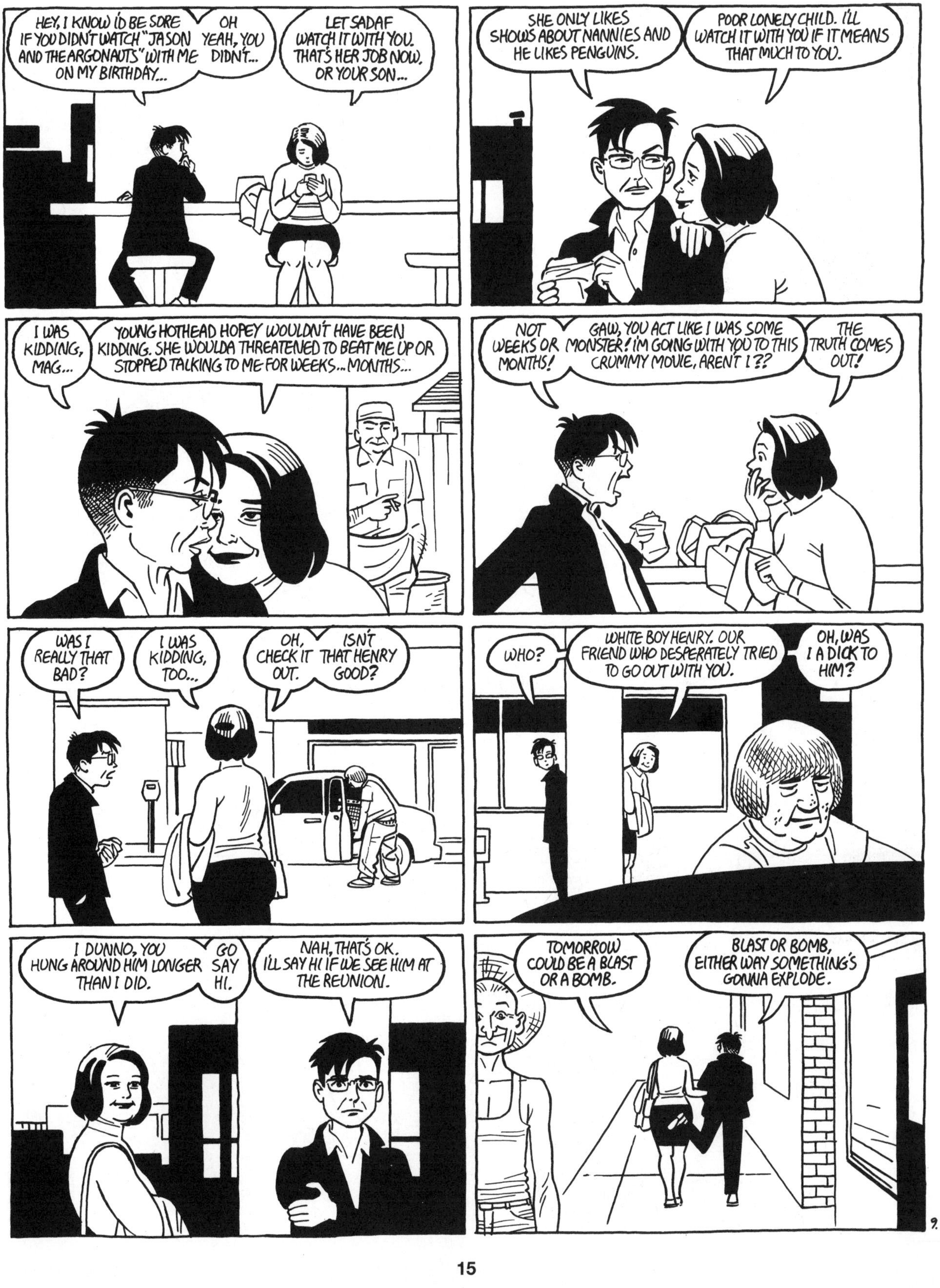
HEY, I KNOW I'D BE SORE IF YOU DIDN'T WATCH "JASON AND THE ARGONAUTS" WITH ME ON MY BIRTHDAY...
OH YEAH, YOU DIDN'T...
LET SADAF WATCH IT WITH YOU. THAT'S HER JOB NOW. OR YOUR SON...
SHE ONLY LIKES SHOWS ABOUT NANNIES AND HE LIKES PENGUINS.
POOR LONELY CHILD. I'LL WATCH IT WITH YOU IF IT MEANS THAT MUCH TO YOU.
I WAS KIDDING, MAG...
YOUNG HOTHEAD HOPEY WOULDN'T HAVE BEEN KIDDING. SHE WOULDA THREATENED TO BEAT ME UP OR STOPPED TALKING TO ME FOR WEEKS... MONTHS...
NOT WEEKS OR MONTHS!
GAW, YOU ACT LIKE I WAS SOME MONSTER! I'M GOING WITH YOU TO THIS CRUMMY MOVIE, AREN'T I??
THE TRUTH COMES OUT!
WAS I REALLY THAT BAD?
I WAS KIDDING, TOO...
OH, CHECK IT OUT.
ISN'T THAT HENRY GOOD?
WHO?
WHITE BOY HENRY. OUR FRIEND WHO DESPERATELY TRIED TO GO OUT WITH YOU.
OH, WAS I A DICK TO HIM?
I DUNNO, YOU HUNG AROUND HIM LONGER THAN I DID.
GO SAY HI.
NAH, THAT'S OK. I'LL SAY HI IF WE SEE HIM AT THE REUNION.
TOMORROW COULD BE A BLAST OR A BOMB.
BLAST OR BOMB, EITHER WAY SOMETHING'S GONNA EXPLODE.
9.

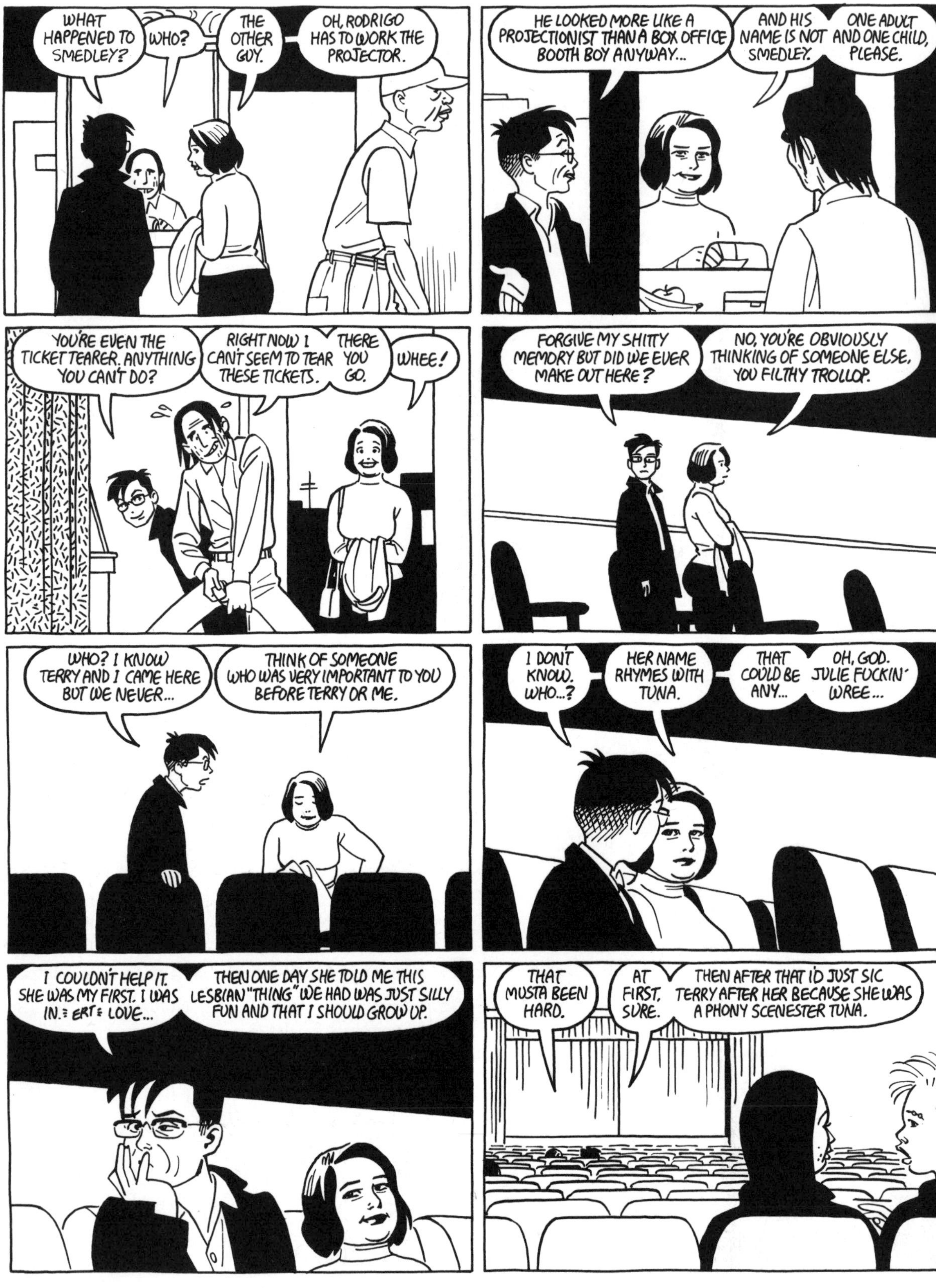
WHAT HAPPENED TO SMEDLEY?
WHO?
THE OTHER GUY.
OH, RODRIGO HAS TO WORK THE PROJECTOR.
HE LOOKED MORE LIKE A PROJECTIONIST THAN A BOX OFFICE BOOTH BOY ANYWAY...
AND HIS NAME IS NOT SMEDLEY.
ONE ADULT AND ONE CHILD, PLEASE.
YOU'RE EVEN THE TICKET TEARER. ANYTHING YOU CAN'T DO?
RIGHT NOW I CAN'T SEEM TO TEAR THESE TICKETS.
THERE YOU GO.
WHEE!
FORGIVE MY SHITTY MEMORY BUT DID WE EVER MAKE OUT HERE?
NO, YOU'RE OBVIOUSLY THINKING OF SOMEONE ELSE, YOU FILTHY TROLLOP.
WHO? I KNOW TERRY AND I CAME HERE BUT WE NEVER...
THINK OF SOMEONE WHO WAS VERY IMPORTANT TO YOU BEFORE TERRY OR ME.
I DON'T KNOW. WHO...?
HER NAME RHYMES WITH TUNA.
THAT COULD BE ANY...
OH, GOD. JULIE FUCKIN' WREE...
I COULDN'T HELP IT. SHE WAS MY FIRST. I WAS IN. ERT LOVE...
THEN ONE DAY SHE TOLD ME THIS LESBIAN "THING" WE HAD WAS JUST SILLY FUN AND THAT I SHOULD GROW UP.
THAT MUSTA BEEN HARD.
AT FIRST, SURE.
THEN AFTER THAT I'D JUST SIC TERRY AFTER HER BECAUSE SHE WAS A PHONY SCENESTER TUNA.

10.

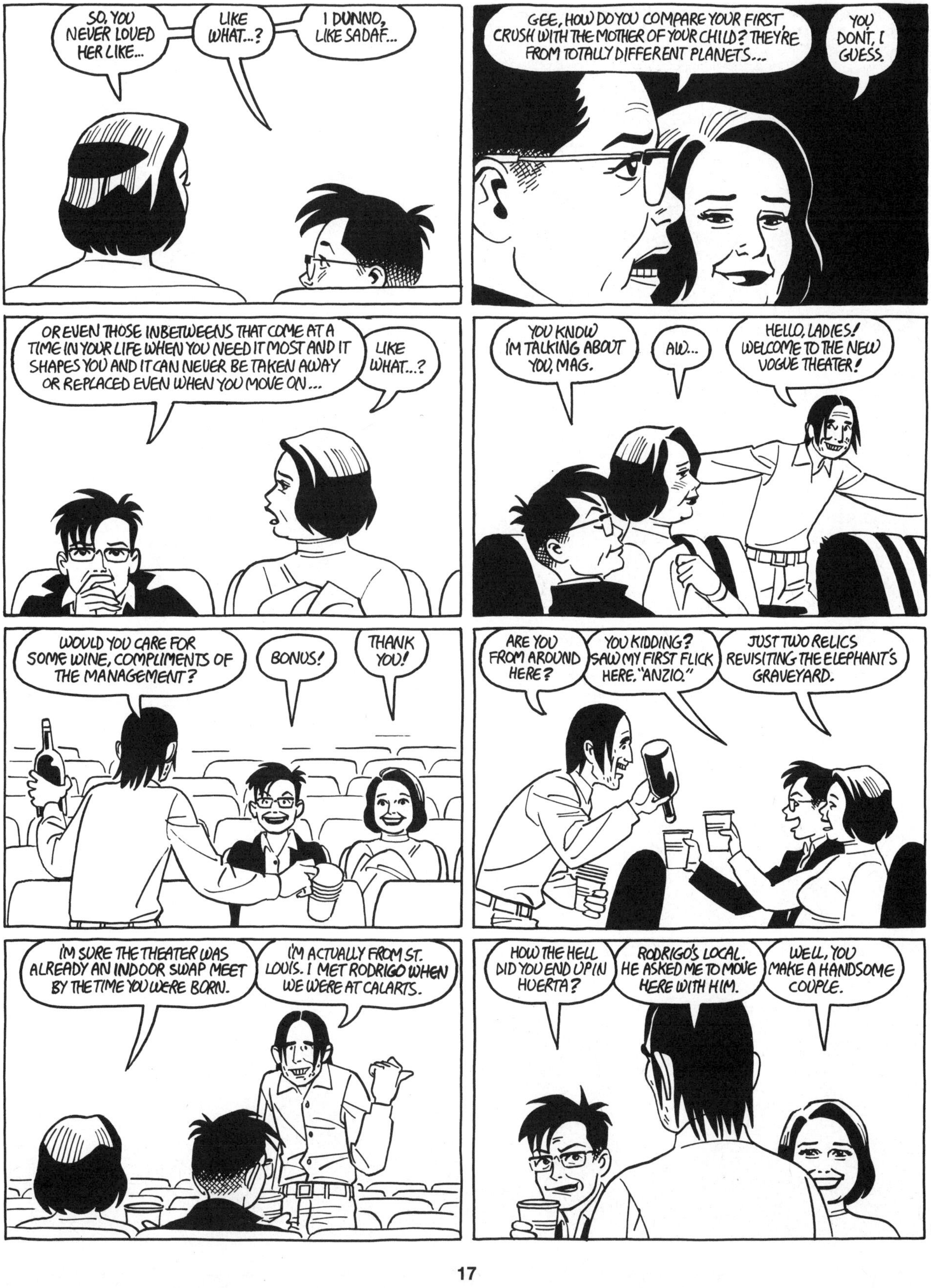
SO, YOU NEVER LOVED HER LIKE...
LIKE WHAT...?
I DUNNO, LIKE SADAF...
GEE, HOW DO YOU COMPARE YOUR FIRST, CRUSH WITH THE MOTHER OF YOUR CHILD? THEY'RE FROM TOTALLY DIFFERENT PLANETS...
YOU DON'T, I GUESS.
OR EVEN THOSE INBETWEENS THAT COME AT A TIME IN YOUR LIFE WHEN YOU NEED IT MOST AND IT SHAPES YOU AND IT CAN NEVER BE TAKEN AWAY OR REPLACED EVEN WHEN YOU MOVE ON...
LIKE WHAT...?
YOU KNOW I'M TALKING ABOUT YOU, MAG.
AW...
HELLO, LADIES! WELCOME TO THE NEW VOGUE THEATER!
WOULD YOU CARE FOR SOME WINE, COMPLIMENTS OF THE MANAGEMENT?
BONUS!
THANK YOU!
ARE YOU FROM AROUND HERE?
YOU KIDDING? SAW MY FIRST FLICK HERE. "ANZIO."
JUST TWO RELICS REVISITING THE ELEPHANT'S GRAVEYARD.
I'M SURE THE THEATER WAS ALREADY AN INDOOR SWAP MEET BY THE TIME YOU WERE BORN.
I'M ACTUALLY FROM ST. LOUIS. I MET RODRIGO WHEN WE WERE AT CALARTS.
HOW THE HELL DID YOU END UP IN HUERTA?
RODRIGO'S LOCAL. HE ASKED ME TO MOVE HERE WITH HIM.
WELL, YOU MAKE A HANDSOME COUPLE.
11.

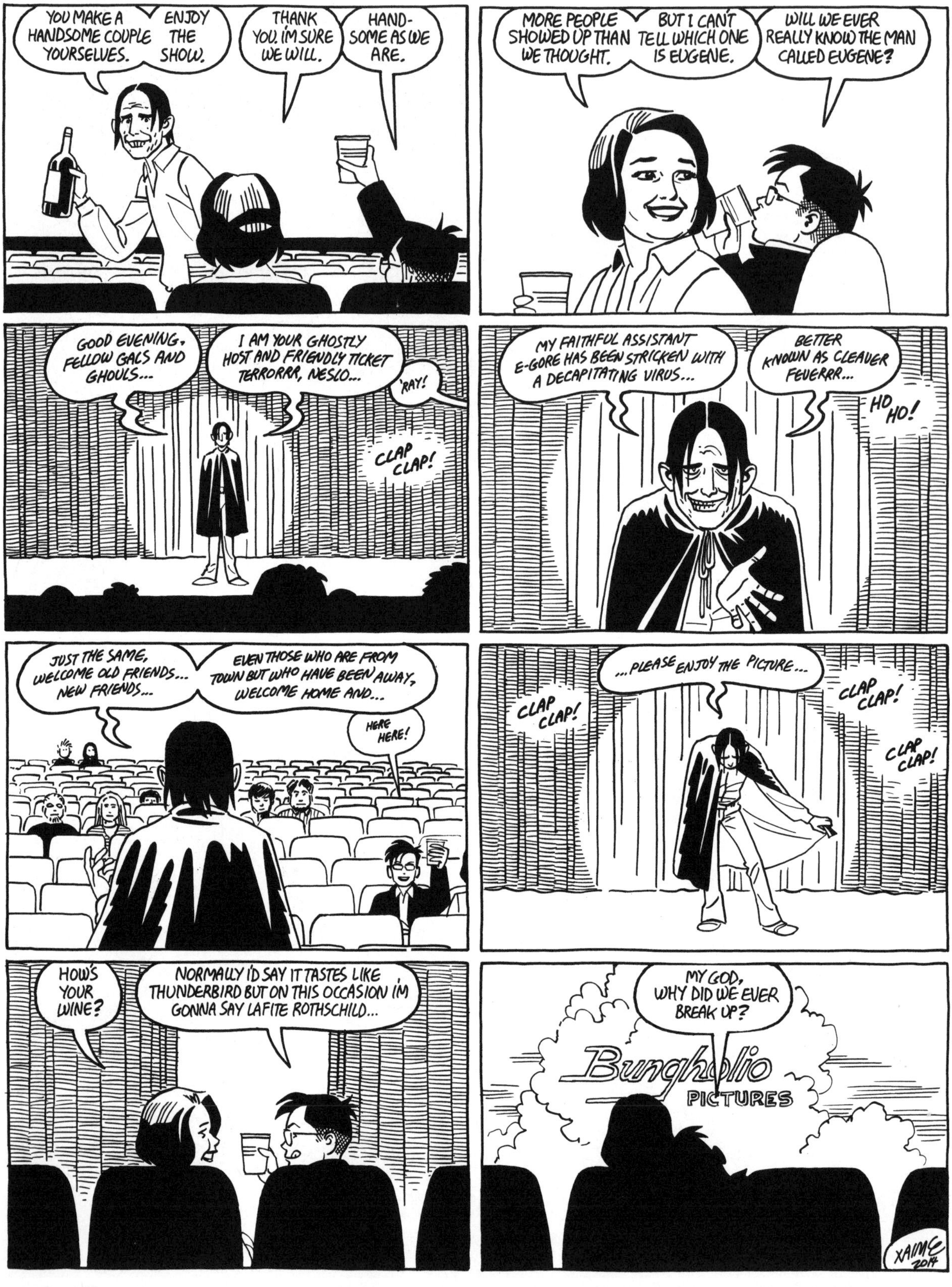

YOU MAKE A HANDSOME COUPLE YOURSELVES.
ENJOY THE SHOW.
THANK YOU. I'M SURE WE WILL.
HAND-SOME AS WE ARE.
MORE PEOPLE SHOWED UP THAN WE THOUGHT.
BUT I CAN'T TELL WHICH ONE IS EUGENE.
WILL WE EVER REALLY KNOW THE MAN CALLED EUGENE?
GOOD EVENING, FELLOW GALS AND GHOULS...
I AM YOUR GHOSTLY HOST AND FRIENDLY TICKET TERRORRR, NESCO...
'RAY!
CLAP CLAP!
MY FAITHFUL ASSISTANT E-GORE HAS BEEN STRICKEN WITH A DECAPITATING VIRUS...
BETTER KNOWN AS CLEAVER FEVERRR...
HO HO!
JUST THE SAME, WELCOME OLD FRIENDS... NEW FRIENDS...
EVEN THOSE WHO ARE FROM TOWN BUT WHO HAVE BEEN AWAY, WELCOME HOME AND...
HERE HERE!
...PLEASE ENJOY THE PICTURE...
CLAP CLAP!
CLAP CLAP!
CLAP CLAP!
HOW'S YOUR WINE?
NORMALLY I'D SAY IT TASTES LIKE THUNDERBIRD BUT ON THIS OCCASION I'M GONNA SAY LAFITE ROTHSCHILD...
MY GOD, WHY DID WE EVER BREAK UP?
Bungholio PICTURES
XAIME 2014
12.

FRITZ.
DAUGHTERS AND MOTHERS AND DAUGHTERS
FRITZ.
< YOUR FATHER'S SILLY NAME FOR YOU.
< YOU'RE ROSALBA, JUST LIKE YOUR GRANDMOTHER.>
FRITZ...
< LET'S WATCH ME IN A MOVIE WITH PING PONG.
< I WAS IN TWO MOVIES WITH HIM.>
< I'M IN THIS MOVIE A LITTLE MORE THAN THE OTHER ONE.
< I NEVER TOLD ANYBODY I WAS IN MOVIES.
< WHAT FOR?>
PING PONG
NI DE AQUI, NI DE ALLÁ
CON
· DIANA SANDOVAL · PETRONIO MAGAÑA · MARIA RODRIGUEZ ·

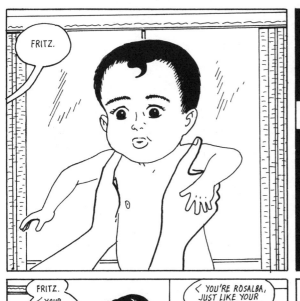

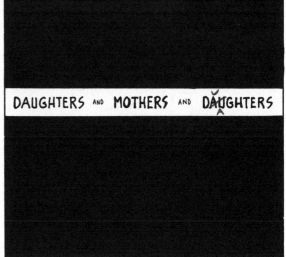

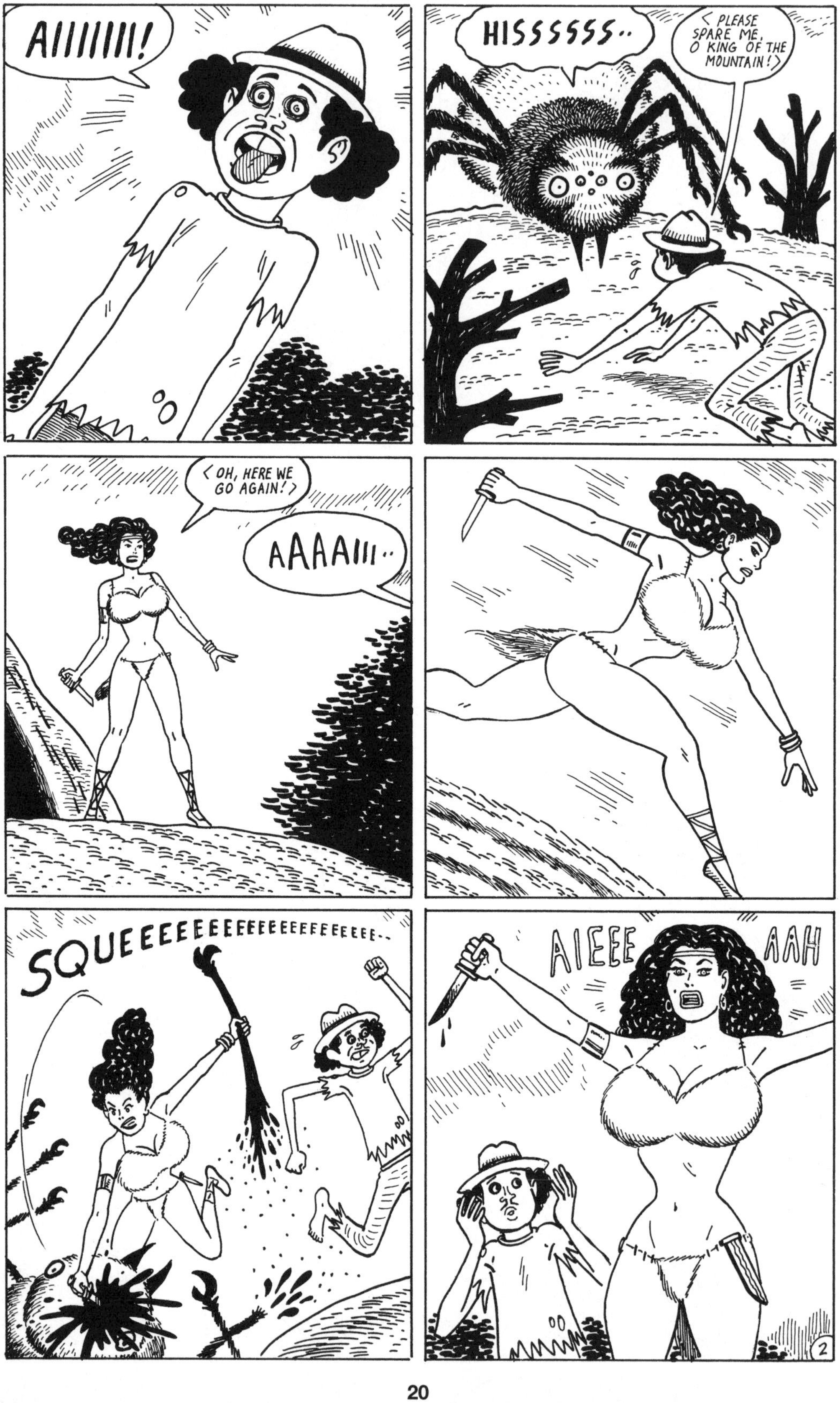
AIIIIIII!
HISSSSSS..
< PLEASE SPARE ME, O KING OF THE MOUNTAIN! >
< OH, HERE WE GO AGAIN! >
AAAAIII..
SQUEEEEEEEEEEEEEEEEEEEEEEE--
AIEEE AAH
2

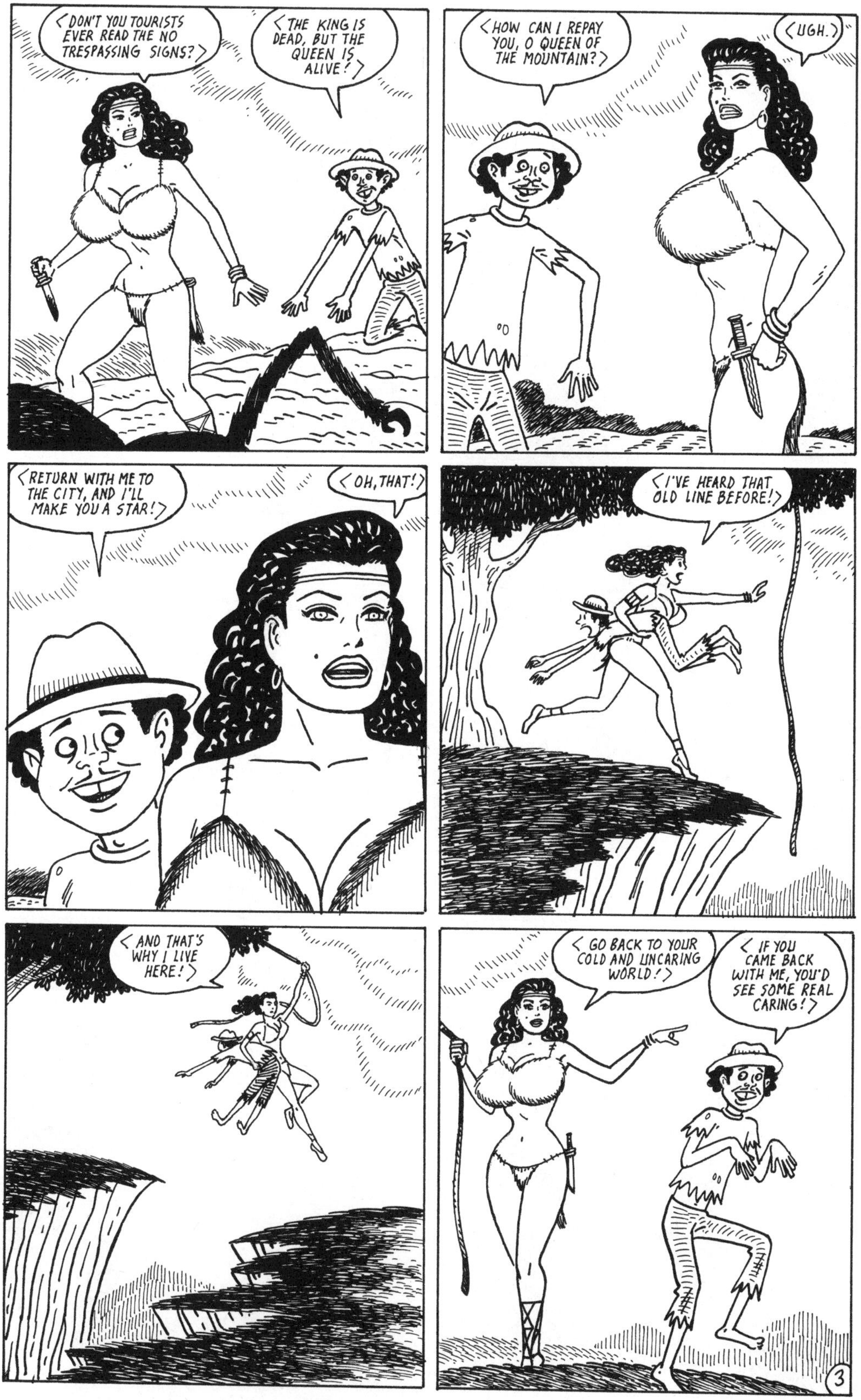
< DON'T YOU TOURISTS EVER READ THE NO TRESPASSING SIGNS? >
< THE KING IS DEAD, BUT THE QUEEN IS ALIVE! >
< HOW CAN I REPAY YOU, O QUEEN OF THE MOUNTAIN? >
< UGH. >
< RETURN WITH ME TO THE CITY, AND I'LL MAKE YOU A STAR! >
< OH, THAT! >
< I'VE HEARD THAT OLD LINE BEFORE! >
< AND THAT'S WHY I LIVE HERE! >
< GO BACK TO YOUR COLD AND UNCARING WORLD! >
< IF YOU CAME BACK WITH ME, YOU'D SEE SOME REAL CARING! >
3

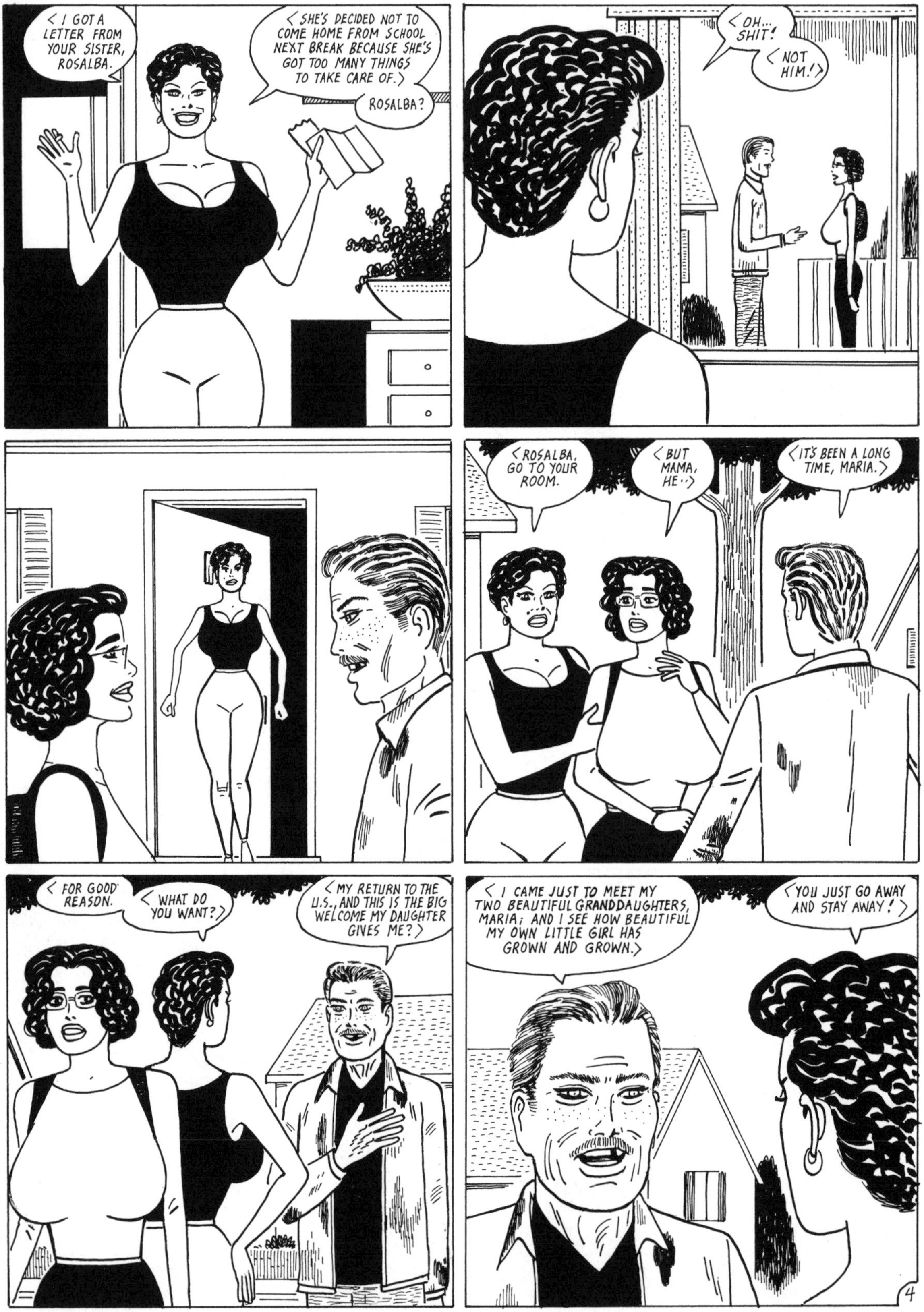

< I GOT A LETTER FROM YOUR SISTER, ROSALBA.
< SHE'S DECIDED NOT TO COME HOME FROM SCHOOL NEXT BREAK BECAUSE SHE'S GOT TOO MANY THINGS TO TAKE CARE OF. >
ROSALBA?
< OH... SHIT!
< NOT HIM! >
< ROSALBA, GO TO YOUR ROOM.
< BUT MAMA, HE··>
< IT'S BEEN A LONG TIME, MARIA. >
< FOR GOOD REASON.
< WHAT DO YOU WANT? >
< MY RETURN TO THE U.S., AND THIS IS THE BIG WELCOME MY DAUGHTER GIVES ME? >
< I CAME JUST TO MEET MY TWO BEAUTIFUL GRANDDAUGHTERS, MARIA; AND I SEE HOW BEAUTIFUL MY OWN LITTLE GIRL HAS GROWN AND GROWN. >
< YOU JUST GO AWAY AND STAY AWAY! >
4

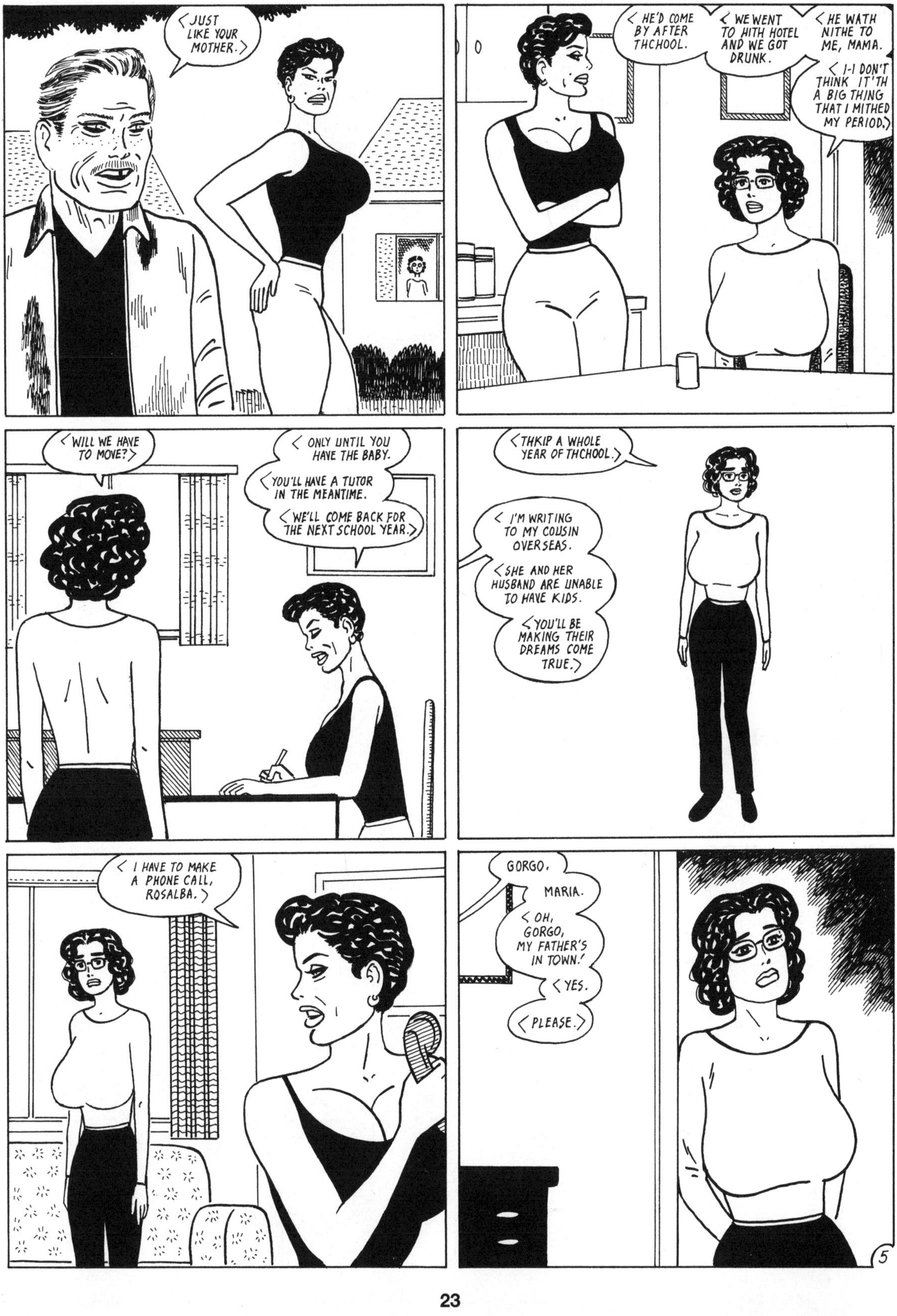
< JUST LIKE YOUR MOTHER. >
< HE'D COME BY AFTER THCHOOL.
< WE WENT TO HITH HOTEL AND WE GOT DRUNK.
< HE WATH NITHE TO ME, MAMA.
< I-I DON'T THINK IT'TH A BIG THING THAT I MITHED MY PERIOD. >
< WILL WE HAVE TO MOVE? >
< ONLY UNTIL YOU HAVE THE BABY.
< YOU'LL HAVE A TUTOR IN THE MEANTIME.
< WE'LL COME BACK FOR THE NEXT SCHOOL YEAR. >
< THKIP A WHOLE YEAR OF THCHOOL. >
< I'M WRITING TO MY COUSIN OVERSEAS.
< SHE AND HER HUSBAND ARE UNABLE TO HAVE KIDS.
< YOU'LL BE MAKING THEIR DREAMS COME TRUE. >
< I HAVE TO MAKE A PHONE CALL, ROSALBA. >
GORGO.
MARIA.
< OH, GORGO, MY FATHER'S IN TOWN.'
< YES.
< PLEASE. >
5

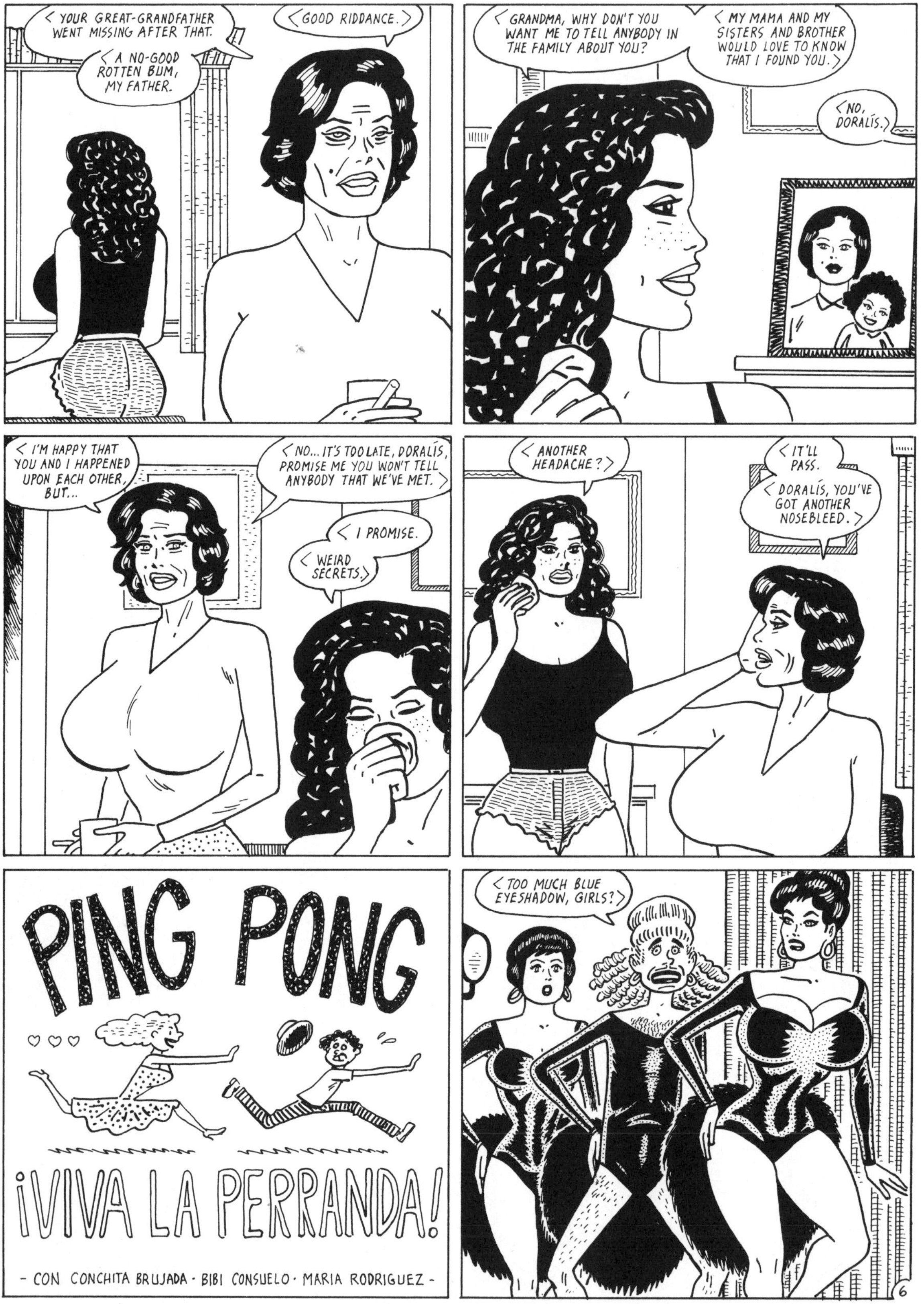

< YOUR GREAT-GRANDFATHER WENT MISSING AFTER THAT.
< A NO-GOOD ROTTEN BUM, MY FATHER.
< GOOD RIDDANCE. >
< GRANDMA, WHY DON'T YOU WANT ME TO TELL ANYBODY IN THE FAMILY ABOUT YOU?
< MY MAMA AND MY SISTERS AND BROTHER WOULD LOVE TO KNOW THAT I FOUND YOU. >
< NO, DORALÍS. >
< I'M HAPPY THAT YOU AND I HAPPENED UPON EACH OTHER, BUT...
< NO... IT'S TOO LATE, DORALÍS, PROMISE ME YOU WON'T TELL ANYBODY THAT WE'VE MET. >
< I PROMISE.
< WEIRD SECRETS. >
< ANOTHER HEADACHE? >
< IT'LL PASS.
< DORALÍS, YOU'VE GOT ANOTHER NOSEBLEED. >
PING PONG
¡VIVA LA PERRANDA!
- CON CONCHITA BRUJADA · BIBI CONSUELO · MARIA RODRIGUEZ -
< TOO MUCH BLUE EYESHADOW, GIRLS? >
6

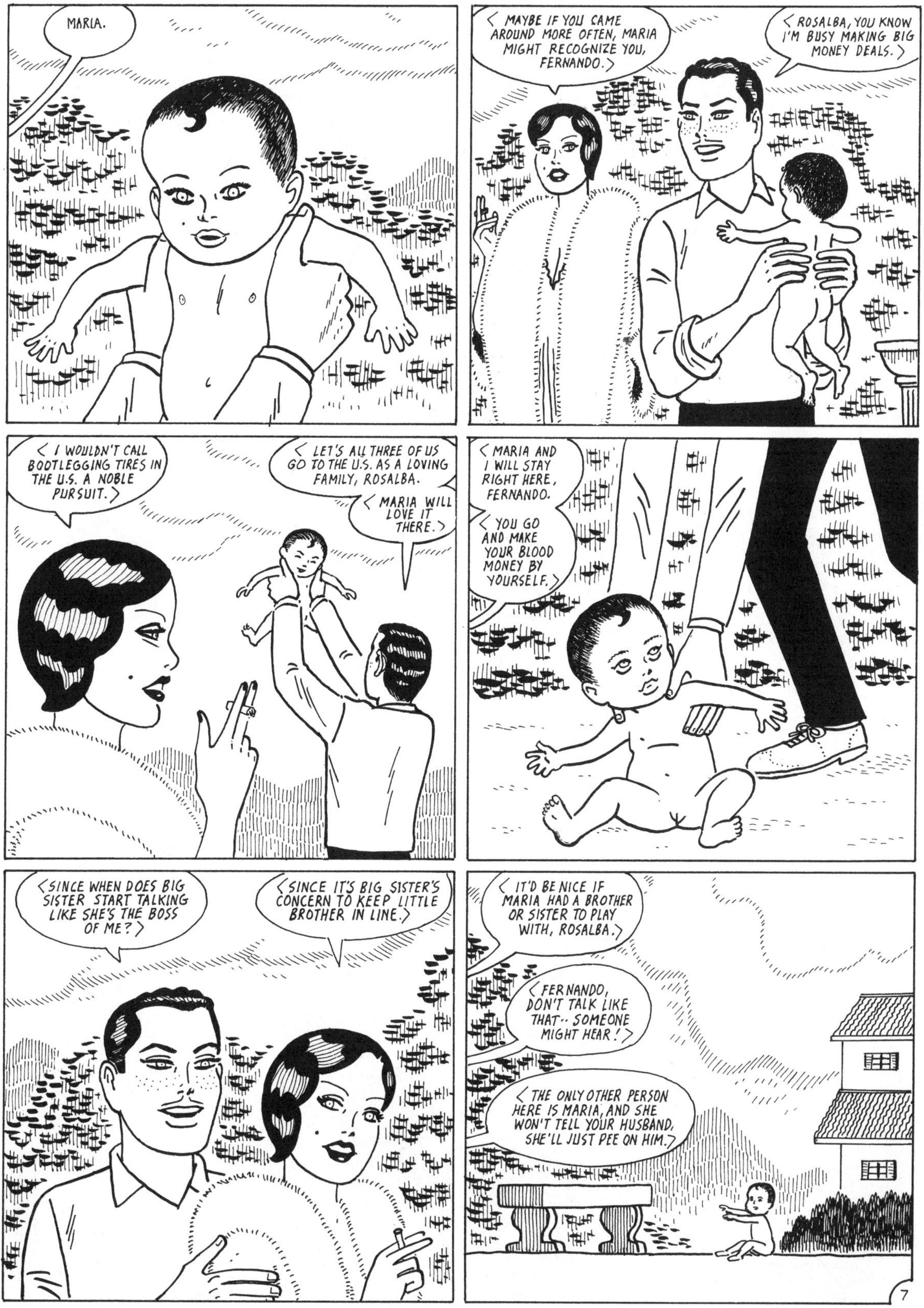
MARIA.
< MAYBE IF YOU CAME AROUND MORE OFTEN, MARIA MIGHT RECOGNIZE YOU, FERNANDO. >
< ROSALBA, YOU KNOW I'M BUSY MAKING BIG MONEY DEALS. >
< I WOULDN'T CALL BOOTLEGGING TIRES IN THE U.S. A NOBLE PURSUIT. >
< LET'S ALL THREE OF US GO TO THE U.S. AS A LOVING FAMILY, ROSALBA. >
< MARIA WILL LOVE IT THERE. >
< MARIA AND I WILL STAY RIGHT HERE, FERNANDO.
< YOU GO AND MAKE YOUR BLOOD MONEY BY YOURSELF. >
<SINCE WHEN DOES BIG SISTER START TALKING LIKE SHE'S THE BOSS OF ME? >
<SINCE IT'S BIG SISTER'S CONCERN TO KEEP LITTLE BROTHER IN LINE. >
< IT'D BE NICE IF MARIA HAD A BROTHER OR SISTER TO PLAY WITH, ROSALBA. >
< FERNANDO, DON'T TALK LIKE THAT.. SOMEONE MIGHT HEAR! >
< THE ONLY OTHER PERSON HERE IS MARIA, AND SHE WON'T TELL YOUR HUSBAND. SHE'LL JUST PEE ON HIM. >
7

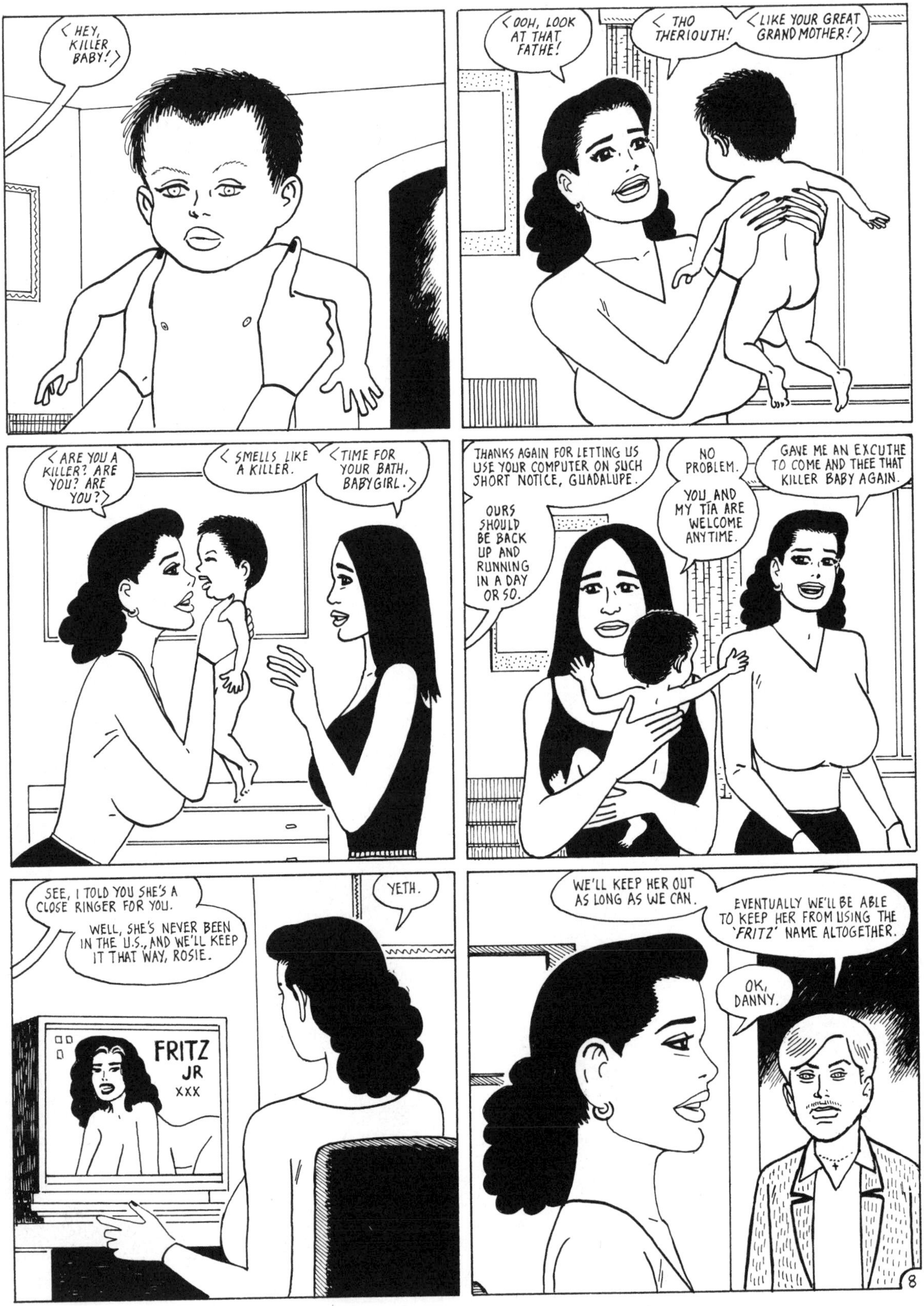

< HEY, KILLER BABY! >
< OOH, LOOK AT THAT FATHE!
< THO THERIOUTH!
< LIKE YOUR GREAT GRANDMOTHER! >
< ARE YOU A KILLER? ARE YOU? ARE YOU? >
< SMELLS LIKE A KILLER.
< TIME FOR YOUR BATH, BABYGIRL. >
THANKS AGAIN FOR LETTING US USE YOUR COMPUTER ON SUCH SHORT NOTICE, GUADALUPE.
OURS SHOULD BE BACK UP AND RUNNING IN A DAY OR SO.
NO PROBLEM.
YOU AND MY TÍA ARE WELCOME ANYTIME.
GAVE ME AN EXCUTHE TO COME AND THEE THAT KILLER BABY AGAIN.
SEE, I TOLD YOU SHE'S A CLOSE RINGER FOR YOU.
WELL, SHE'S NEVER BEEN IN THE U.S., AND WE'LL KEEP IT THAT WAY, ROSIE.
YETH.
FRITZ
JR
XXX
WE'LL KEEP HER OUT AS LONG AS WE CAN.
EVENTUALLY WE'LL BE ABLE TO KEEP HER FROM USING THE 'FRITZ' NAME ALTOGETHER.
OK, DANNY.
8

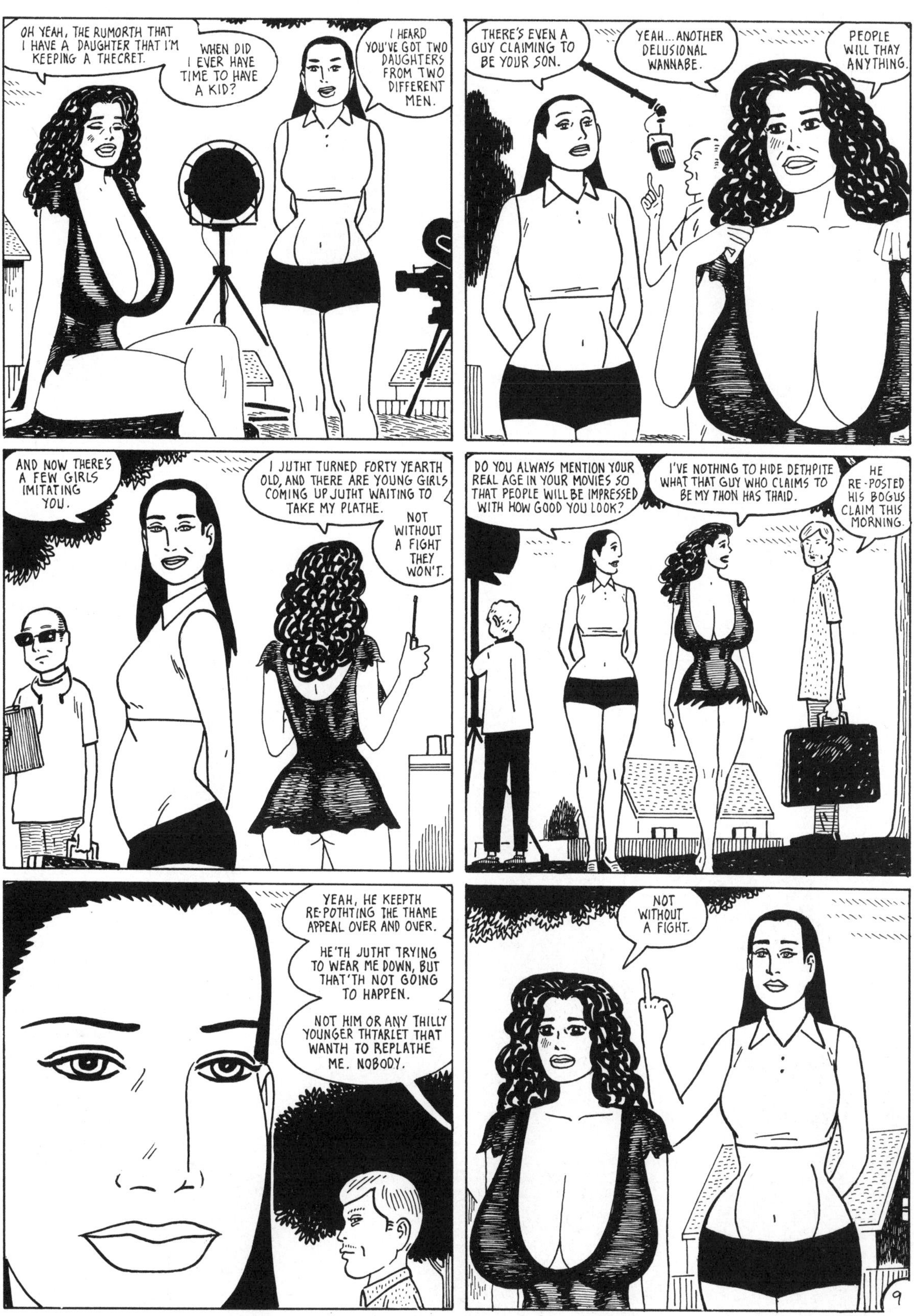
OH YEAH, THE RUMORTH THAT I HAVE A DAUGHTER THAT I'M KEEPING A THECRET.
WHEN DID I EVER HAVE TIME TO HAVE A KID?
I HEARD YOU'VE GOT TWO DAUGHTERS FROM TWO DIFFERENT MEN.
THERE'S EVEN A GUY CLAIMING TO BE YOUR SON.
YEAH... ANOTHER DELUSIONAL WANNABE.
PEOPLE WILL THAY ANYTHING.
AND NOW THERE'S A FEW GIRLS IMITATING YOU.
I JUTHT TURNED FORTY YEARTH OLD, AND THERE ARE YOUNG GIRLS COMING UP JUTHT WAITING TO TAKE MY PLATHE.
NOT WITHOUT A FIGHT THEY WON'T.
DO YOU ALWAYS MENTION YOUR REAL AGE IN YOUR MOVIES SO THAT PEOPLE WILL BE IMPRESSED WITH HOW GOOD YOU LOOK?
I'VE NOTHING TO HIDE DETHPITE WHAT THAT GUY WHO CLAIMS TO BE MY THON HAS THAID.
HE RE-POSTED HIS BOGUS CLAIM THIS MORNING.
YEAH, HE KEEPTH RE-POTHTING THE THAME APPEAL OVER AND OVER.
HE'TH JUTHT TRYING TO WEAR ME DOWN, BUT THAT'TH NOT GOING TO HAPPEN.
NOT HIM OR ANY THILLY YOUNGER THTARLET THAT WANTH TO REPLATHE ME. NOBODY.
NOT WITHOUT A FIGHT.
9

YOU'VE MADE MORE THAN A FEW FACES, AND SOME HAVE EVEN CAUSED YOU GRIEF.

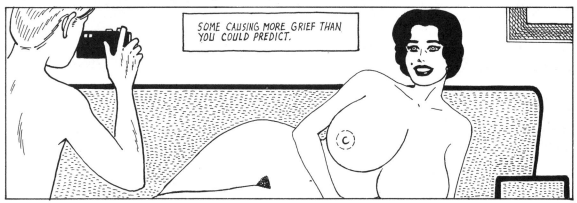

SOME CAUSING MORE GRIEF THAN YOU COULD PREDICT.

OTHER FACES ENDEARING YOU TO SO MANY.

BUT THE HURT CAN DARKEN THE LIGHT OF LOVE, HOWEVER TRUE AND BRILLIANT THE LOVE IS.

AS MINE ENDURES FOR YOU ALL.

The End

YOU AND HOPEY

YOU AND HOPEY. DID SHE REALLY SAY THAT? THAT'S WHAT IT SOUNDED LIKE. YOU AND HOPEY. YOU AND HOPEY BOTH LIKE ME TO KEEP MY UNDERWEAR ON WHEN WE START TO JIG. YOU AND HOPEY. WHAT DO YOU MEAN YOU AND HOPEY?

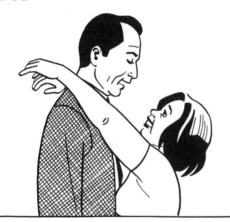

OK, SO SHE WAS TALKING ABOUT HOPEY IN THE PAST. SHE STILL SAID IT, LIKE IT'S STILL HERE IN THE PRESENT AND SHE SAID IT ONE HOUR BEFORE THE TWO OF THEM ARE OFF ON A TWO-DAY TRIP TOGETHER.

INSTEAD OF CALLING HER OUT ON IT I JUST LET HER WISH ME LUCK WITH MY INTERVIEW AND I WAS ON MY WAY. NO SENSE IN PUTTING A DAMPER ON HER WEEKEND EVEN IF MINE WAS ALREADY DAMP AS THE DEW.

AND WHAT'S THIS SHIT ABOUT A THIRD INTERVIEW? WHO HAS A THIRD INTERVIEW FOR A LIFE-DRAWING TEACHING POSITION? BUT THEY WERE NICE, I GOT THE JOB AND THEY TOOK ME OUT FOR MARGARITAS. MY DAMPENED SPIRITS WERE MOMENTARILY LIFTED.

I TEXTED MAGGIE THE GOOD NEWS BUT LEFT OUT THE MARGARITAS PART. SHE WORRIES ABOUT ME AND WANTS ME TO LIVE FOREVER SO WE CAN WATCH RERUNS OF OUR LIFE TOGETHER WHEN WE'RE 90. TAKE THAT, YOU AND HOPEY.

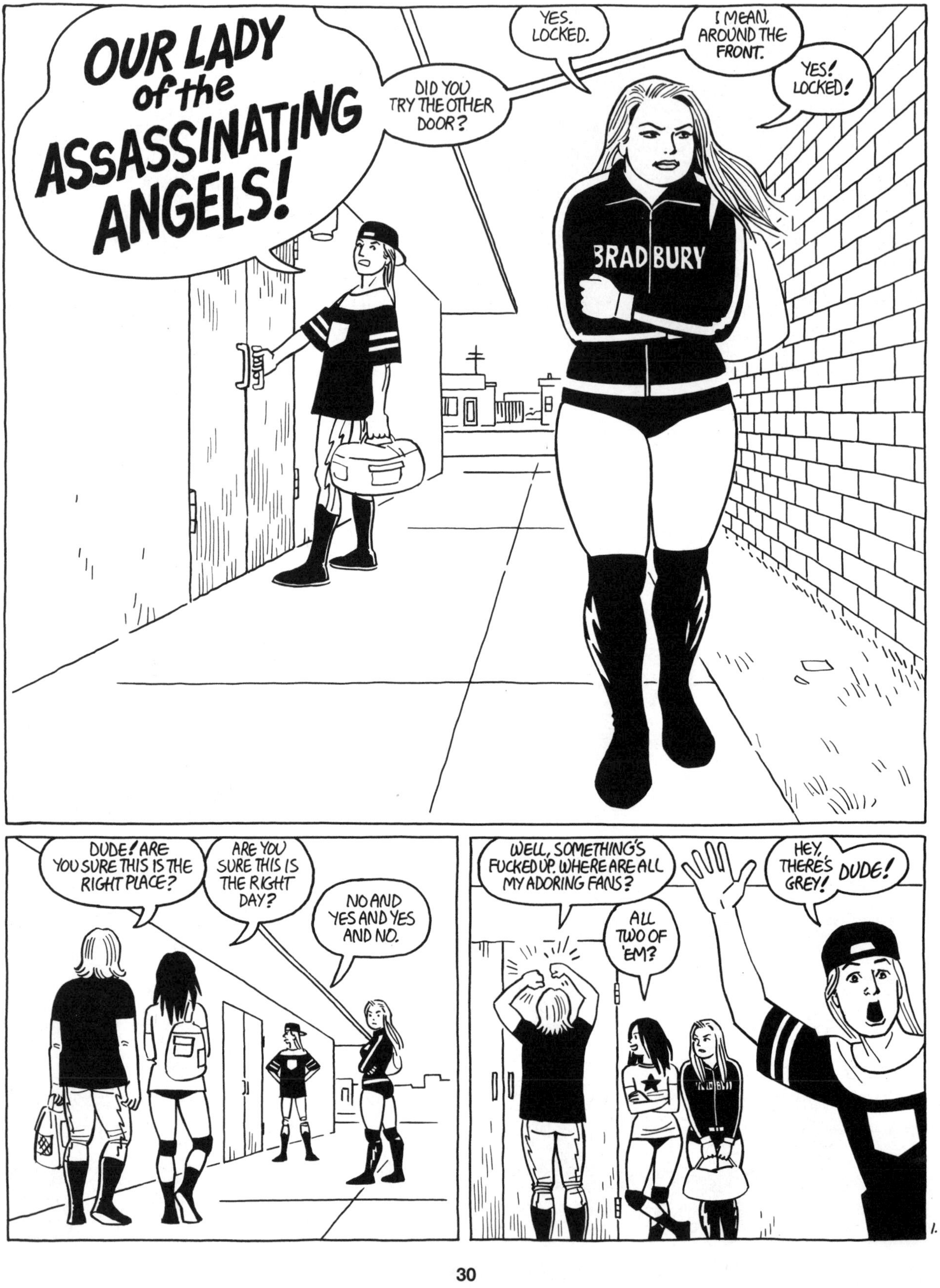
OUR LADY of the ASSASSINATING ANGELS!
DID YOU TRY THE OTHER DOOR?
YES. LOCKED.
I MEAN, AROUND THE FRONT.
YES! LOCKED!
BRADBURY
DUDE! ARE YOU SURE THIS IS THE RIGHT PLACE?
ARE YOU SURE THIS IS THE RIGHT DAY?
NO AND YES AND YES AND NO.
WELL, SOMETHING'S FUCKED UP. WHERE ARE ALL MY ADORING FANS?
ALL TWO OF 'EM?
HEY, THERE'S GREY!
DUDE!
1.

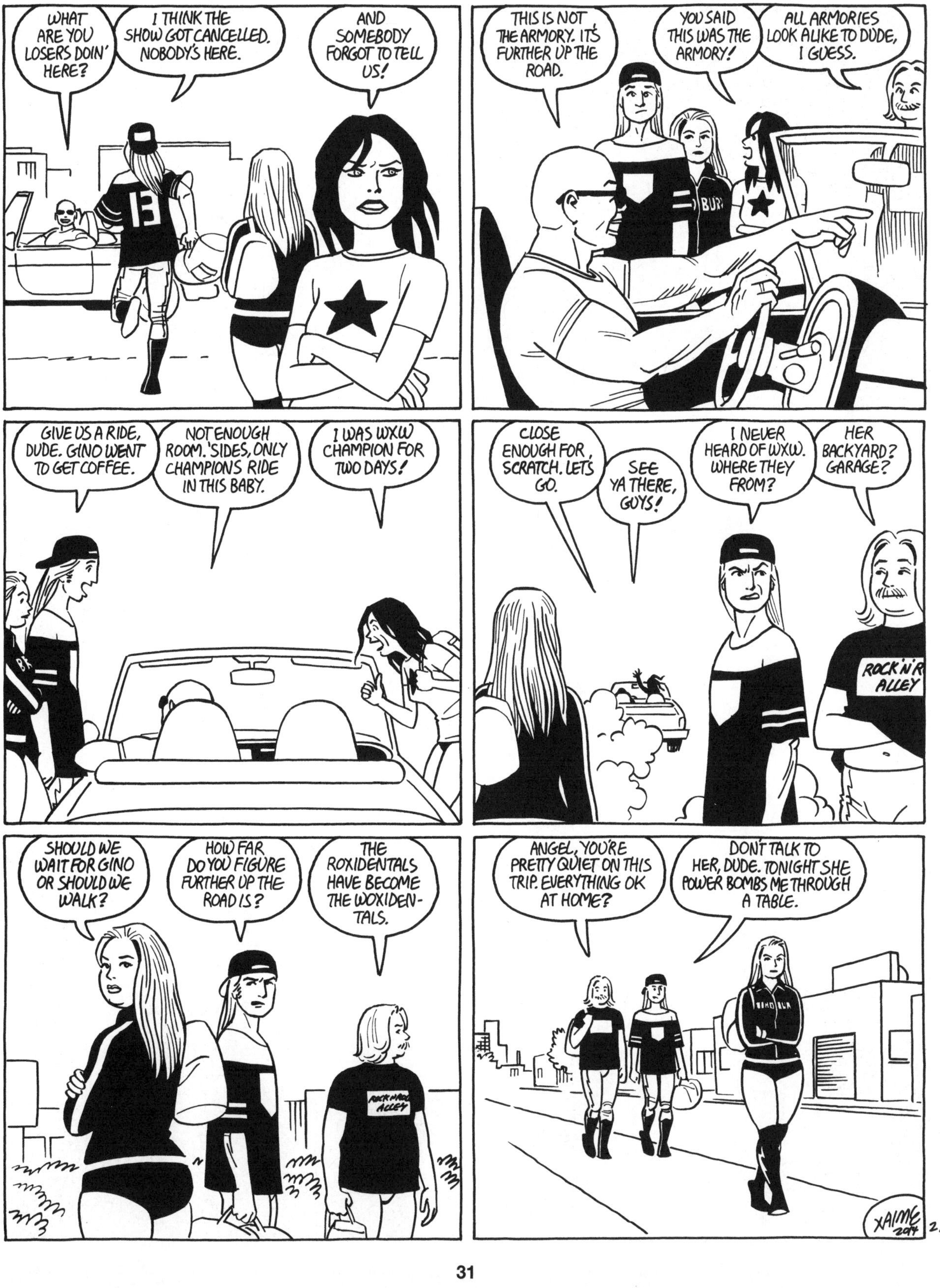
WHAT ARE YOU LOSERS DOIN' HERE?
I THINK THE SHOW GOT CANCELLED. NOBODY'S HERE.
AND SOMEBODY FORGOT TO TELL US!
THIS IS NOT THE ARMORY. IT'S FURTHER UP THE ROAD.
YOU SAID THIS WAS THE ARMORY!
ALL ARMORIES LOOK ALIKE TO DUDE, I GUESS.
GIVE US A RIDE, DUDE. GINO WENT TO GET COFFEE.
NOT ENOUGH ROOM. 'SIDES, ONLY CHAMPIONS RIDE IN THIS BABY.
I WAS WXW CHAMPION FOR TWO DAYS!
CLOSE ENOUGH FOR SCRATCH. LET'S GO.
SEE YA THERE, GUYS!
I NEVER HEARD OF WXW. WHERE THEY FROM?
HER BACKYARD? GARAGE?
ROCK 'N' R ALLEY
SHOULD WE WAIT FOR GINO OR SHOULD WE WALK?
HOW FAR DO YOU FIGURE FURTHER UP THE ROAD IS?
THE ROXIDENTALS HAVE BECOME THE WOXIDENTALS.
ROCK 'N' ROLL ALLEY
ANGEL, YOU'RE PRETTY QUIET ON THIS TRIP. EVERYTHING OK AT HOME?
DON'T TALK TO HER, DUDE. TONIGHT SHE POWER BOMBS ME THROUGH A TABLE.
XAIME 2014
2.

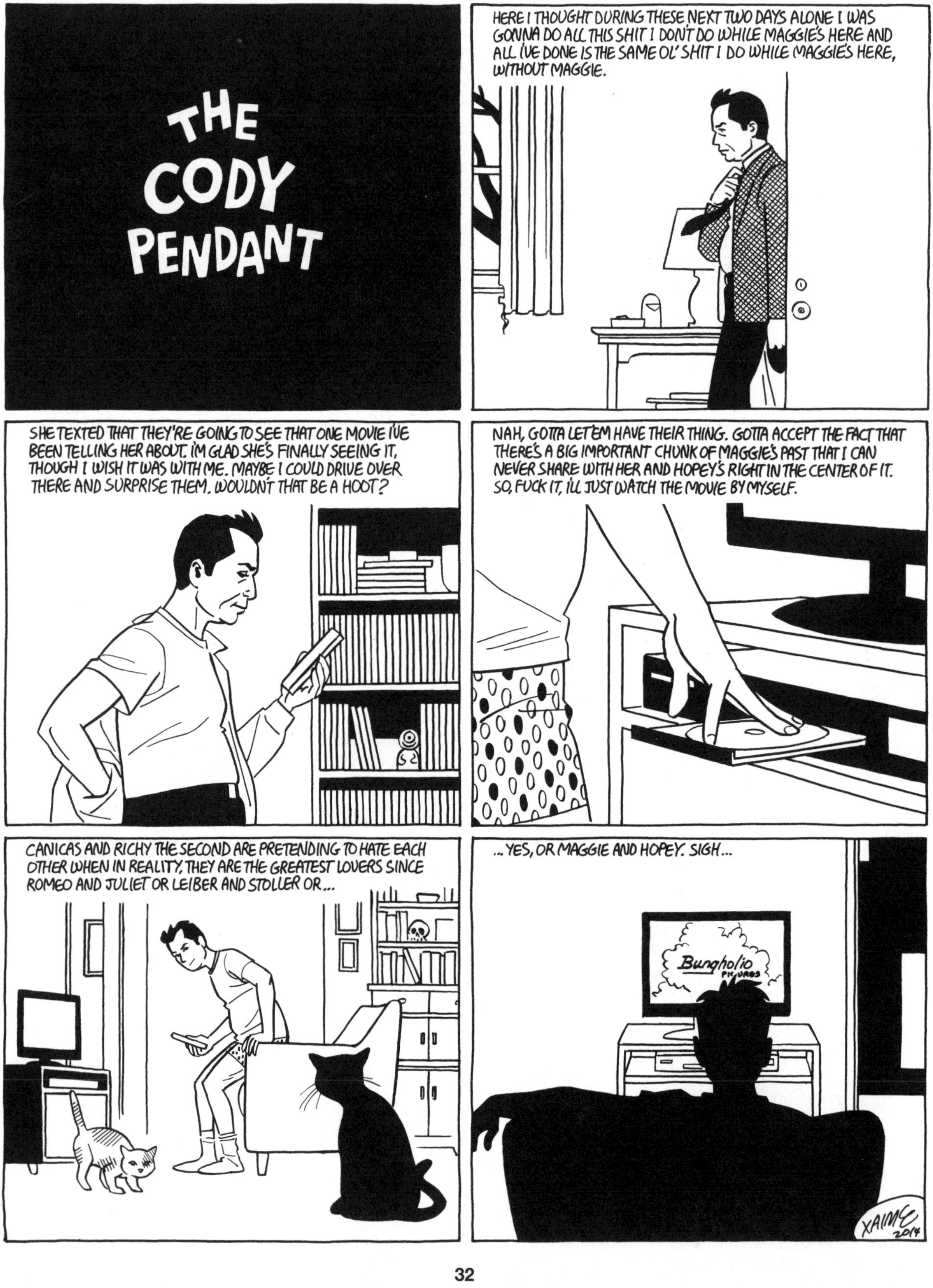
THE CODY PENDANT
HERE I THOUGHT DURING THESE NEXT TWO DAYS ALONE I WAS GONNA DO ALL THIS SHIT I DON'T DO WHILE MAGGIE'S HERE AND ALL I'VE DONE IS THE SAME OL' SHIT I DO WHILE MAGGIE'S HERE, WITHOUT MAGGIE.
SHE TEXTED THAT THEY'RE GOING TO SEE THAT ONE MOVIE I'VE BEEN TELLING HER ABOUT. I'M GLAD SHE'S FINALLY SEEING IT, THOUGH I WISH IT WAS WITH ME. MAYBE I COULD DRIVE OVER THERE AND SURPRISE THEM. WOULDN'T THAT BE A HOOT?
NAH, GOTTA LET'EM HAVE THEIR THING. GOTTA ACCEPT THE FACT THAT THERE'S A BIG IMPORTANT CHUNK OF MAGGIE'S PAST THAT I CAN NEVER SHARE WITH HER AND HOPEY'S RIGHT IN THE CENTER OF IT. SO, FUCK IT, I'LL JUST WATCH THE MOVIE BY MYSELF.
CANICAS AND RICHY THE SECOND ARE PRETENDING TO HATE EACH OTHER WHEN IN REALITY, THEY ARE THE GREATEST LOVERS SINCE ROMEO AND JULIET OR LEIBER AND STOLLER OR...
...YES, OR MAGGIE AND HOPEY. SIGH...
Bungholio PICTURES
XAIME 2014

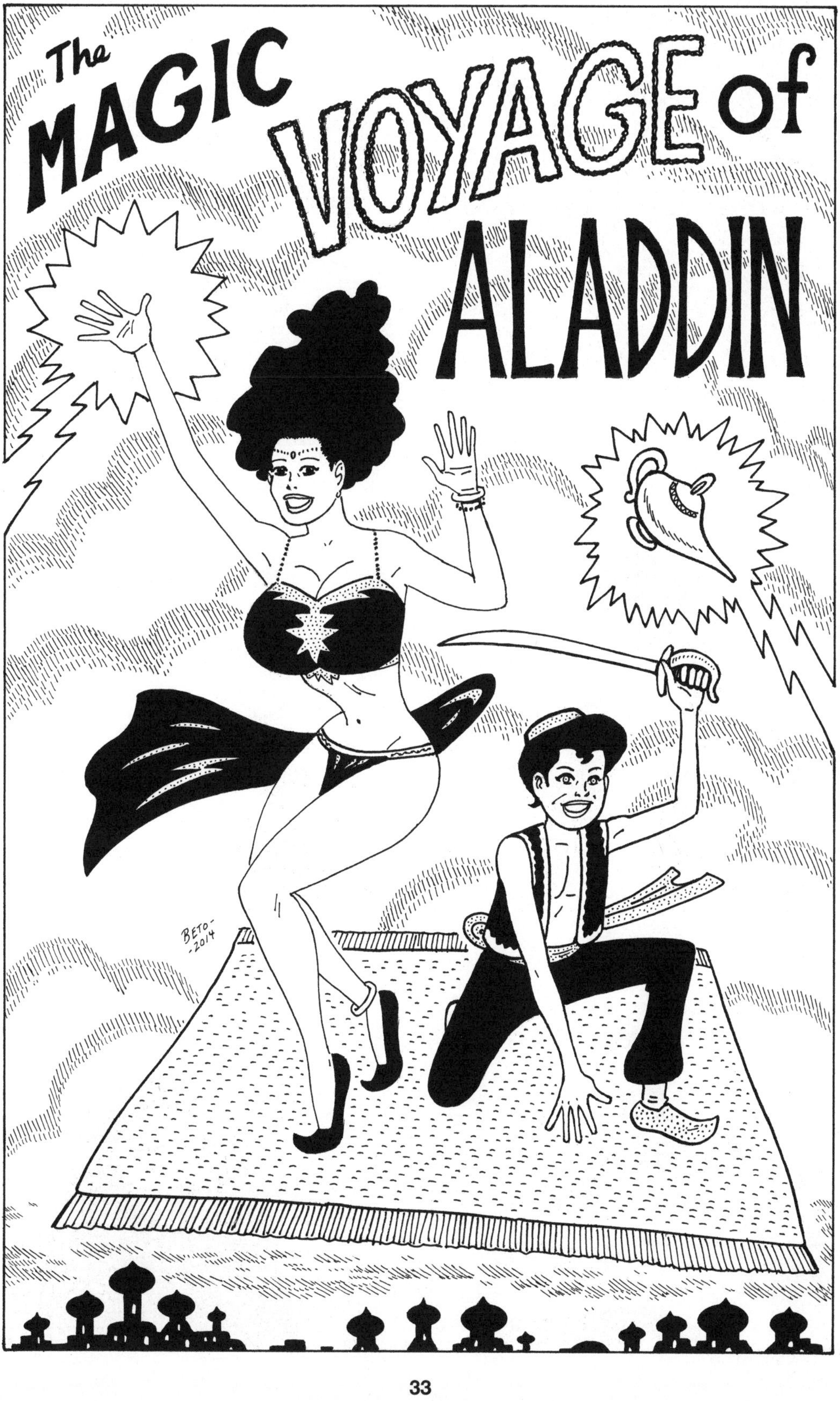
The MAGIC VOYAGE of ALADDIN
BETO -2014

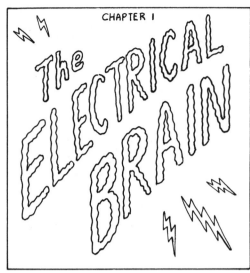

CHAPTER I

The ELECTRICAL BRAIN

FLYING CARPET, COME TO ME!

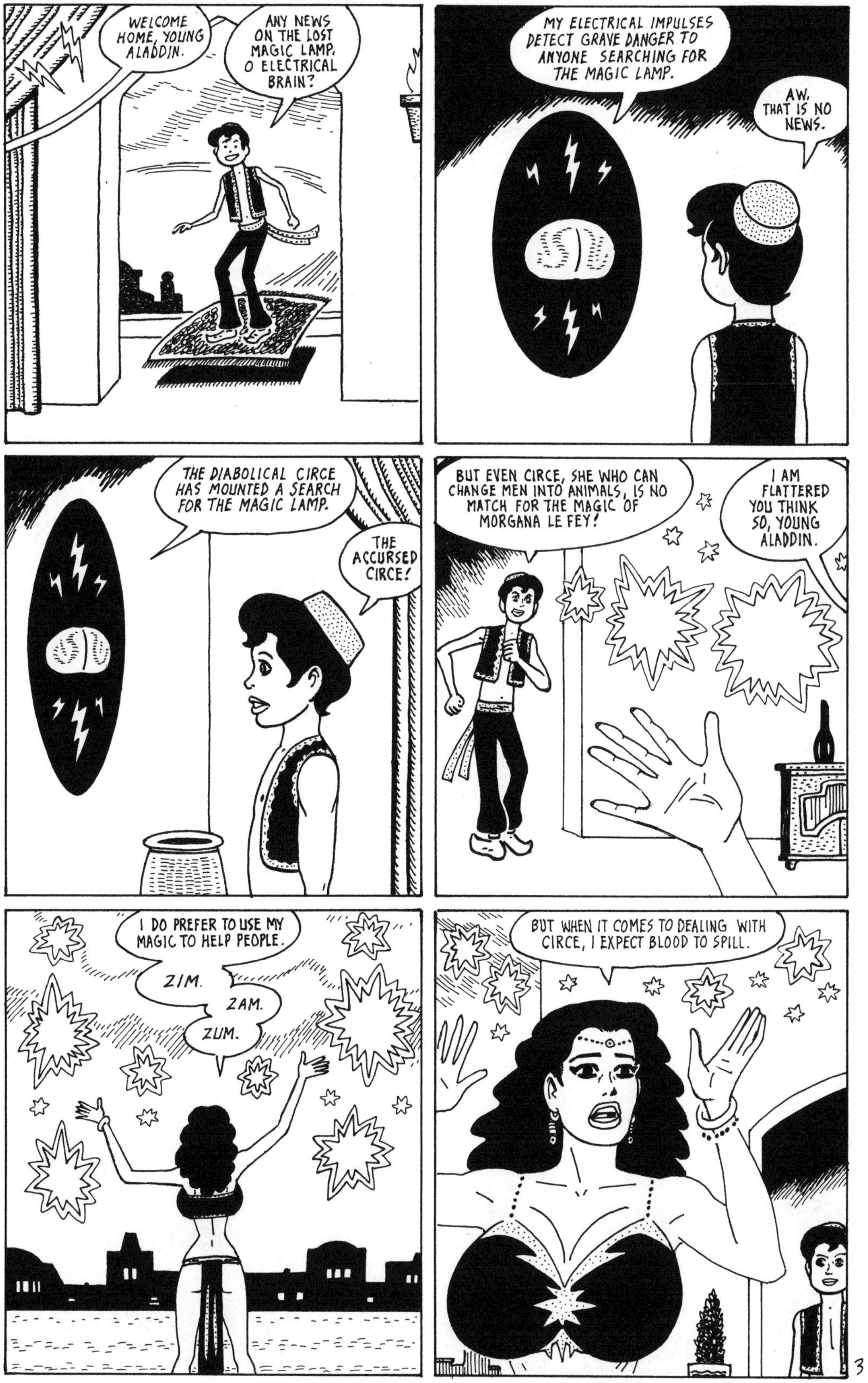
WELCOME HOME, YOUNG ALADDIN.
ANY NEWS ON THE LOST MAGIC LAMP, O ELECTRICAL BRAIN?
MY ELECTRICAL IMPULSES DETECT GRAVE DANGER TO ANYONE SEARCHING FOR THE MAGIC LAMP.
AW, THAT IS NO NEWS.
THE DIABOLICAL CIRCE HAS MOUNTED A SEARCH FOR THE MAGIC LAMP.
THE ACCURSED CIRCE!
BUT EVEN CIRCE, SHE WHO CAN CHANGE MEN INTO ANIMALS, IS NO MATCH FOR THE MAGIC OF MORGANA LE FEY!
I AM FLATTERED YOU THINK SO, YOUNG ALADDIN.
I DO PREFER TO USE MY MAGIC TO HELP PEOPLE.
ZIM.
ZAM.
ZUM.
BUT WHEN IT COMES TO DEALING WITH CIRCE, I EXPECT BLOOD TO SPILL.
3

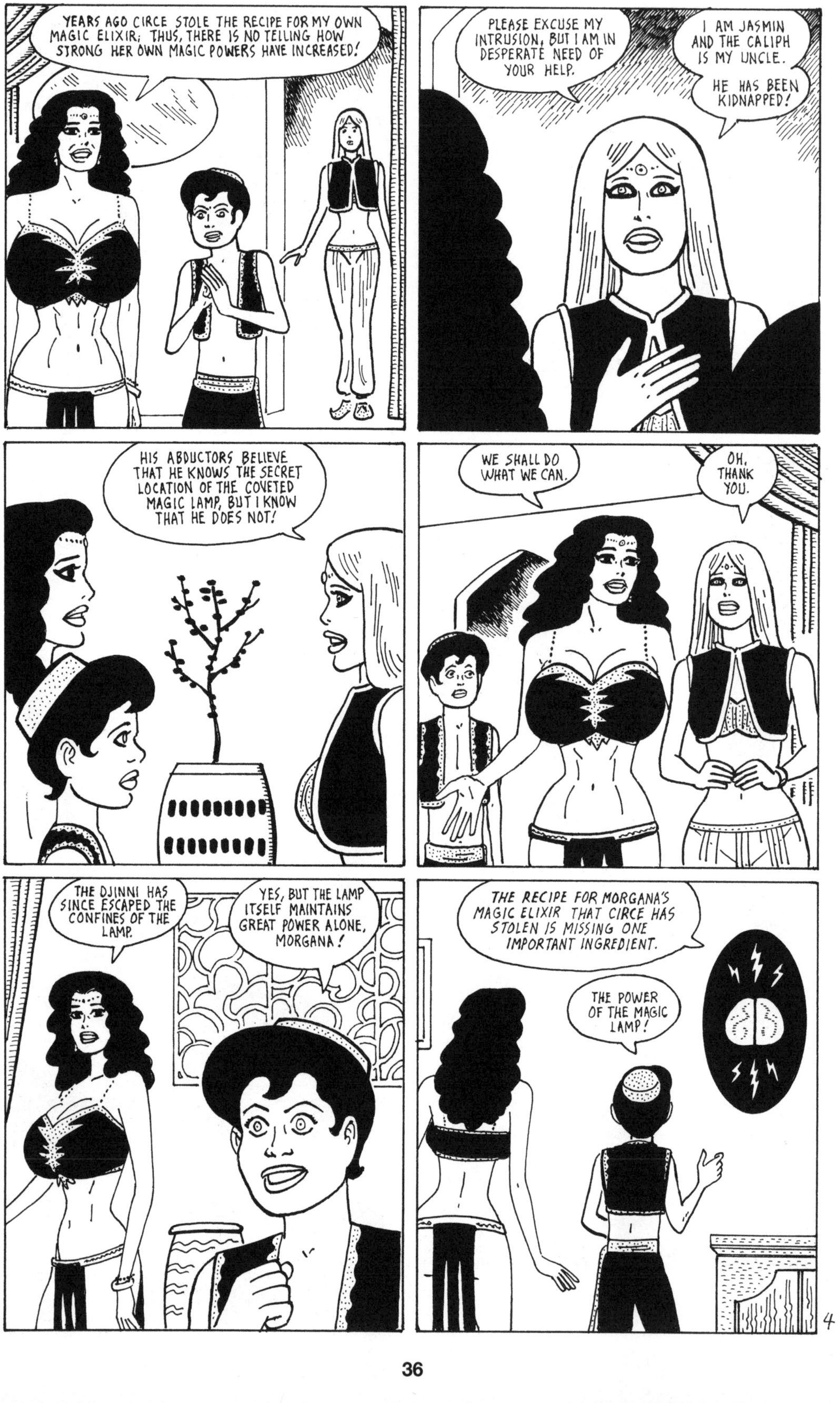
YEARS AGO CIRCE STOLE THE RECIPE FOR MY OWN MAGIC ELIXIR; THUS, THERE IS NO TELLING HOW STRONG HER OWN MAGIC POWERS HAVE INCREASED!
PLEASE EXCUSE MY INTRUSION, BUT I AM IN DESPERATE NEED OF YOUR HELP.
I AM JASMIN AND THE CALIPH IS MY UNCLE.
HE HAS BEEN KIDNAPPED!
HIS ABDUCTORS BELIEVE THAT HE KNOWS THE SECRET LOCATION OF THE COVETED MAGIC LAMP, BUT I KNOW THAT HE DOES NOT!
WE SHALL DO WHAT WE CAN.
OH, THANK YOU.
THE DJINNI HAS SINCE ESCAPED THE CONFINES OF THE LAMP.
YES, BUT THE LAMP ITSELF MAINTAINS GREAT POWER ALONE, MORGANA!
THE RECIPE FOR MORGANA'S MAGIC ELIXIR THAT CIRCE HAS STOLEN IS MISSING ONE IMPORTANT INGREDIENT.
THE POWER OF THE MAGIC LAMP!
4

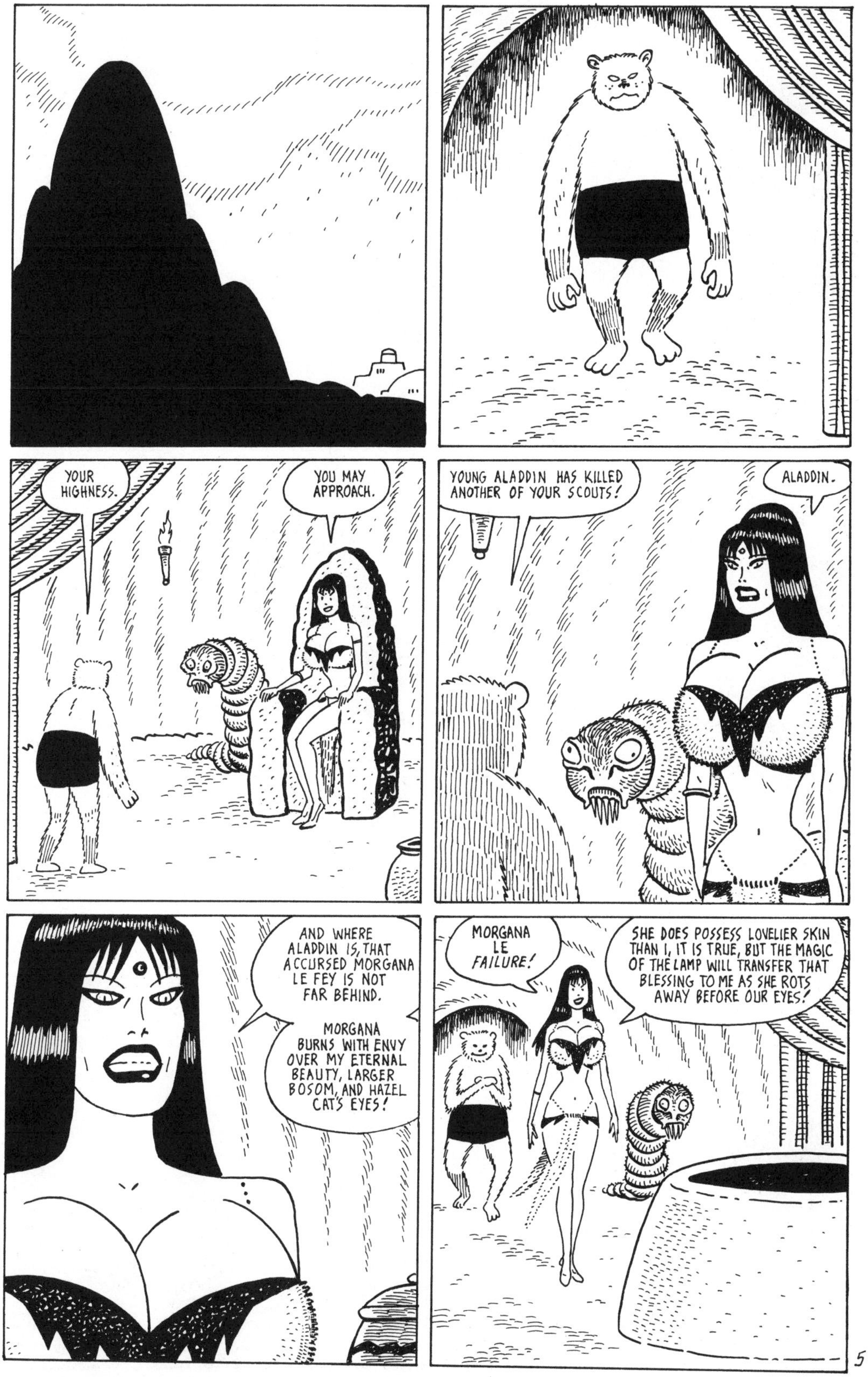
YOUR HIGHNESS.
YOU MAY APPROACH.
YOUNG ALADDIN HAS KILLED ANOTHER OF YOUR SCOUTS!
ALADDIN.
AND WHERE ALADDIN IS, THAT ACCURSED MORGANA LE FEY IS NOT FAR BEHIND.
MORGANA BURNS WITH ENVY OVER MY ETERNAL BEAUTY, LARGER BOSOM, AND HAZEL CAT'S EYES!
MORGANA LE *FAILURE*!
SHE DOES POSSESS LOVELIER SKIN THAN I, IT IS TRUE, BUT THE MAGIC OF THE LAMP WILL TRANSFER THAT BLESSING TO ME AS SHE ROTS AWAY BEFORE OUR EYES!
5

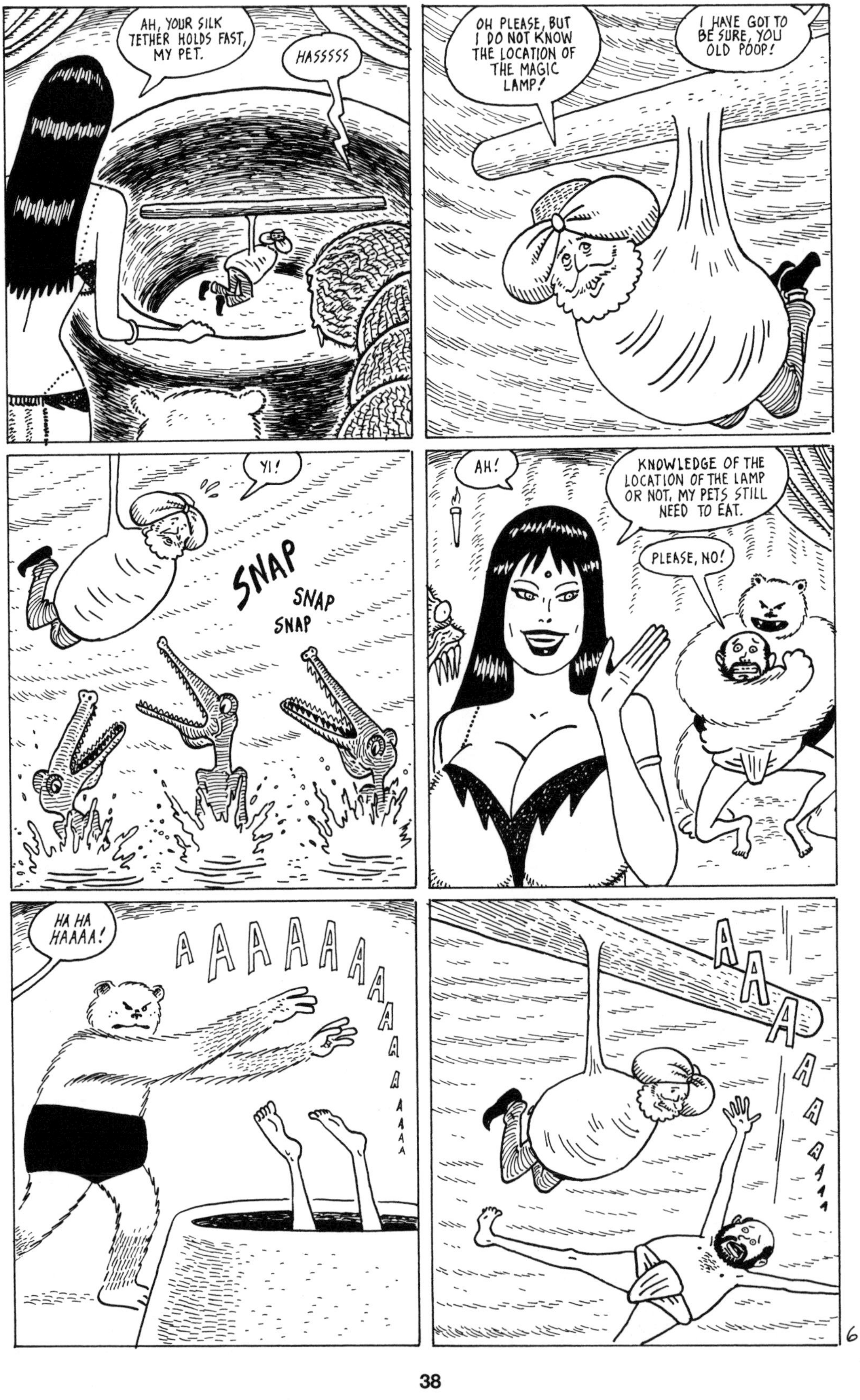
AH, YOUR SILK TETHER HOLDS FAST, MY PET.
HASSSSS
OH PLEASE, BUT I DO NOT KNOW THE LOCATION OF THE MAGIC LAMP!
I HAVE GOT TO BE SURE, YOU OLD POOP!
YI!
SNAP
SNAP
SNAP
AH!
KNOWLEDGE OF THE LOCATION OF THE LAMP OR NOT, MY PETS STILL NEED TO EAT.
PLEASE, NO!
HA HA HAAAA!
AAAAAAAAAAAAAAAA
AAAAAAAAAAA
6

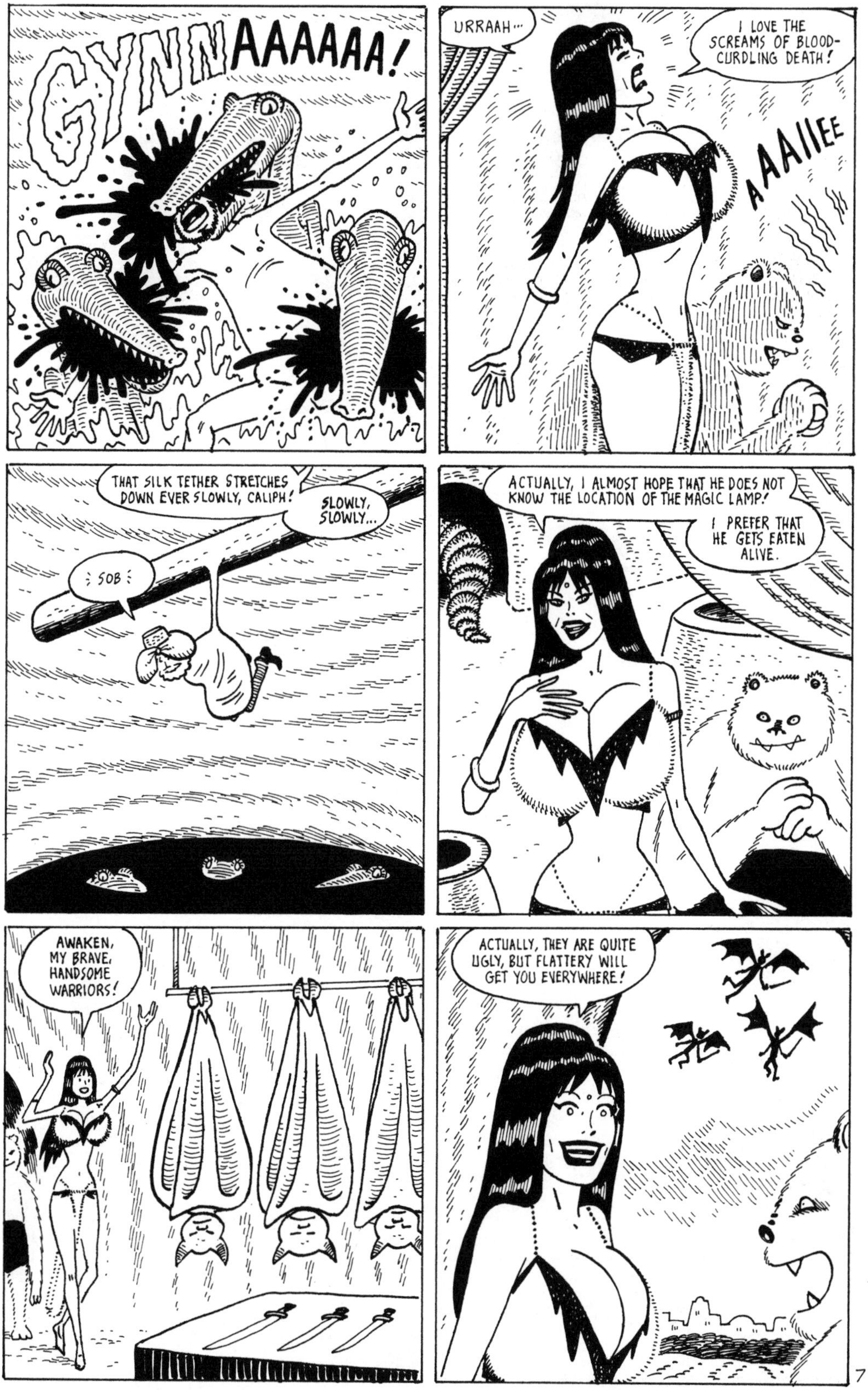
GYNNAAAAAA!
URRAAH...
I LOVE THE SCREAMS OF BLOOD-CURDLING DEATH!
AAAIIEE
THAT SILK TETHER STRETCHES DOWN EVER SLOWLY, CALIPH!
SLOWLY, SLOWLY...
SOB
ACTUALLY, I ALMOST HOPE THAT HE DOES NOT KNOW THE LOCATION OF THE MAGIC LAMP!
I PREFER THAT HE GETS EATEN ALIVE.
AWAKEN, MY BRAVE, HANDSOME WARRIORS!
ACTUALLY, THEY ARE QUITE UGLY, BUT FLATTERY WILL GET YOU EVERYWHERE!
7

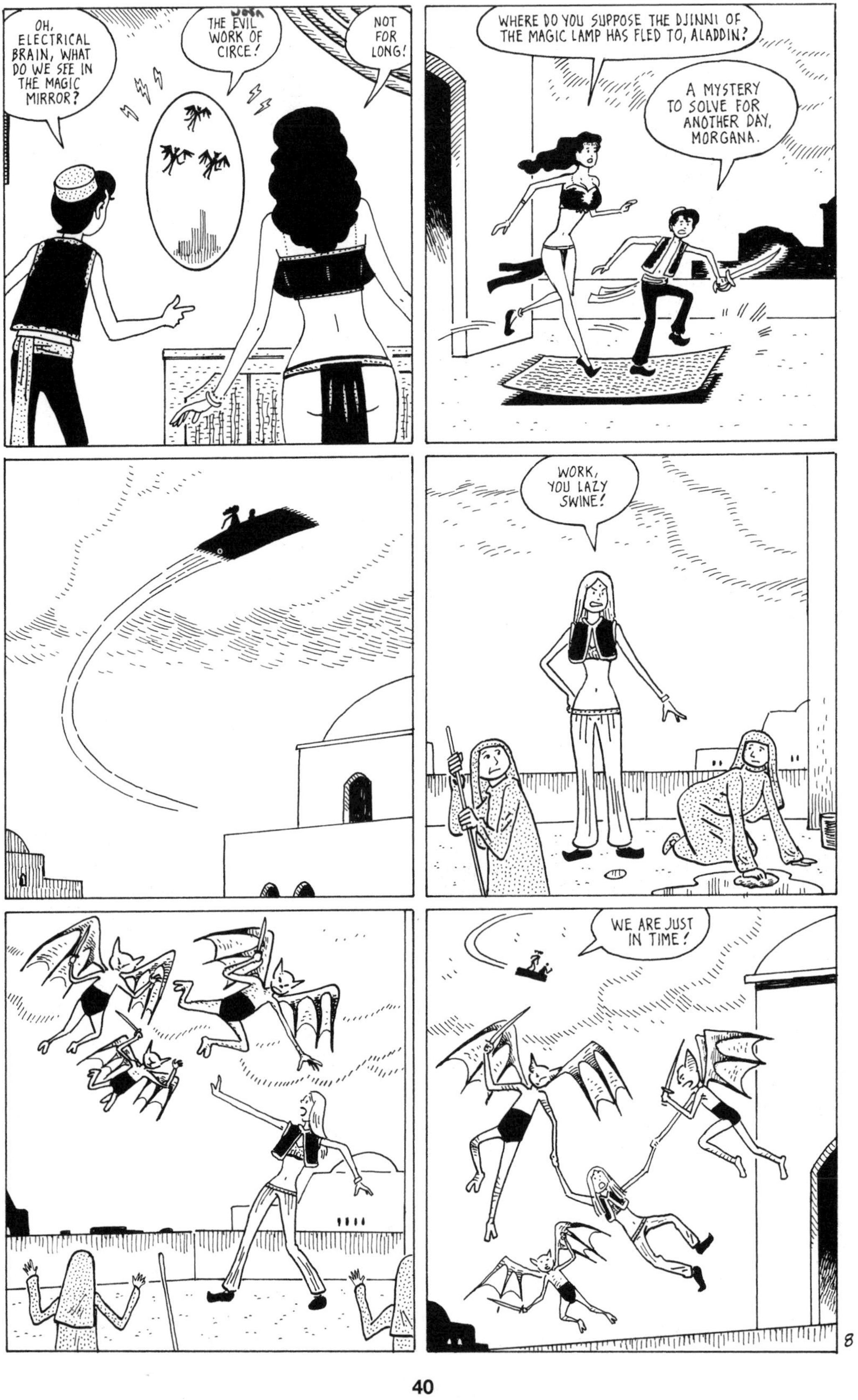
OH, ELECTRICAL BRAIN, WHAT DO WE SEE IN THE MAGIC MIRROR?
THE EVIL WORK OF CIRCE!
NOT FOR LONG!
WHERE DO YOU SUPPOSE THE DJINNI OF THE MAGIC LAMP HAS FLED TO, ALADDIN?
A MYSTERY TO SOLVE FOR ANOTHER DAY, MORGANA.
WORK, YOU LAZY SWINE!
WE ARE JUST IN TIME!
8

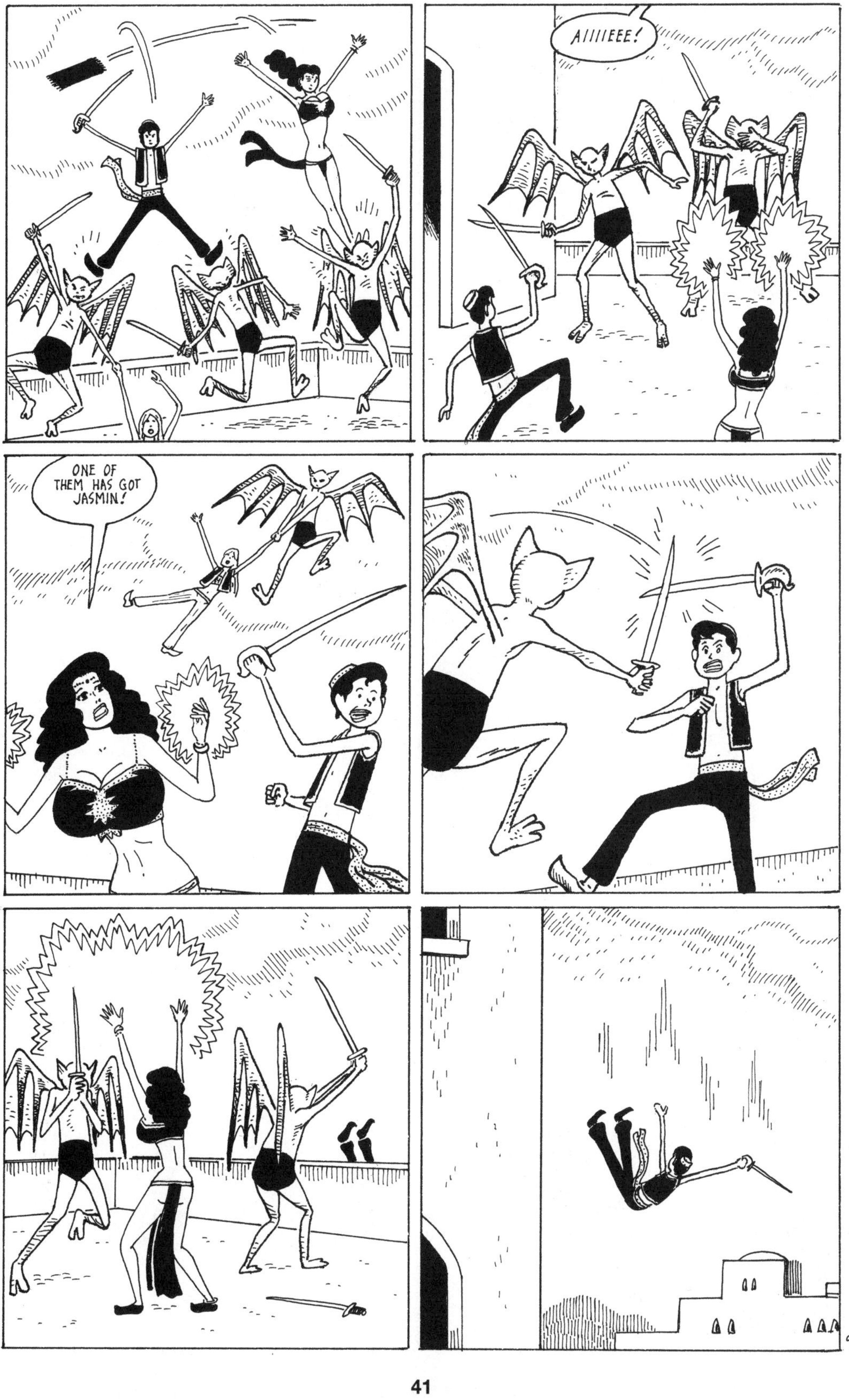
AIIIIEEE!
ONE OF THEM HAS GOT JASMIN!
9

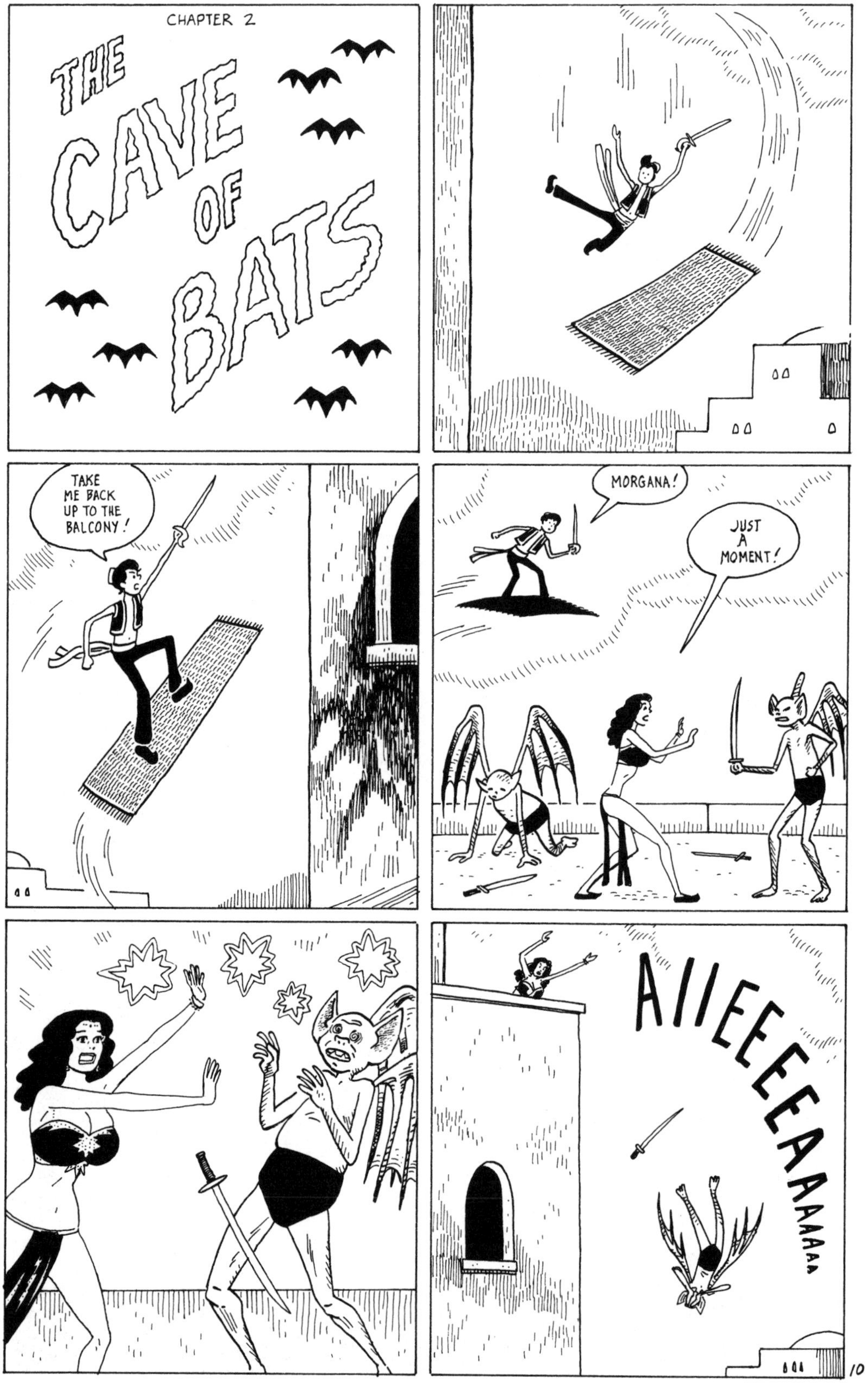
CHAPTER 2
THE CAVE OF BATS
TAKE ME BACK UP TO THE BALCONY!
MORGANA!
JUST A MOMENT!
AIIEEEEAAAAaaa
10

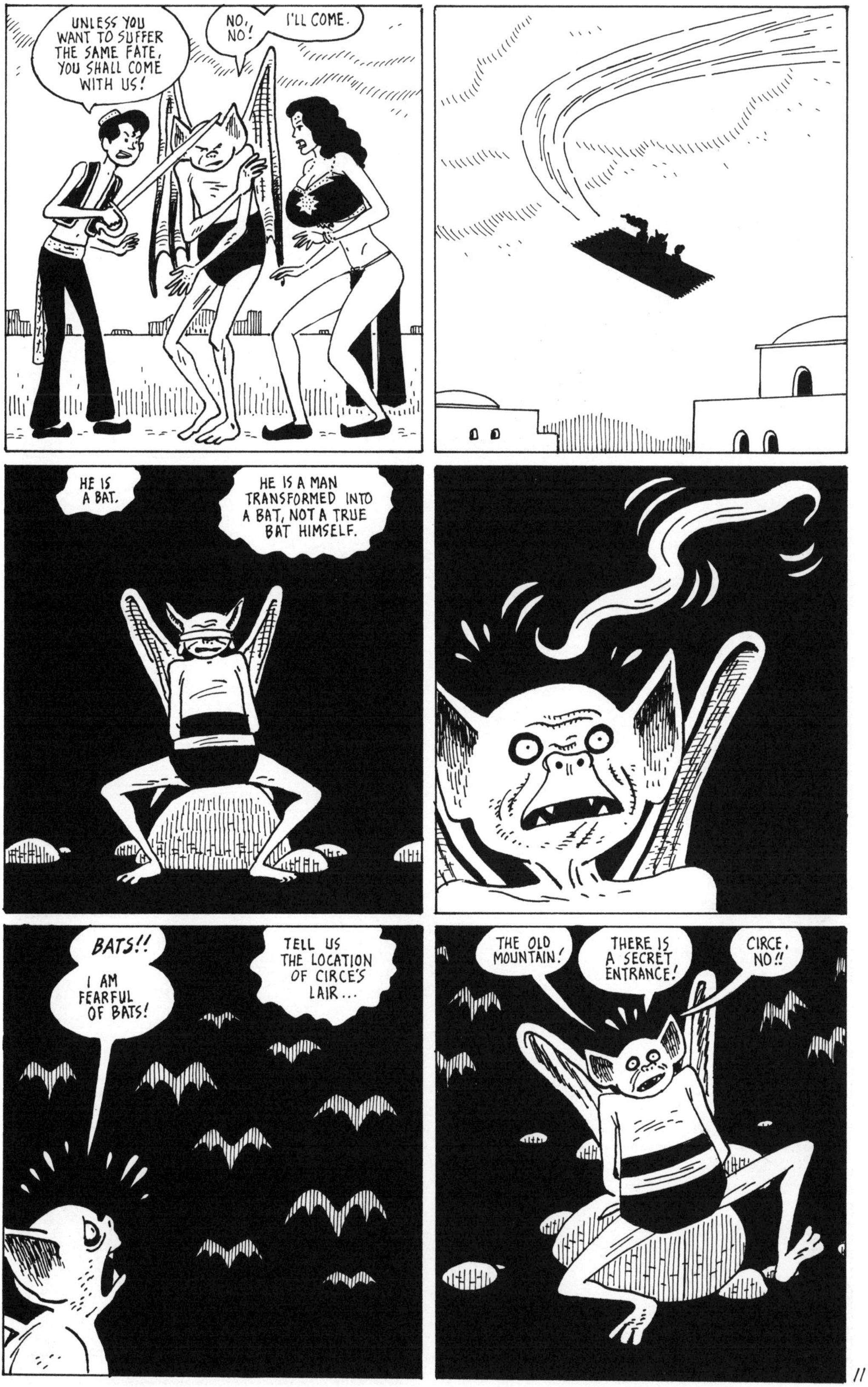
UNLESS YOU WANT TO SUFFER THE SAME FATE, YOU SHALL COME WITH US!
NO, NO!
I'LL COME.
HE IS A BAT.
HE IS A MAN TRANSFORMED INTO A BAT, NOT A TRUE BAT HIMSELF.
BATS!!
I AM FEARFUL OF BATS!
TELL US THE LOCATION OF CIRCE'S LAIR...
THE OLD MOUNTAIN!
THERE IS A SECRET ENTRANCE!
CIRCE, NO!!
11

AAIEEAAOOO
OOOOH, LOST ANOTHER ONE!
TWO IN THE SAME DAY!
AM I SLIPPING?
AHH.
MORGANA'S REJUVENATION ELIXIR.
OH PLEASE, MY UNCLE!
HA!
IF YOUR UNCLE TELLS ME THE LOCATION OF THE MAGIC LAMP, HE CAN GO INSIDE THERE WITH YOU, BRAT!
BUT HE DOESN'T KNOW!
DO YOU WISH THAT YOUR NIECE TRADE PLACES WITH YOU, POPS?
BUT I HAVE NO NIECE!
OH, LISTEN TO HOW MY OLD SWEET UNCLE PROTECTS ME!
SNAP SNAP SNAP SNAP SNAP SNAP SNAP SNAP
CIRCE'S GOTTEN NASTIER.
HE WAS SUPPORTING A LARGE FAMILY.
THE OLD MOUNTAIN!
BUT OF COURSE!
12

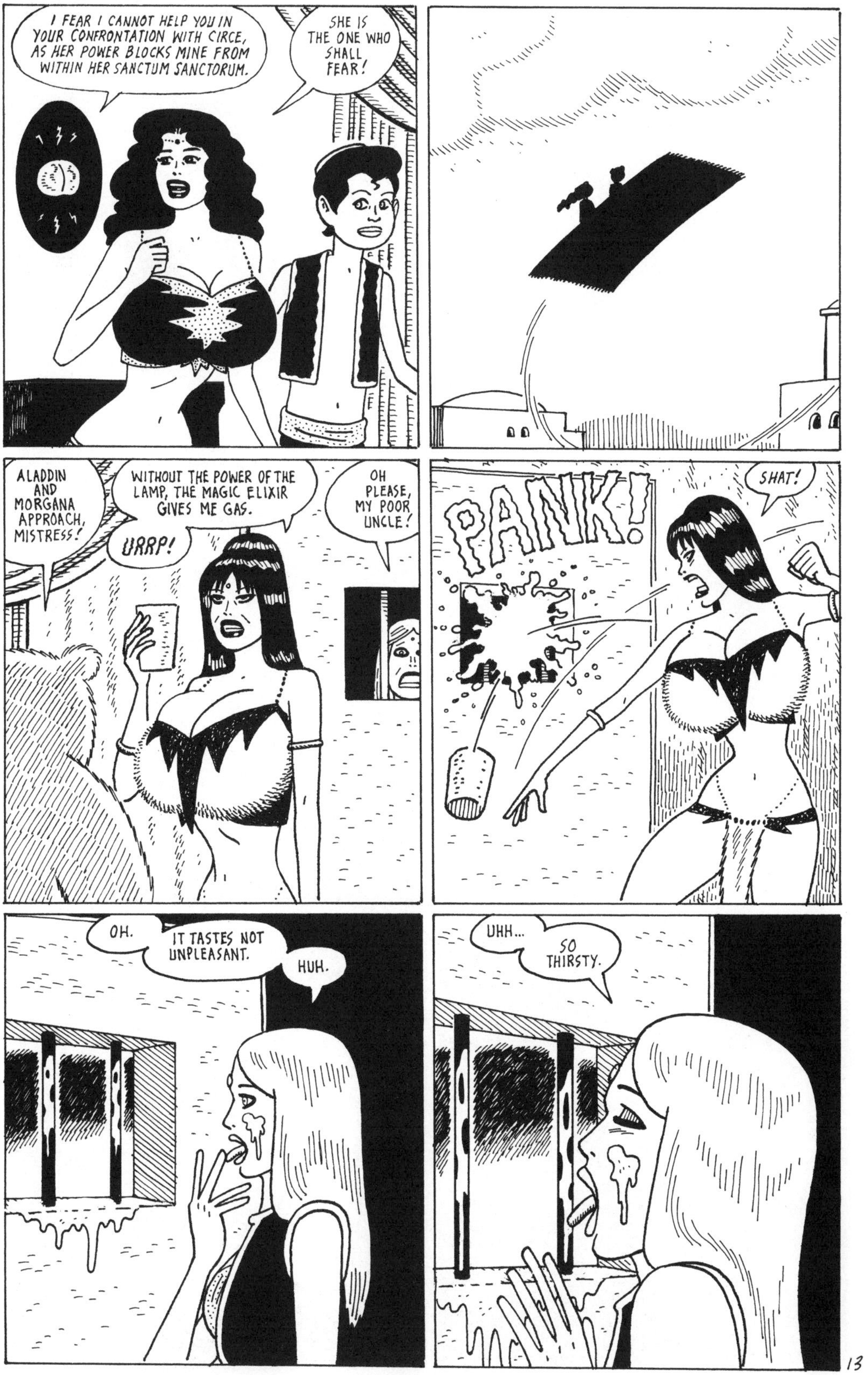
I FEAR I CANNOT HELP YOU IN YOUR CONFRONTATION WITH CIRCE, AS HER POWER BLOCKS MINE FROM WITHIN HER SANCTUM SANCTORUM.
SHE IS THE ONE WHO SHALL FEAR!
ALADDIN AND MORGANA APPROACH, MISTRESS!
WITHOUT THE POWER OF THE LAMP, THE MAGIC ELIXIR GIVES ME GAS.
URRP!
OH PLEASE, MY POOR UNCLE!
PANK!
SHAT!
OH.
IT TASTES NOT UNPLEASANT.
HUH.
UHH...
SO THIRSTY.
13

ARRH, THERE'S THAT GAS.
OH, PLEASE..!
BLAP!
I THIRST SO.
MAY I HAVE MORE OF THE MAGIC ELIXIR?
BUT, I...
I...
....
FILL THE CUP.
FILL...
CUP...
AHHH.
MORE.
THAT IS ALL OF IT.
THERE SHALL NOT BE MORE UNTIL THE MOON IS FULL.

14

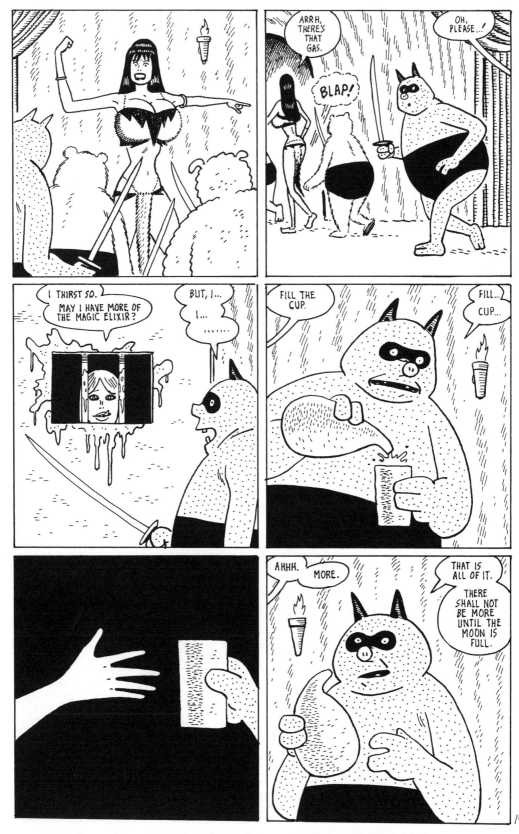

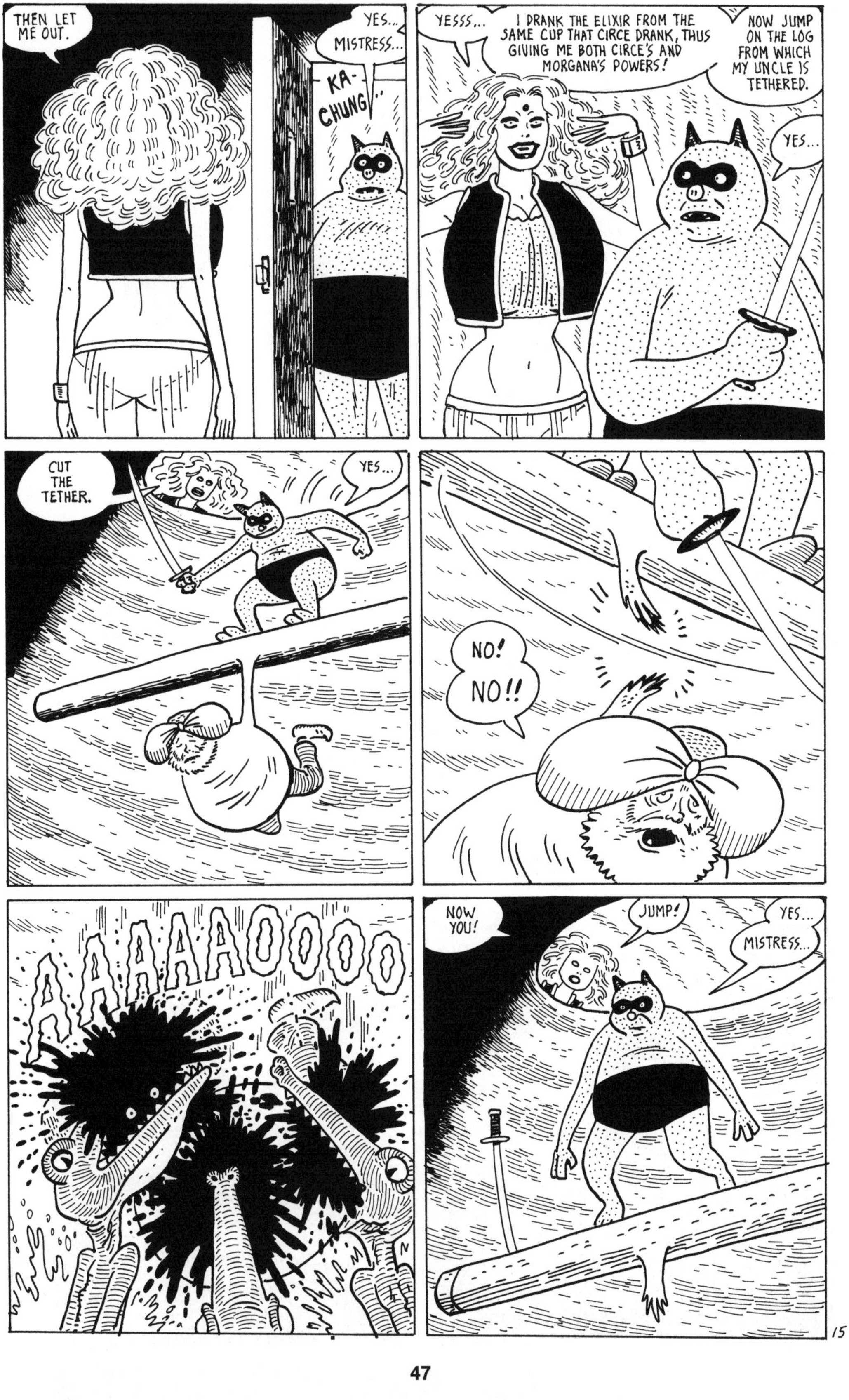
THEN LET ME OUT.
YES... MISTRESS...
KA-CHUNG...
YESSS...
I DRANK THE ELIXIR FROM THE SAME CUP THAT CIRCE DRANK, THUS GIVING ME BOTH CIRCE'S AND MORGANA'S POWERS!
NOW JUMP ON THE LOG FROM WHICH MY UNCLE IS TETHERED.
YES...
CUT THE TETHER.
YES...
NO!
NO!!
AAAAAOOOO
NOW YOU!
JUMP!
YES... MISTRESS...
15

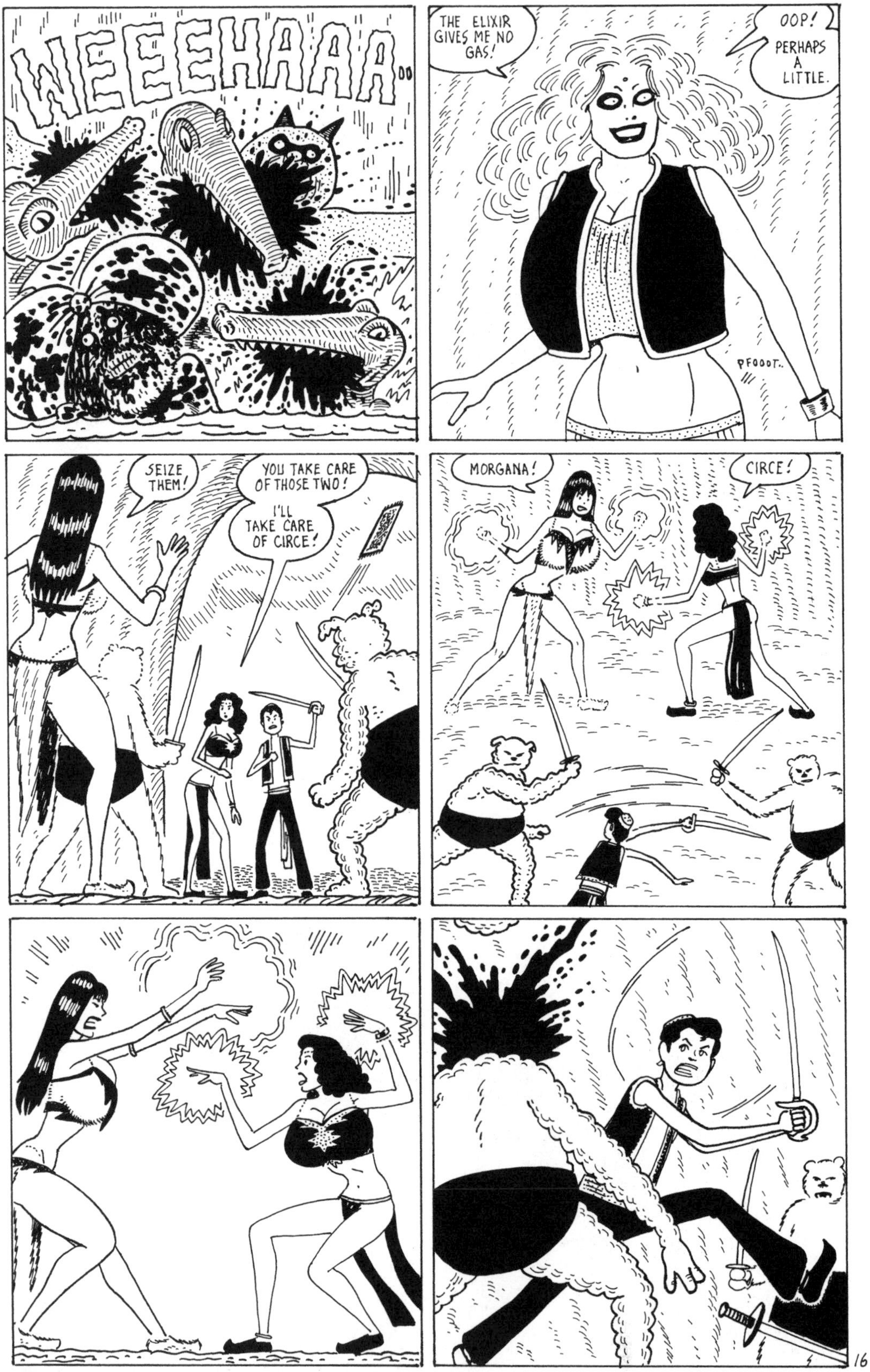
WEEEHAAA..
THE ELIXIR GIVES ME NO GAS!
OOP! PERHAPS A LITTLE.
PFOOOT..
SEIZE THEM!
YOU TAKE CARE OF THOSE TWO!
I'LL TAKE CARE OF CIRCE!
MORGANA!
CIRCE!
16

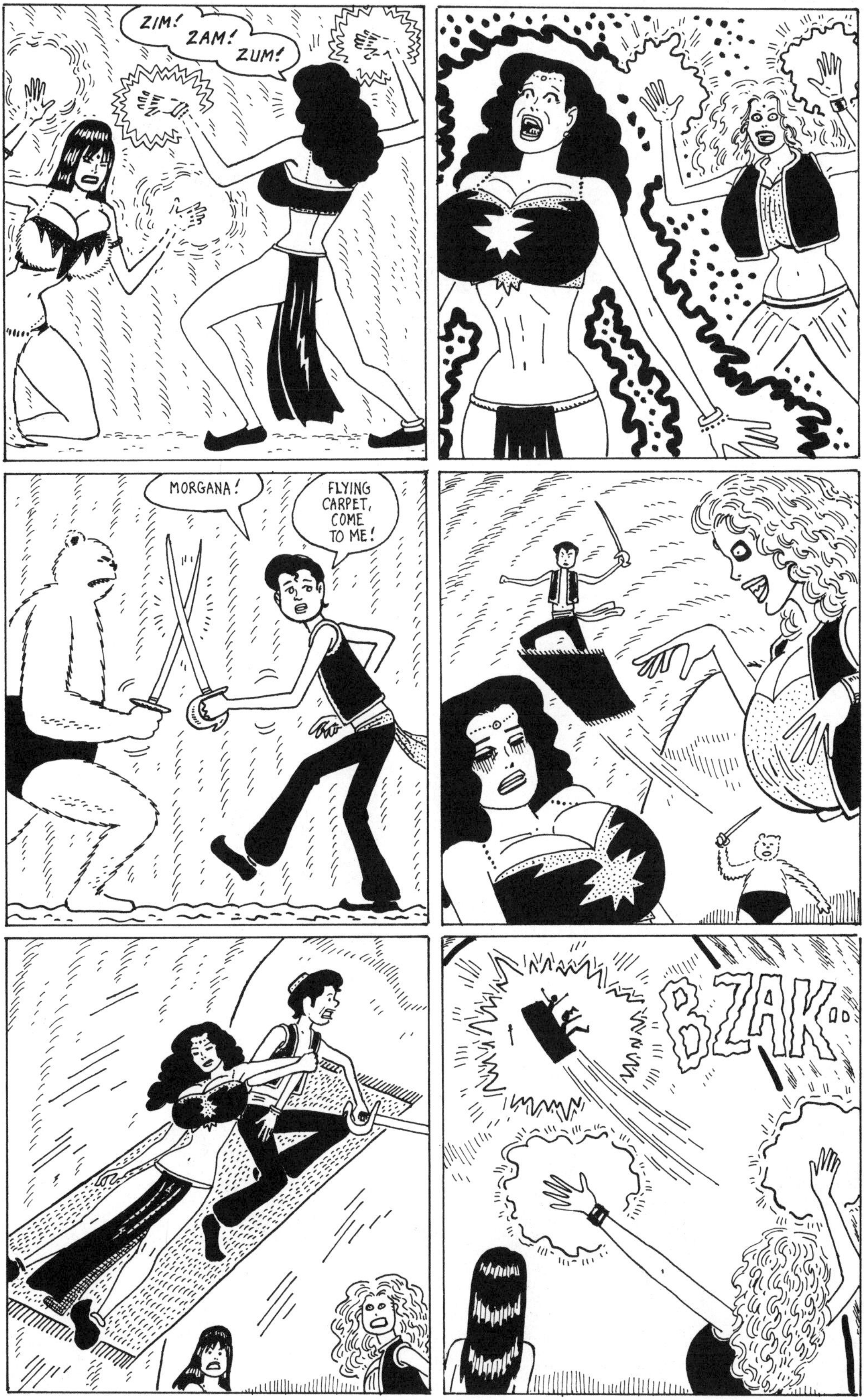
ZIM! ZAM! ZUM!
MORGANA!
FLYING CARPET, COME TO ME!
BZAK..
17

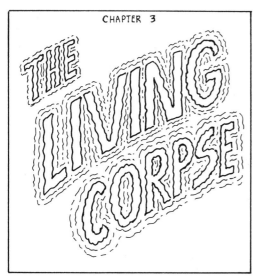

CHAPTER 3

THE LIVING CORPSE

MORGANA...

MOR...

HIS STUPID FLYING CARPET WILL INSTINCTIVELY CARRY HIM TO SAFETY.

AND THE CLOSEST SHELTER IS RIGHT HERE!

WHAT...

ABOUT... MORGANA?

EVEN IF SHE SURVIVED THE FALL, MORGANA WILL BE AT THE MERCY OF THE MONSTERS THAT DWELL IN THE FOREST.

OHHH...

18

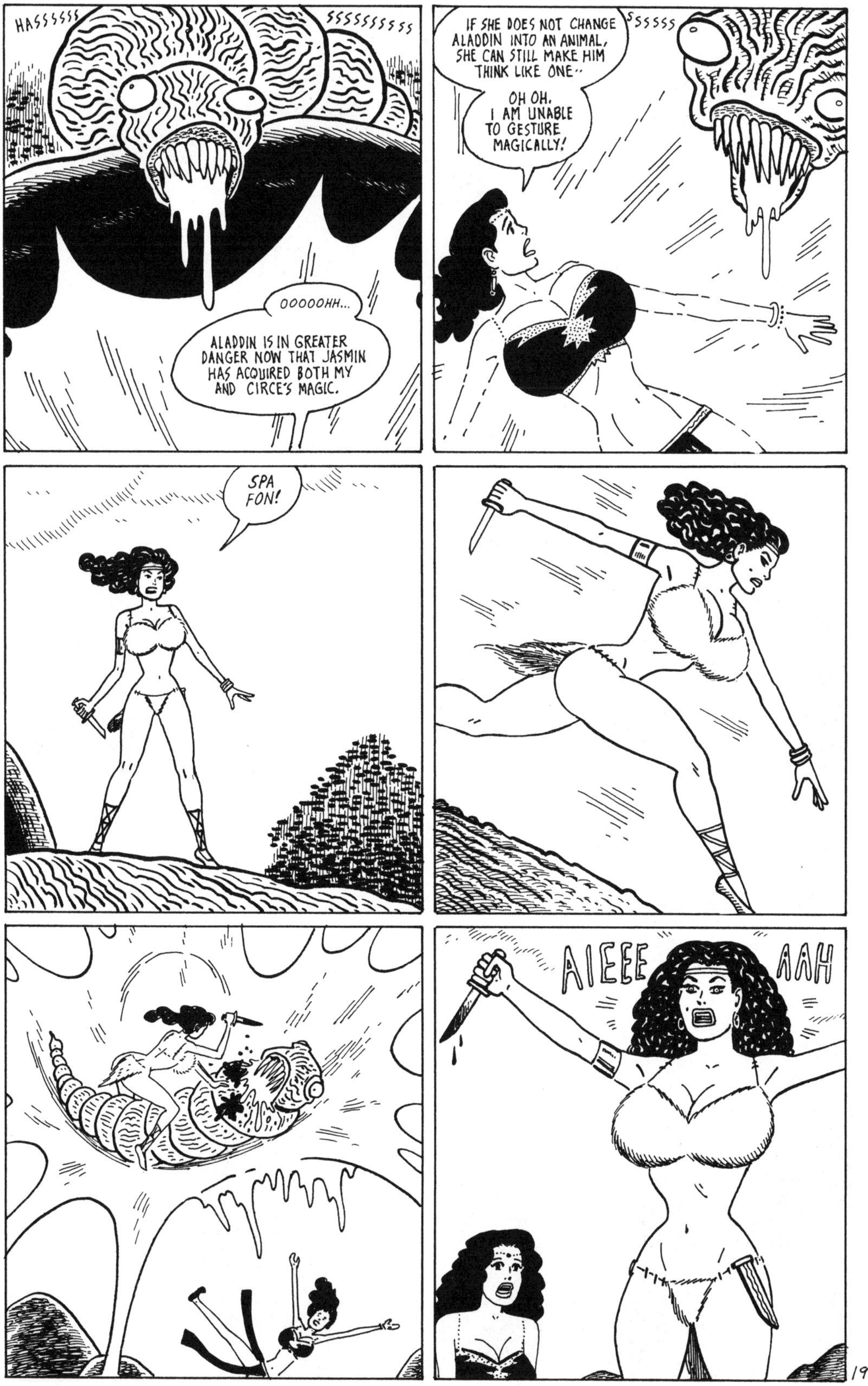
HASSSSSS
SSSSSSSSSSS
OOOOOHH...
ALADDIN IS IN GREATER DANGER NOW THAT JASMIN HAS ACQUIRED BOTH MY AND CIRCE'S MAGIC.
IF SHE DOES NOT CHANGE ALADDIN INTO AN ANIMAL, SHE CAN STILL MAKE HIM THINK LIKE ONE..
SSSSS
OH OH. I AM UNABLE TO GESTURE MAGICALLY!
SPA FON!
AIEEE
AAH
19

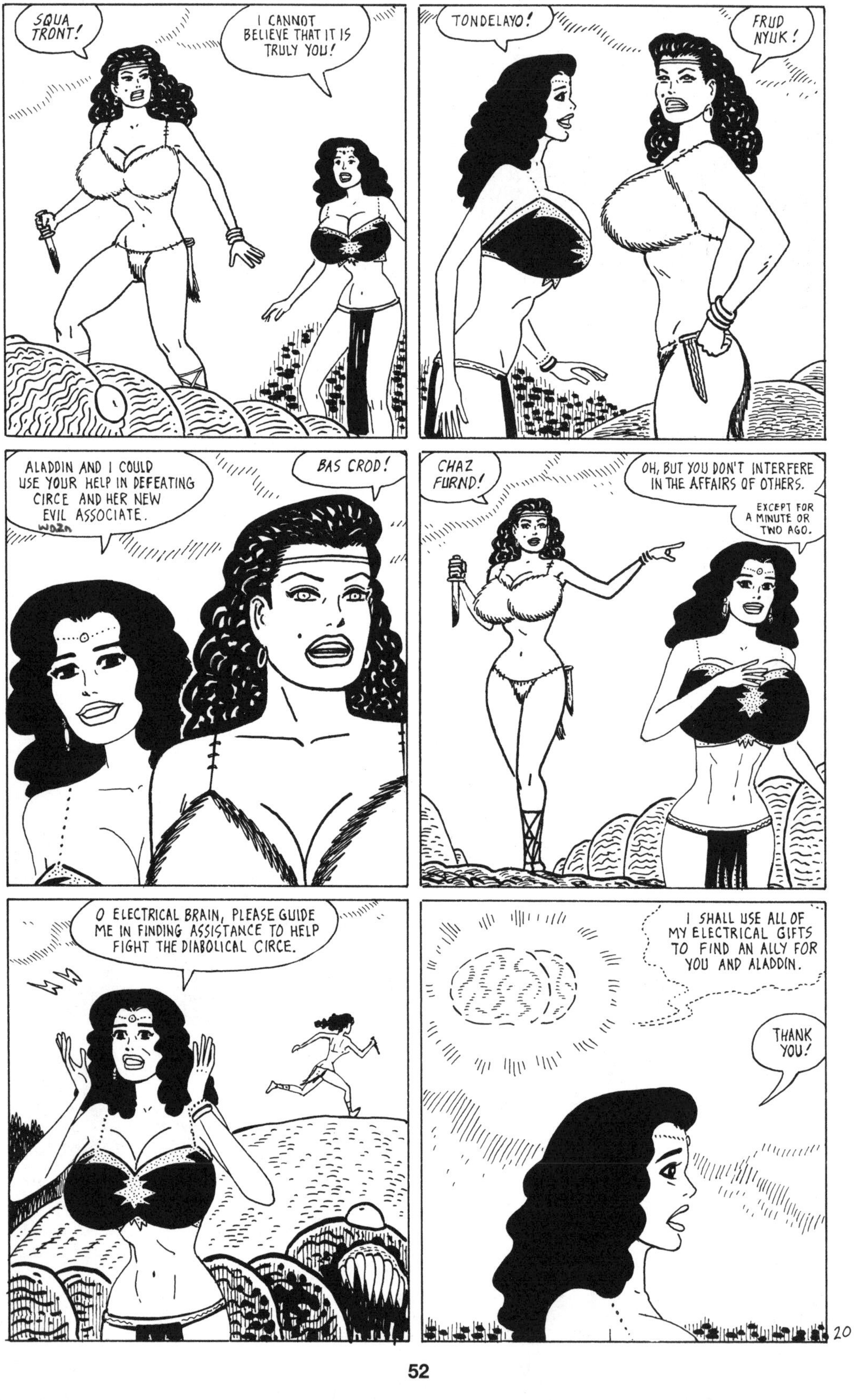
SQUA TRONT!
I CANNOT BELIEVE THAT IT IS TRULY YOU!
TONDELAYO!
FRUD NYUK!
ALADDIN AND I COULD USE YOUR HELP IN DEFEATING CIRCE AND HER NEW EVIL ASSOCIATE.
BAS CROD!
CHAZ FURND!
OH, BUT YOU DON'T INTERFERE IN THE AFFAIRS OF OTHERS.
EXCEPT FOR A MINUTE OR TWO AGO.
O ELECTRICAL BRAIN, PLEASE GUIDE ME IN FINDING ASSISTANCE TO HELP FIGHT THE DIABOLICAL CIRCE.
I SHALL USE ALL OF MY ELECTRICAL GIFTS TO FIND AN ALLY FOR YOU AND ALADDIN.
THANK YOU!
20

WE'RE FINALLY SLOWING DOWN NOW, PROFESSOR ENIGMA!
STEADY, MISSY; STEADY!
THERE IS ONLY ONE ENERGY SOURCE THAT CAN MANIPULATE OUR STAR CRAFT FROM SUCH A FAR DISTANCE, MISSY.
Y-YOU MEAN THE ELECTRICAL BRAIN?
WOW!
...
PROFESSOR ENIGMA AND MISSY TO MY RESCUE!
OUR GOOD FRIEND MORGANA LE FEY, AS I LIVE AND BREATHE!
21

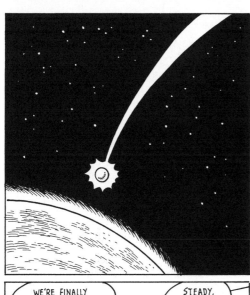

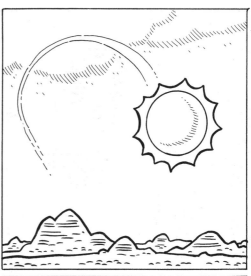

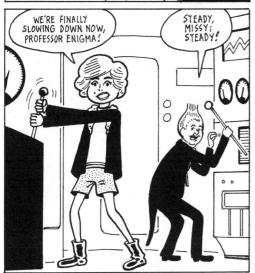

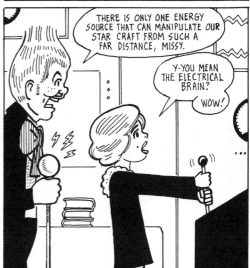

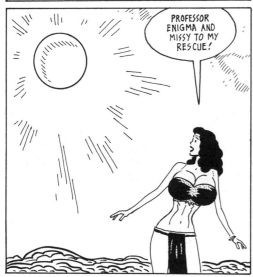

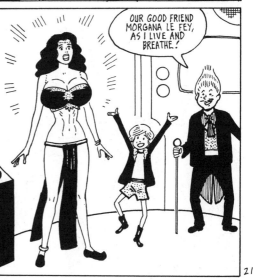

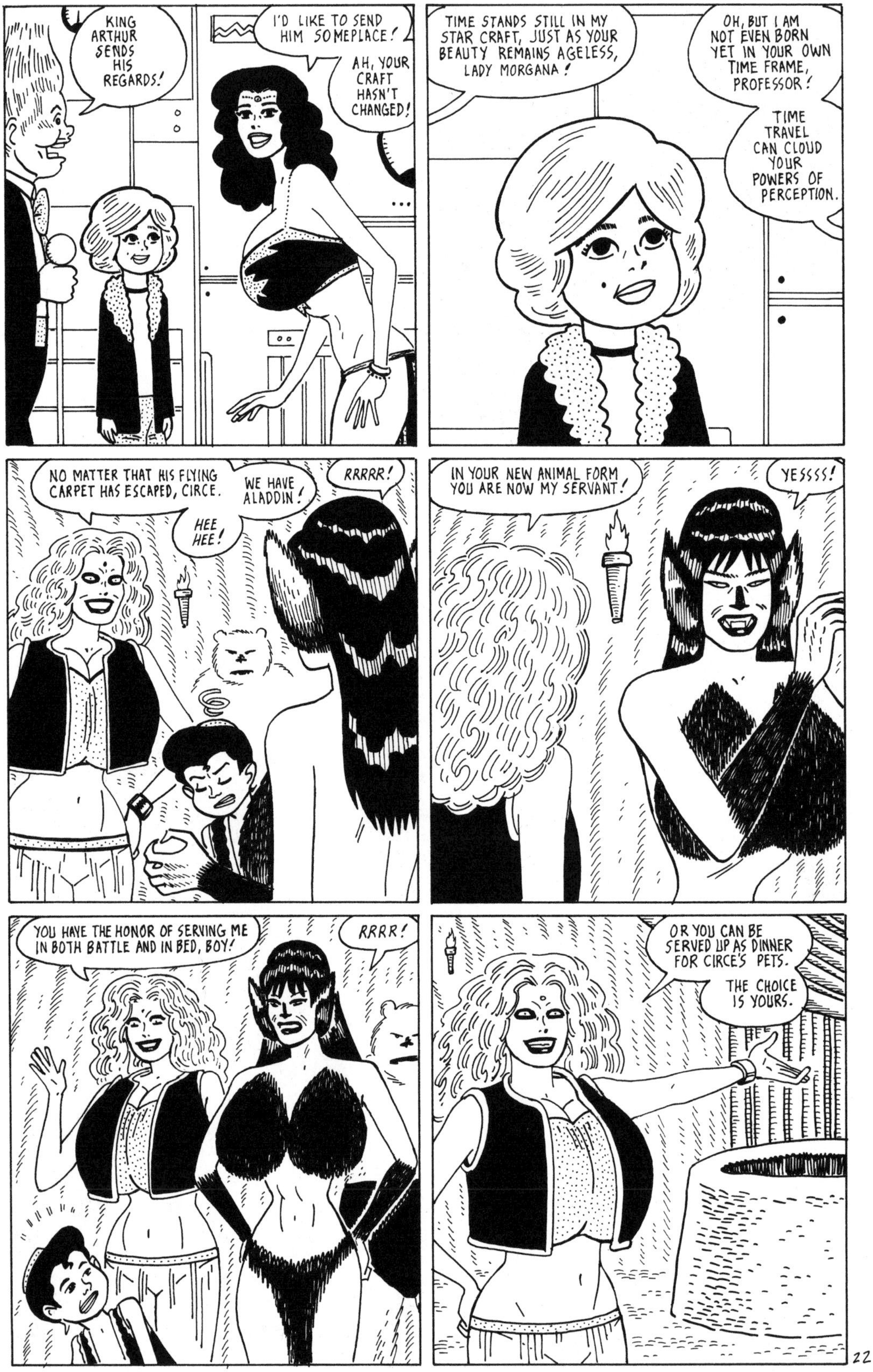
KING ARTHUR SENDS HIS REGARDS!
I'D LIKE TO SEND HIM SOMEPLACE!
AH, YOUR CRAFT HASN'T CHANGED!
TIME STANDS STILL IN MY STAR CRAFT, JUST AS YOUR BEAUTY REMAINS AGELESS, LADY MORGANA!
OH, BUT I AM NOT EVEN BORN YET IN YOUR OWN TIME FRAME, PROFESSOR!
TIME TRAVEL CAN CLOUD YOUR POWERS OF PERCEPTION.
NO MATTER THAT HIS FLYING CARPET HAS ESCAPED, CIRCE.
WE HAVE ALADDIN!
HEE HEE!
RRRRR!
IN YOUR NEW ANIMAL FORM YOU ARE NOW MY SERVANT!
YESSSS!
YOU HAVE THE HONOR OF SERVING ME IN BOTH BATTLE AND IN BED, BOY!
RRRR!
OR YOU CAN BE SERVED UP AS DINNER FOR CIRCE'S PETS.
THE CHOICE IS YOURS.
22

ALADDIN WILL NEVER BETRAY MORGANA LE FEY, MISTRESS!
THAT IS WHAT I WAS HOPING TO BE TRUE!
I POSSESS CIRCE'S MAGIC!
AND HER MAGIC CAN OBSCURE YOUR ABILITY TO RETRIEVE YOUR FLYING CARPET!
ARF?!
THUMM THUMM THUMM THUMM THUMMM
I CAN'T HOLD US HERE MUCH LONGER, PROFESSOR!
I AM SORRY THAT WE CAN'T INTERFERE IN THE AFFAIRS OF OTHERS.
NO HARM IN ME ASKING.
FAREWELL THEN.
23

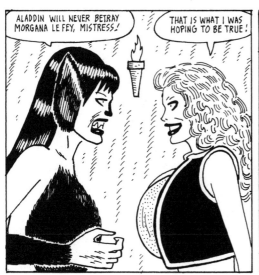

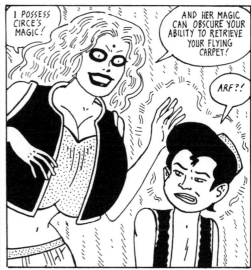

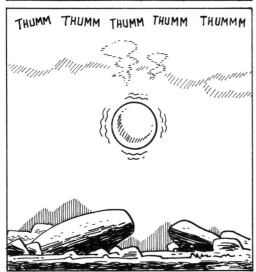

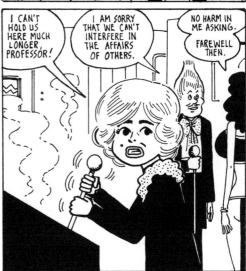

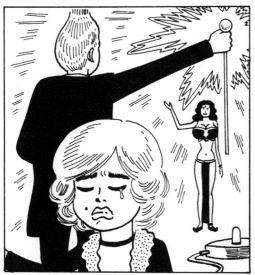

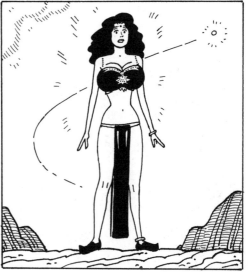

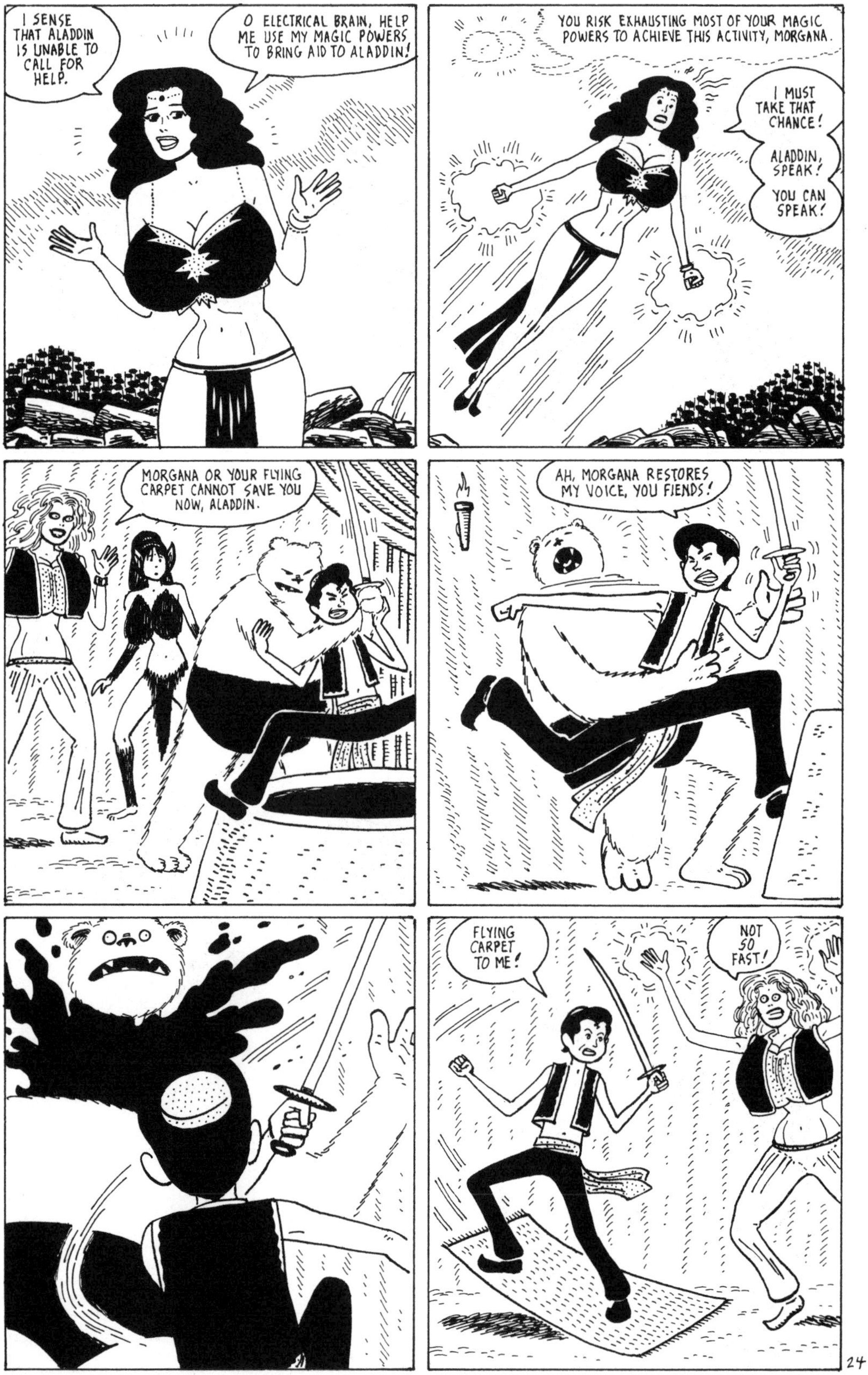
I SENSE THAT ALADDIN IS UNABLE TO CALL FOR HELP.
O ELECTRICAL BRAIN, HELP ME USE MY MAGIC POWERS TO BRING AID TO ALADDIN!
YOU RISK EXHAUSTING MOST OF YOUR MAGIC POWERS TO ACHIEVE THIS ACTIVITY, MORGANA.
I MUST TAKE THAT CHANCE!
ALADDIN, SPEAK!
YOU CAN SPEAK!
MORGANA OR YOUR FLYING CARPET CANNOT SAVE YOU NOW, ALADDIN.
AH, MORGANA RESTORES MY VOICE, YOU FIENDS!
FLYING CARPET TO ME!
NOT SO FAST!
24

MORGANA'S MAGIC POWERS PROTECT ME FROM ANY MAGIC STOLEN FROM HER!

THEN YOU SEIZE HIM, CIRCE!

I HAVE NO MAGIC ABILITIES IN THIS ANIMAL FORM.

YOU CAN STILL WIELD A BLADE, FERAL ONE!

YESSSSS!

SEE WHAT HAPPENS IN THE NEXT CHAPTER OF: The MAGIC VOYAGE OF ALADDIN

25

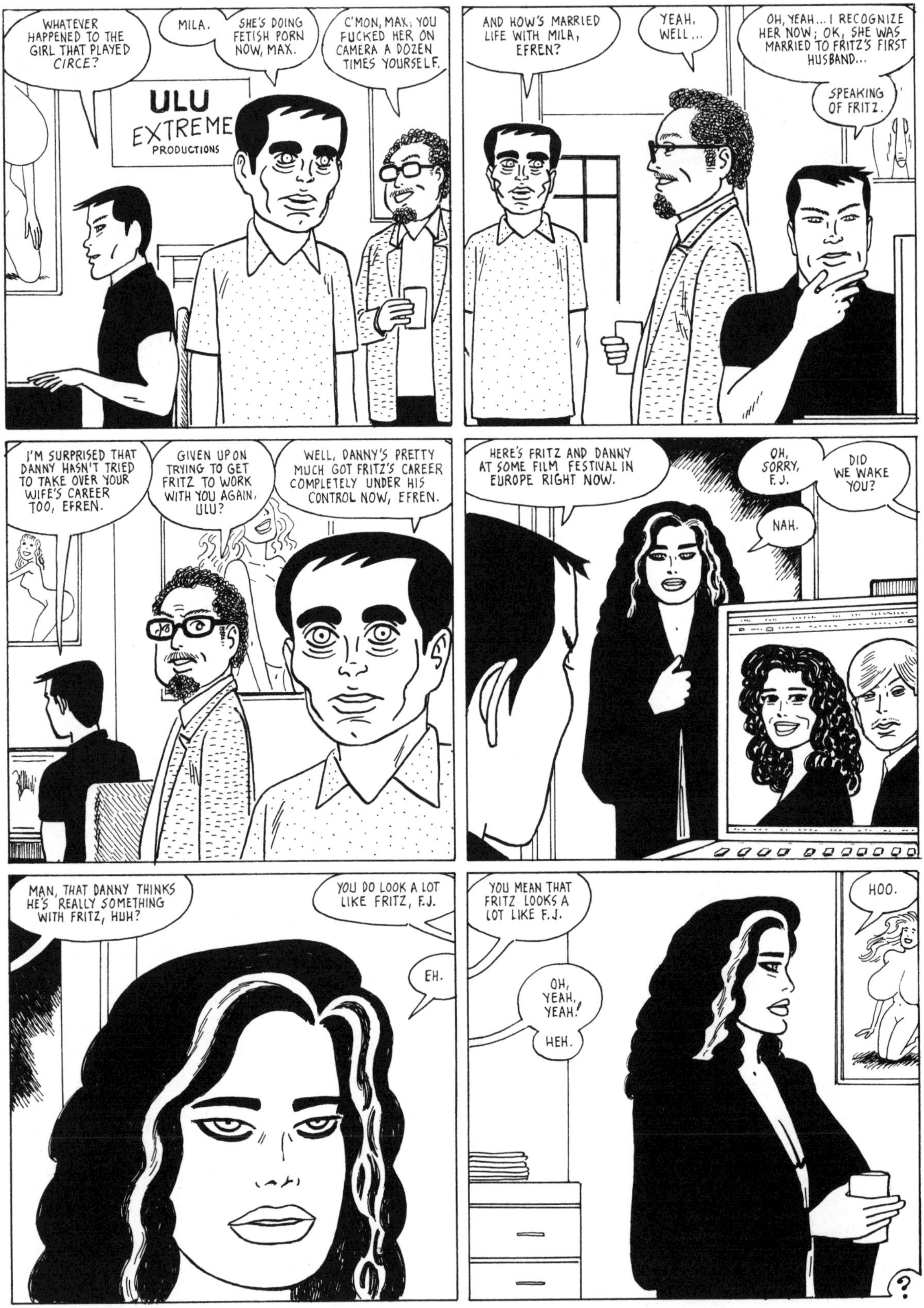
WHATEVER HAPPENED TO THE GIRL THAT PLAYED CIRCE?
MILA.
SHE'S DOING FETISH PORN NOW, MAX.
C'MON, MAX; YOU FUCKED HER ON CAMERA A DOZEN TIMES YOURSELF.
ULU EXTREME PRODUCTIONS
AND HOW'S MARRIED LIFE WITH MILA, EFREN?
YEAH, WELL...
OH, YEAH... I RECOGNIZE HER NOW; OK, SHE WAS MARRIED TO FRITZ'S FIRST HUSBAND...
SPEAKING OF FRITZ.
I'M SURPRISED THAT DANNY HASN'T TRIED TO TAKE OVER YOUR WIFE'S CAREER TOO, EFREN.
GIVEN UP ON TRYING TO GET FRITZ TO WORK WITH YOU AGAIN, ULU?
WELL, DANNY'S PRETTY MUCH GOT FRITZ'S CAREER COMPLETELY UNDER HIS CONTROL NOW, EFREN.
HERE'S FRITZ AND DANNY AT SOME FILM FESTIVAL IN EUROPE RIGHT NOW.
OH, SORRY, F.J.
DID WE WAKE YOU?
NAH.
MAN, THAT DANNY THINKS HE'S REALLY SOMETHING WITH FRITZ, HUH?
YOU DO LOOK A LOT LIKE FRITZ, F.J.
EH.
YOU MEAN THAT FRITZ LOOKS A LOT LIKE F.J.
OH, YEAH, YEAH!
HEH.
HOO.

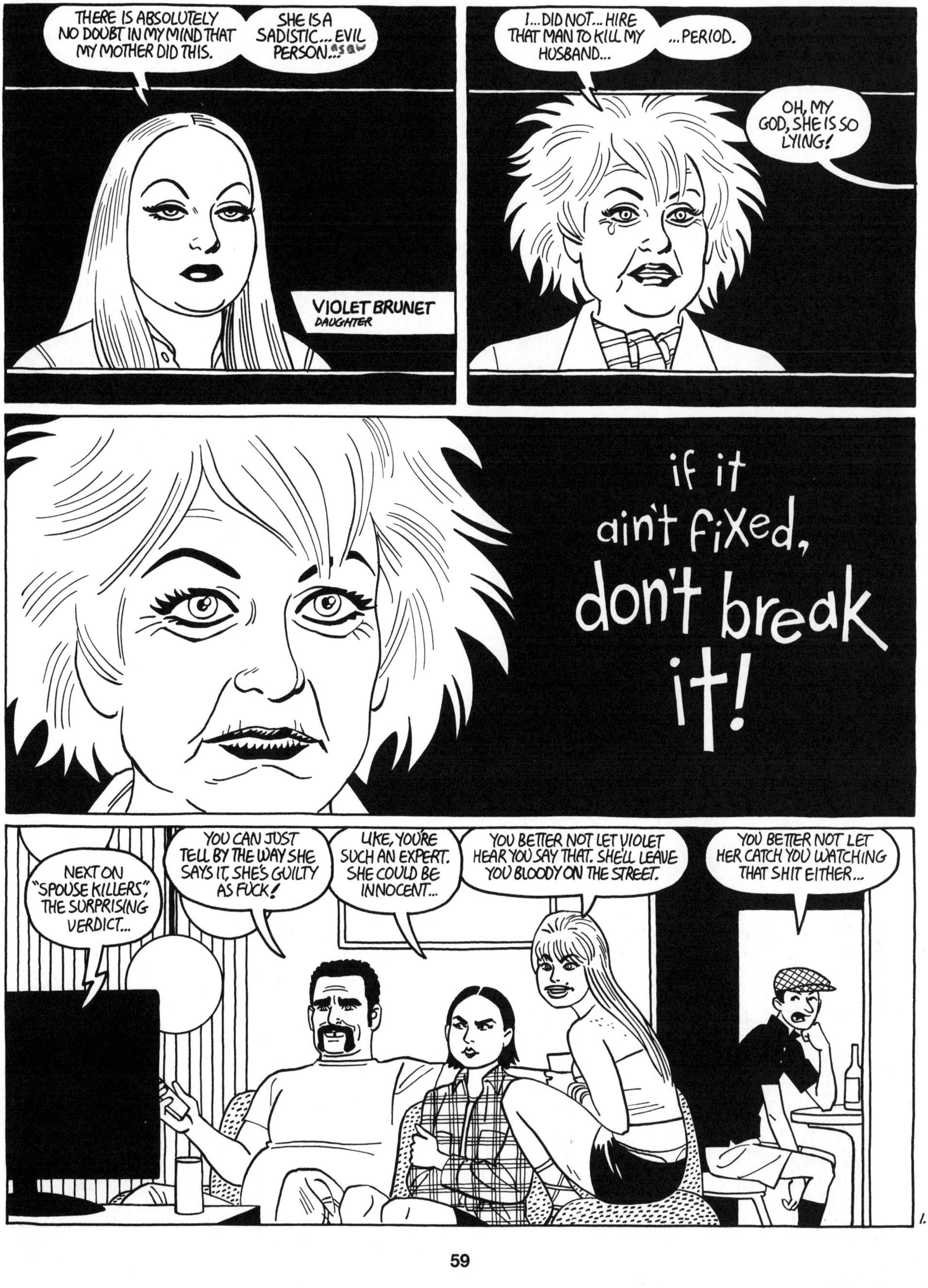
THERE IS ABSOLUTELY NO DOUBT IN MY MIND THAT MY MOTHER DID THIS.
SHE IS A SADISTIC... EVIL PERSON...
VIOLET BRUNET
DAUGHTER
I... DID NOT... HIRE THAT MAN TO KILL MY HUSBAND...
...PERIOD.
OH, MY GOD, SHE IS SO LYING!
if it ain't fixed, don't break it!
NEXT ON "SPOUSE KILLERS", THE SURPRISING VERDICT...
YOU CAN JUST TELL BY THE WAY SHE SAYS IT, SHE'S GUILTY AS FUCK!
LIKE, YOU'RE SUCH AN EXPERT. SHE COULD BE INNOCENT...
YOU BETTER NOT LET VIOLET HEAR YOU SAY THAT. SHE'LL LEAVE YOU BLOODY ON THE STREET.
YOU BETTER NOT LET HER CATCH YOU WATCHING THAT SHIT EITHER...
1.

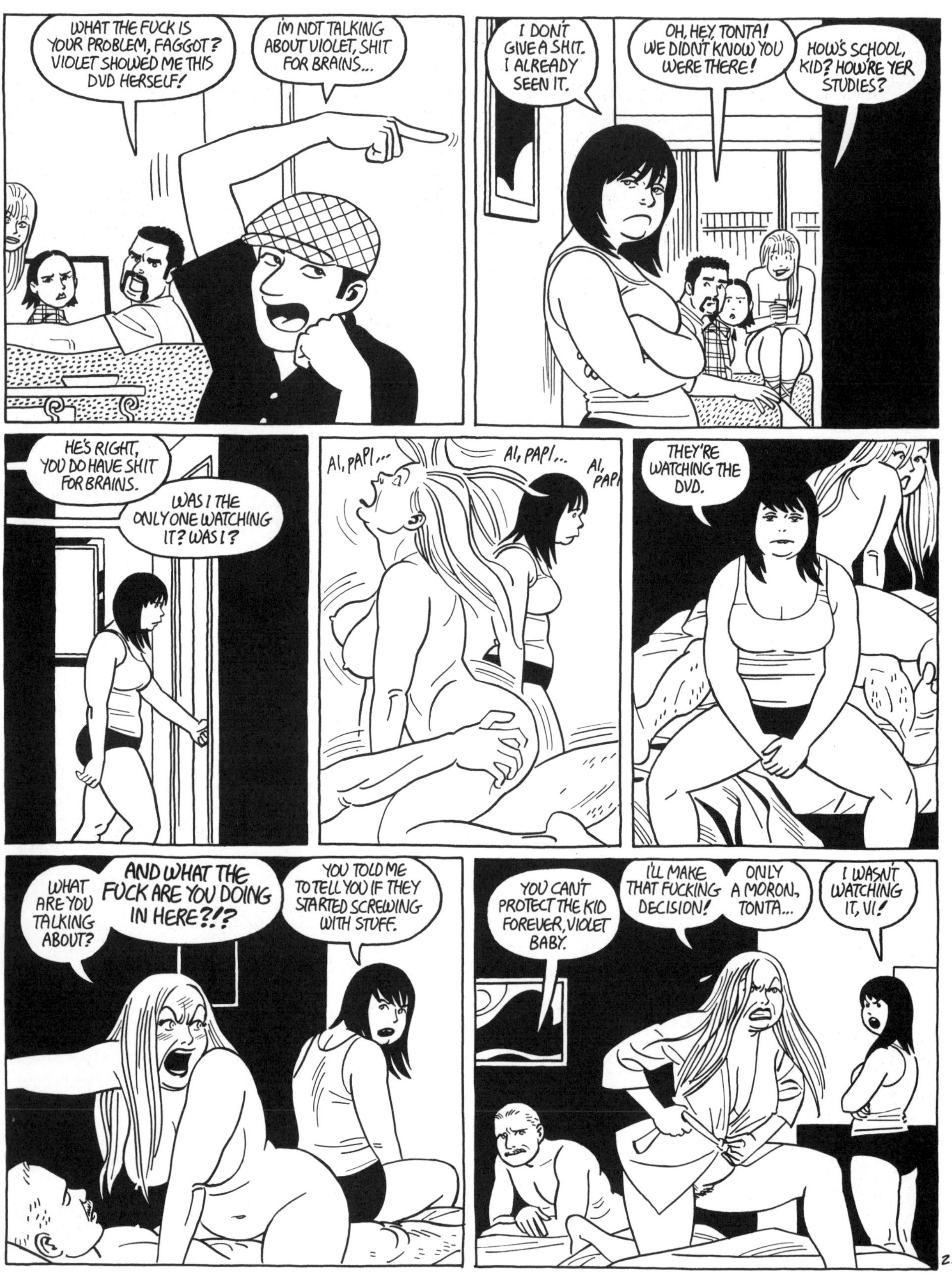

WHAT THE FUCK IS YOUR PROBLEM, FAGGOT? VIOLET SHOWED ME THIS DVD HERSELF!
I'M NOT TALKING ABOUT VIOLET, SHIT FOR BRAINS...
I DON'T GIVE A SHIT. I ALREADY SEEN IT.
OH, HEY, TONTA! WE DIDN'T KNOW YOU WERE THERE!
HOW'S SCHOOL, KID? HOW'RE YER STUDIES?
HE'S RIGHT, YOU DO HAVE SHIT FOR BRAINS.
WAS I THE ONLY ONE WATCHING IT? WAS I?
AI, PAPI...
AI, PAPI...
AI, PAPI
THEY'RE WATCHING THE DVD.
WHAT ARE YOU TALKING ABOUT?
AND WHAT THE FUCK ARE YOU DOING IN HERE?!?
YOU TOLD ME TO TELL YOU IF THEY STARTED SCREWING WITH STUFF.
YOU CAN'T PROTECT THE KID FOREVER, VIOLET BABY.
I'LL MAKE THAT FUCKING DECISION!
ONLY A MORON, TONTA...
I WASN'T WATCHING IT, VI!
2.

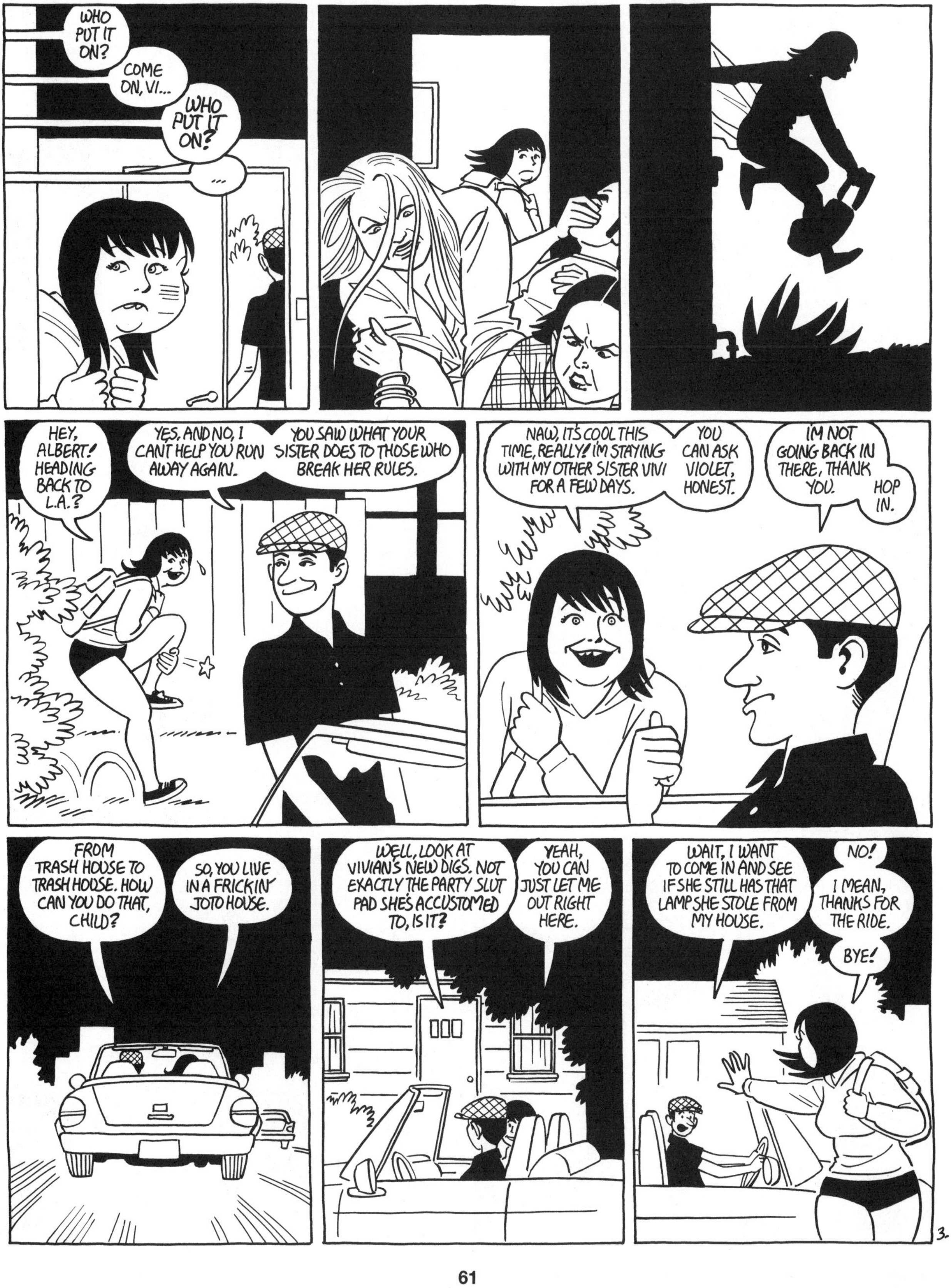
WHO PUT IT ON?
COME ON, VI...
WHO PUT IT ON?
...
HEY, ALBERT! HEADING BACK TO L.A.?
YES, AND NO, I CAN'T HELP YOU RUN AWAY AGAIN.
YOU SAW WHAT YOUR SISTER DOES TO THOSE WHO BREAK HER RULES.
NAW, IT'S COOL THIS TIME, REALLY! I'M STAYING WITH MY OTHER SISTER VIVI FOR A FEW DAYS.
YOU CAN ASK VIOLET, HONEST.
I'M NOT GOING BACK IN THERE, THANK YOU.
HOP IN.
FROM TRASH HOUSE TO TRASH HOUSE. HOW CAN YOU DO THAT, CHILD?
SO, YOU LIVE IN A FRICKIN' JOTO HOUSE.
WELL, LOOK AT VIVIAN'S NEW DIGS. NOT EXACTLY THE PARTY SLUT PAD SHE'S ACCUSTOMED TO, IS IT?
YEAH, YOU CAN JUST LET ME OUT RIGHT HERE.
WAIT, I WANT TO COME IN AND SEE IF SHE STILL HAS THAT LAMP SHE STOLE FROM MY HOUSE.
NO!
I MEAN, THANKS FOR THE RIDE.
BYE!
3.

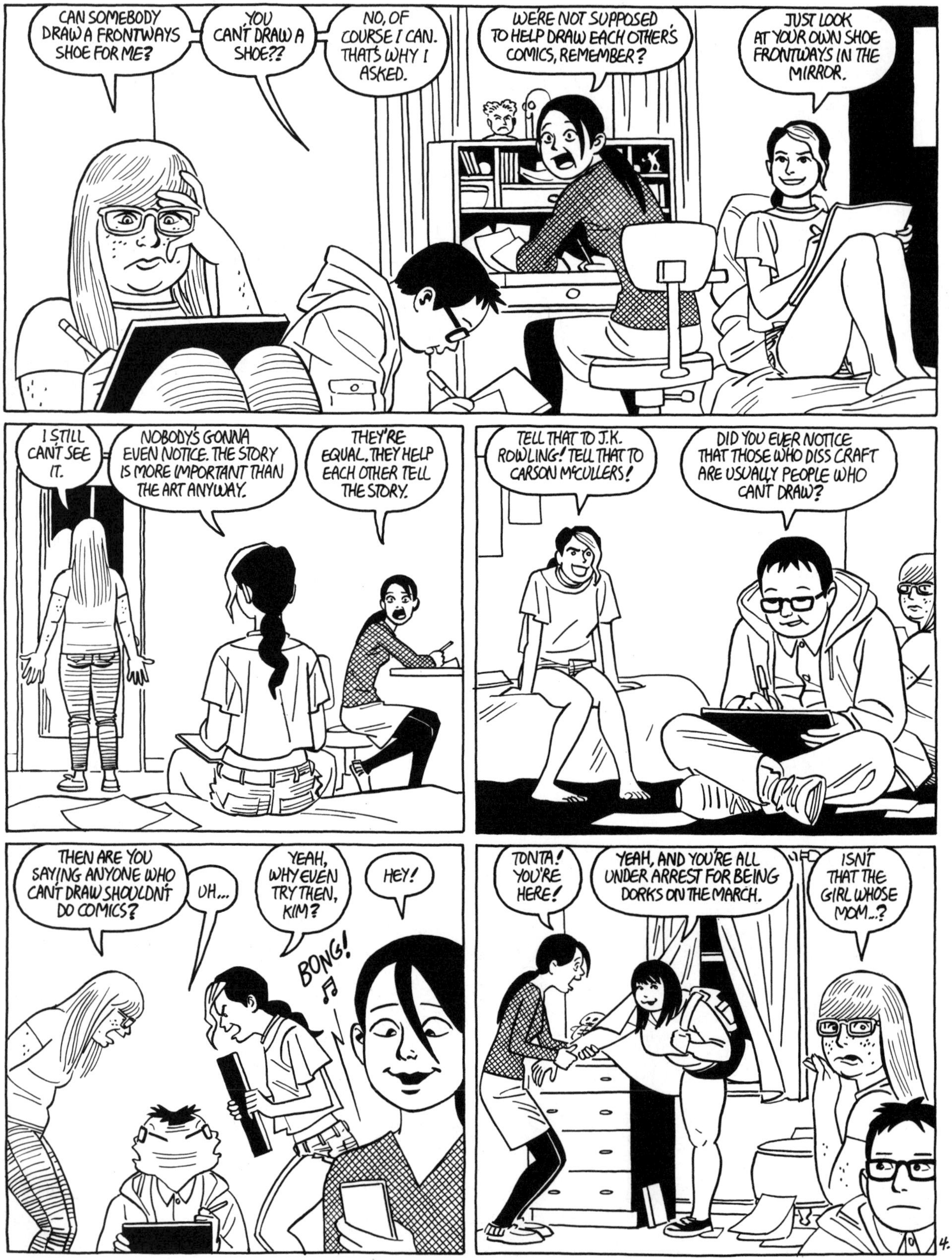
CAN SOMEBODY DRAW A FRONTWAYS SHOE FOR ME?
YOU CAN'T DRAW A SHOE??
NO, OF COURSE I CAN. THAT'S WHY I ASKED.
WE'RE NOT SUPPOSED TO HELP DRAW EACH OTHER'S COMICS, REMEMBER?
JUST LOOK AT YOUR OWN SHOE FRONTWAYS IN THE MIRROR.
I STILL CAN'T SEE IT.
NOBODY'S GONNA EVEN NOTICE. THE STORY IS MORE IMPORTANT THAN THE ART ANYWAY.
THEY'RE EQUAL. THEY HELP EACH OTHER TELL THE STORY.
TELL THAT TO J.K. ROWLING! TELL THAT TO CARSON McCULLERS!
DID YOU EVER NOTICE THAT THOSE WHO DISS CRAFT ARE USUALLY PEOPLE WHO CAN'T DRAW?
THEN ARE YOU SAYING ANYONE WHO CAN'T DRAW SHOULDN'T DO COMICS?
UH...
YEAH, WHY EVEN TRY THEN, KIM?
HEY!
BONG!
TONTA! YOU'RE HERE!
YEAH, AND YOU'RE ALL UNDER ARREST FOR BEING DORKS ON THE MARCH.
ISN'T THAT THE GIRL WHOSE MOM...?
4.

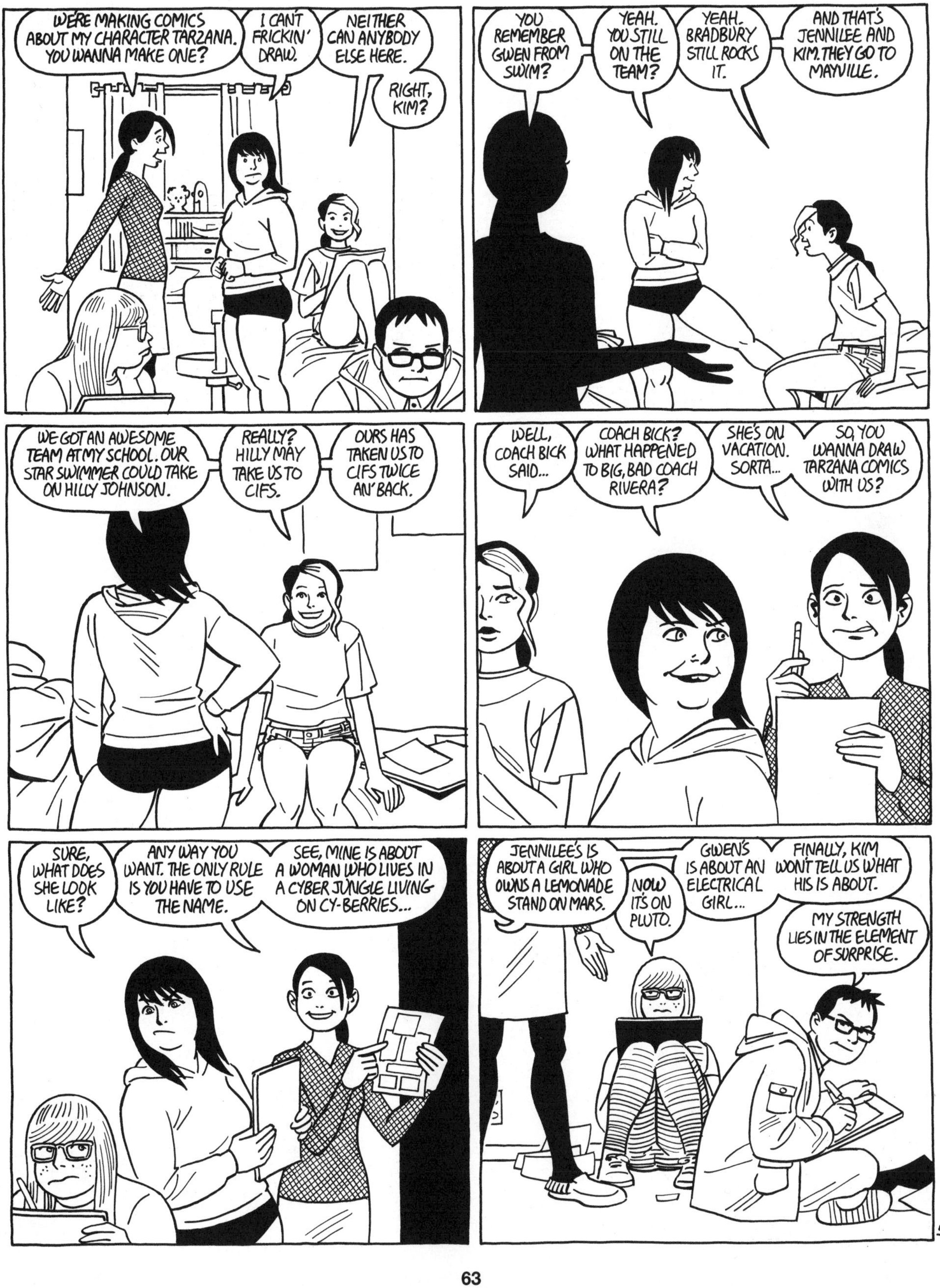
WE'RE MAKING COMICS ABOUT MY CHARACTER TARZANA. YOU WANNA MAKE ONE?
I CAN'T FRICKIN' DRAW.
NEITHER CAN ANYBODY ELSE HERE.
RIGHT, KIM?
YOU REMEMBER GWEN FROM SWIM?
YEAH. YOU STILL ON THE TEAM?
YEAH. BRADBURY STILL ROCKS IT.
AND THAT'S JENNILEE AND KIM. THEY GO TO MAYVILLE.
WE GOT AN AWESOME TEAM AT MY SCHOOL. OUR STAR SWIMMER COULD TAKE ON HILLY JOHNSON.
REALLY? HILLY MAY TAKE US TO CIFS.
OURS HAS TAKEN US TO CIFS TWICE AN' BACK.
WELL, COACH BICK SAID...
COACH BICK? WHAT HAPPENED TO BIG, BAD COACH RIVERA?
SHE'S ON VACATION. SORTA...
SO, YOU WANNA DRAW TARZANA COMICS WITH US?
SURE, WHAT DOES SHE LOOK LIKE?
ANY WAY YOU WANT. THE ONLY RULE IS YOU HAVE TO USE THE NAME.
SEE, MINE IS ABOUT A WOMAN WHO LIVES IN A CYBER JUNGLE LIVING ON CY-BERRIES...
JENNILEE'S IS ABOUT A GIRL WHO OWNS A LEMONADE STAND ON MARS.
NOW IT'S ON PLUTO.
GWEN'S IS ABOUT AN ELECTRICAL GIRL...
FINALLY, KIM WON'T TELL US WHAT HIS IS ABOUT.
MY STRENGTH LIES IN THE ELEMENT OF SURPRISE.
5.

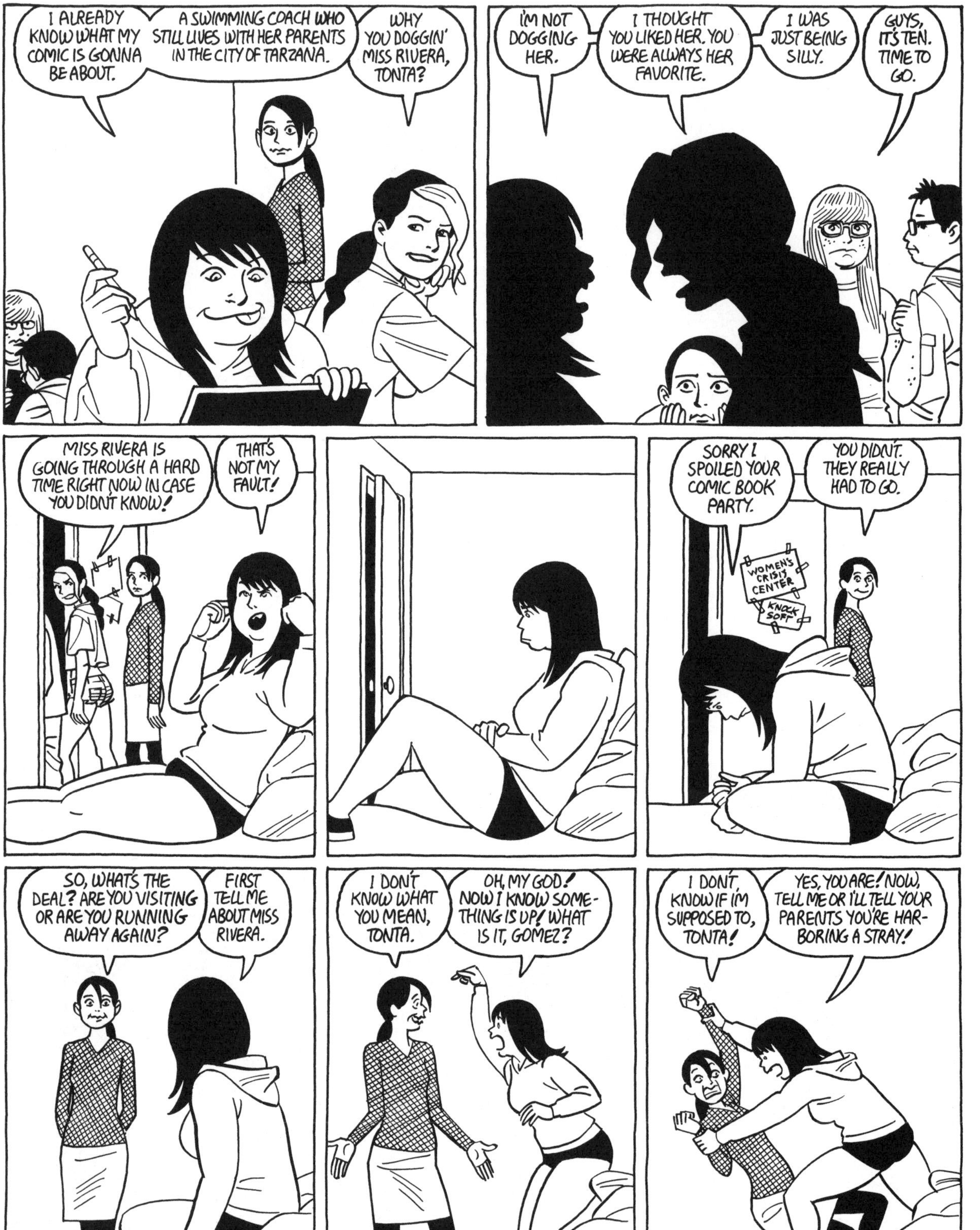
I ALREADY KNOW WHAT MY COMIC IS GONNA BE ABOUT.
A SWIMMING COACH WHO STILL LIVES WITH HER PARENTS IN THE CITY OF TARZANA.
WHY YOU DOGGIN' MISS RIVERA, TONTA?
I'M NOT DOGGING HER.
I THOUGHT YOU LIKED HER. YOU WERE ALWAYS HER FAVORITE.
I WAS JUST BEING SILLY.
GUYS, IT'S TEN. TIME TO GO.
MISS RIVERA IS GOING THROUGH A HARD TIME RIGHT NOW IN CASE YOU DIDN'T KNOW!
THAT'S NOT MY FAULT!
SORRY I SPOILED YOUR COMIC BOOK PARTY.
YOU DIDN'T. THEY REALLY HAD TO GO.
WOMEN'S CRISIS CENTER
KNOCK SOFT
SO, WHAT'S THE DEAL? ARE YOU VISITING OR ARE YOU RUNNING AWAY AGAIN?
FIRST TELL ME ABOUT MISS RIVERA.
I DON'T KNOW WHAT YOU MEAN, TONTA.
OH, MY GOD! NOW I KNOW SOME-THING IS UP! WHAT IS IT, GOMEZ?
I DON'T KNOW IF I'M SUPPOSED TO, TONTA!
YES, YOU ARE! NOW, TELL ME OR I'LL TELL YOUR PARENTS YOU'RE HAR-BORING A STRAY!
6.

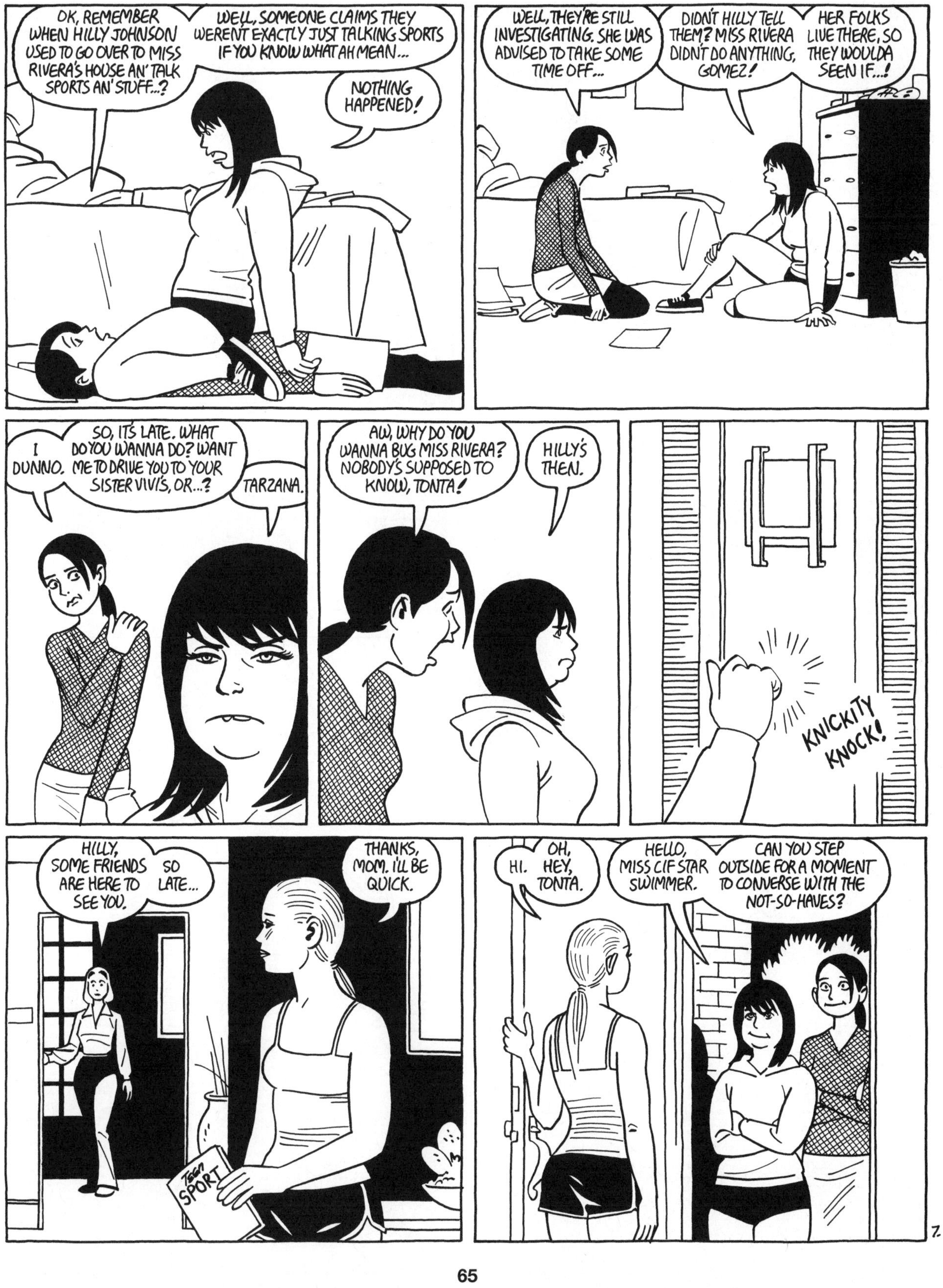

OK, REMEMBER WHEN HILLY JOHNSON USED TO GO OVER TO MISS RIVERA'S HOUSE AN' TALK SPORTS AN' STUFF...?
WELL, SOMEONE CLAIMS THEY WEREN'T EXACTLY JUST TALKING SPORTS IF YOU KNOW WHAT AH MEAN...
NOTHING HAPPENED!
WELL, THEY'RE STILL INVESTIGATING. SHE WAS ADVISED TO TAKE SOME TIME OFF...
DIDN'T HILLY TELL THEM? MISS RIVERA DIDN'T DO ANYTHING, GOMEZ!
HER FOLKS LIVE THERE, SO THEY WOULDA SEEN IF...!
SO, IT'S LATE. WHAT DO YOU WANNA DO? WANT ME TO DRIVE YOU TO YOUR SISTER VIVI'S, OR...?
I DUNNO.
TARZANA.
AW, WHY DO YOU WANNA BUG MISS RIVERA? NOBODY'S SUPPOSED TO KNOW, TONTA!
HILLY'S THEN.
KNICKITY KNOCK!
HILLY, SOME FRIENDS ARE HERE TO SEE YOU.
SO LATE...
THANKS, MOM. I'LL BE QUICK.
SPORT
HI.
OH, HEY, TONTA.
HELLO, MISS CIF STAR SWIMMER.
CAN YOU STEP OUTSIDE FOR A MOMENT TO CONVERSE WITH THE NOT-SO-HAVES?
7.

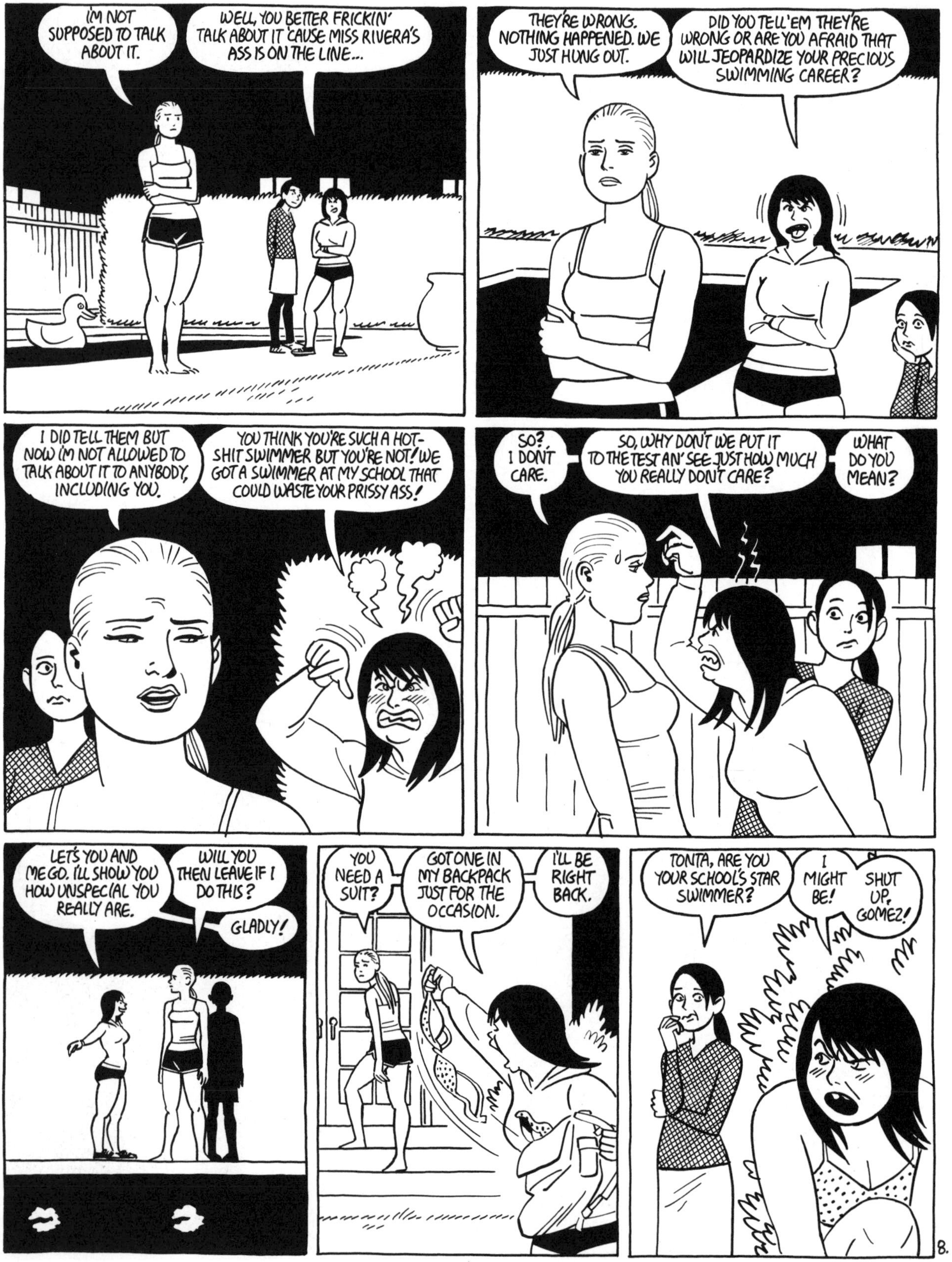

I'M NOT SUPPOSED TO TALK ABOUT IT.
WELL, YOU BETTER FRICKIN' TALK ABOUT IT 'CAUSE MISS RIVERA'S ASS IS ON THE LINE...
THEY'RE WRONG. NOTHING HAPPENED. WE JUST HUNG OUT.
DID YOU TELL 'EM THEY'RE WRONG OR ARE YOU AFRAID THAT WILL JEOPARDIZE YOUR PRECIOUS SWIMMING CAREER?
I DID TELL THEM BUT NOW I'M NOT ALLOWED TO TALK ABOUT IT TO ANYBODY, INCLUDING YOU.
YOU THINK YOU'RE SUCH A HOT-SHIT SWIMMER BUT YOU'RE NOT! WE GOT A SWIMMER AT MY SCHOOL THAT COULD WASTE YOUR PRISSY ASS!
SO? I DON'T CARE.
SO, WHY DON'T WE PUT IT TO THE TEST AN' SEE JUST HOW MUCH YOU REALLY DON'T CARE?
WHAT DO YOU MEAN?
LET'S YOU AND ME GO. I'LL SHOW YOU HOW UNSPECIAL YOU REALLY ARE.
WILL YOU THEN LEAVE IF I DO THIS?
GLADLY!
YOU NEED A SUIT?
GOT ONE IN MY BACKPACK JUST FOR THE OCCASION.
I'LL BE RIGHT BACK.
TONTA, ARE YOU YOUR SCHOOL'S STAR SWIMMER?
I MIGHT BE!
SHUT UP, GOMEZ!
8.

OK, ONE LENGTH OF THE POOL AND BACK.
READY...
SET... UH, GO.
?!
??
!!!
BRRRRRRR
BRRRRRRB
IT'S LATE. I HAVE TO GO IN NOW.
BYE, HILLY.
DO YOU THINK THOSE WERE TEARS IN HILLY'S EYES OR JUST POOL WATER?
I DUNNO, BUT I DO KNOW SHE PROBABLY HATES ME NOW...
...AND HILLY JOHNSON DOESN'T HATE ANYBODY!
AND YOU, THINK IT'S FUNNY?
YES!
DID YOU SEE HOW FAST HILLY SWAM??
IT WAS STRAIGHT OUT OF GILLIGAN'S ISLAND!
9.

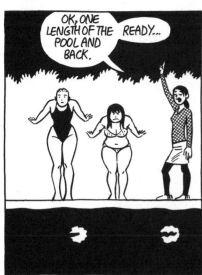

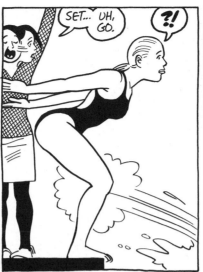

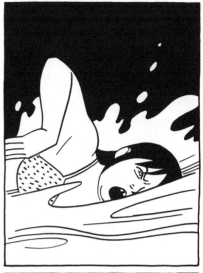

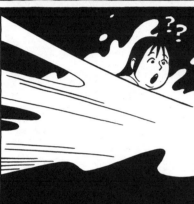

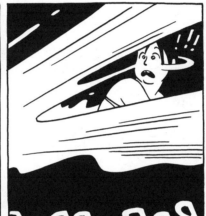

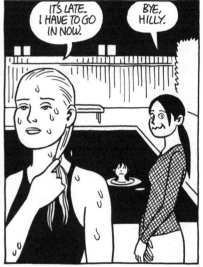

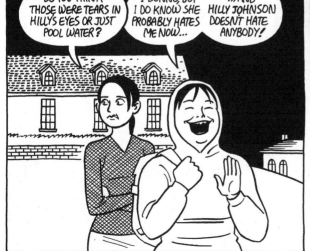

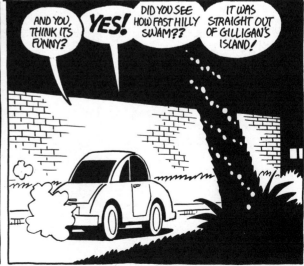

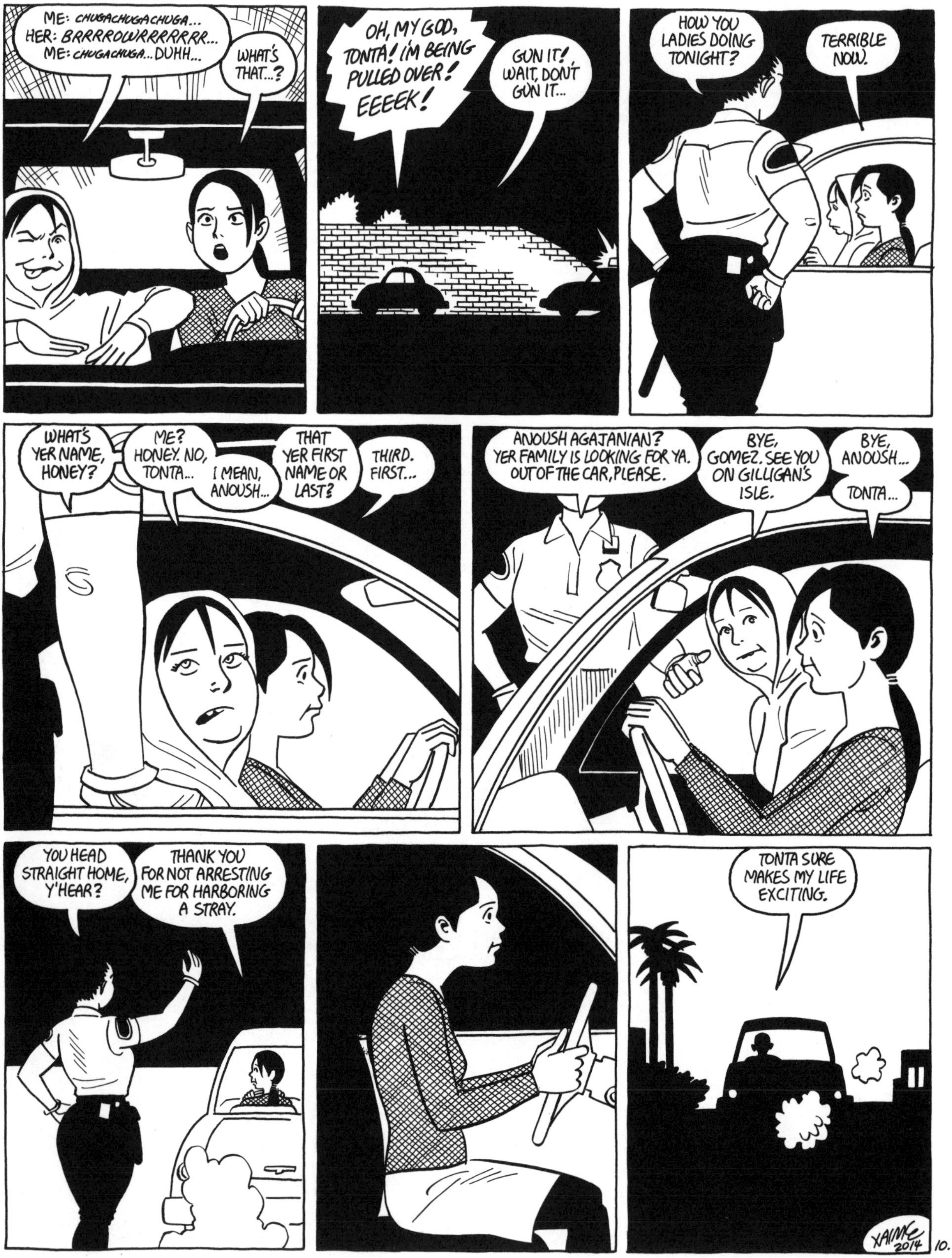
ME: CHUGACHUGACHUGA...
HER: BRRRROWRRRRRR...
ME: CHUGACHUGA... DUHH...
WHAT'S THAT...?
OH, MY GOD, TONTA! I'M BEING PULLED OVER! EEEEK!
GUN IT! WAIT, DON'T GUN IT...
HOW YOU LADIES DOING TONIGHT?
TERRIBLE NOW.
WHAT'S YER NAME, HONEY?
ME? HONEY. NO, TONTA...
I MEAN, ANOUSH...
THAT YER FIRST NAME OR LAST?
THIRD. FIRST...
ANOUSH AGAJANIAN? YER FAMILY IS LOOKING FOR YA. OUT OF THE CAR, PLEASE.
BYE, GOMEZ. SEE YOU ON GILLIGAN'S ISLE.
BYE, ANOUSH...
TONTA...
YOU HEAD STRAIGHT HOME, Y'HEAR?
THANK YOU FOR NOT ARRESTING ME FOR HARBORING A STRAY.
TONTA SURE MAKES MY LIFE EXCITING.
XAIME 2014
10.

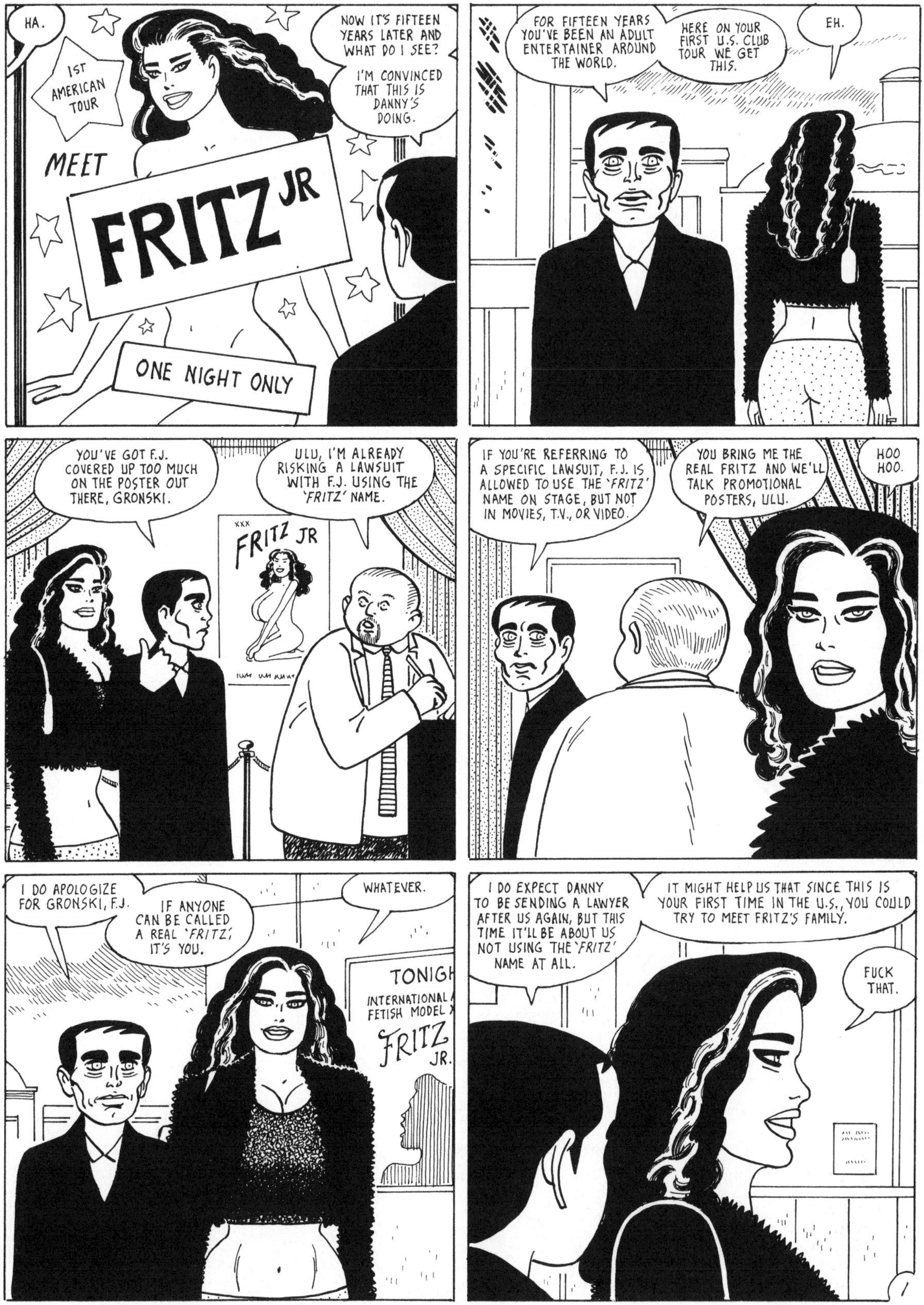
HA.
1ST AMERICAN TOUR
MEET FRITZ JR
ONE NIGHT ONLY
NOW IT'S FIFTEEN YEARS LATER AND WHAT DO I SEE?
I'M CONVINCED THAT THIS IS DANNY'S DOING.
FOR FIFTEEN YEARS YOU'VE BEEN AN ADULT ENTERTAINER AROUND THE WORLD.
HERE ON YOUR FIRST U.S. CLUB TOUR WE GET THIS.
EH.
YOU'VE GOT F.J. COVERED UP TOO MUCH ON THE POSTER OUT THERE, GRONSKI.
ULU, I'M ALREADY RISKING A LAWSUIT WITH F.J. USING THE 'FRITZ' NAME.
XXX
FRITZ JR
IF YOU'RE REFERRING TO A SPECIFIC LAWSUIT, F.J. IS ALLOWED TO USE THE 'FRITZ' NAME ON STAGE, BUT NOT IN MOVIES, T.V., OR VIDEO.
YOU BRING ME THE REAL FRITZ AND WE'LL TALK PROMOTIONAL POSTERS, ULU.
HOO HOO.
I DO APOLOGIZE FOR GRONSKI, F.J.
IF ANYONE CAN BE CALLED A REAL 'FRITZ,' IT'S YOU.
WHATEVER.
TONIGH
INTERNATIONAL
FETISH MODEL
FRITZ JR.
I DO EXPECT DANNY TO BE SENDING A LAWYER AFTER US AGAIN, BUT THIS TIME IT'LL BE ABOUT US NOT USING THE 'FRITZ' NAME AT ALL.
IT MIGHT HELP US THAT SINCE THIS IS YOUR FIRST TIME IN THE U.S., YOU COULD TRY TO MEET FRITZ'S FAMILY.
FUCK THAT.

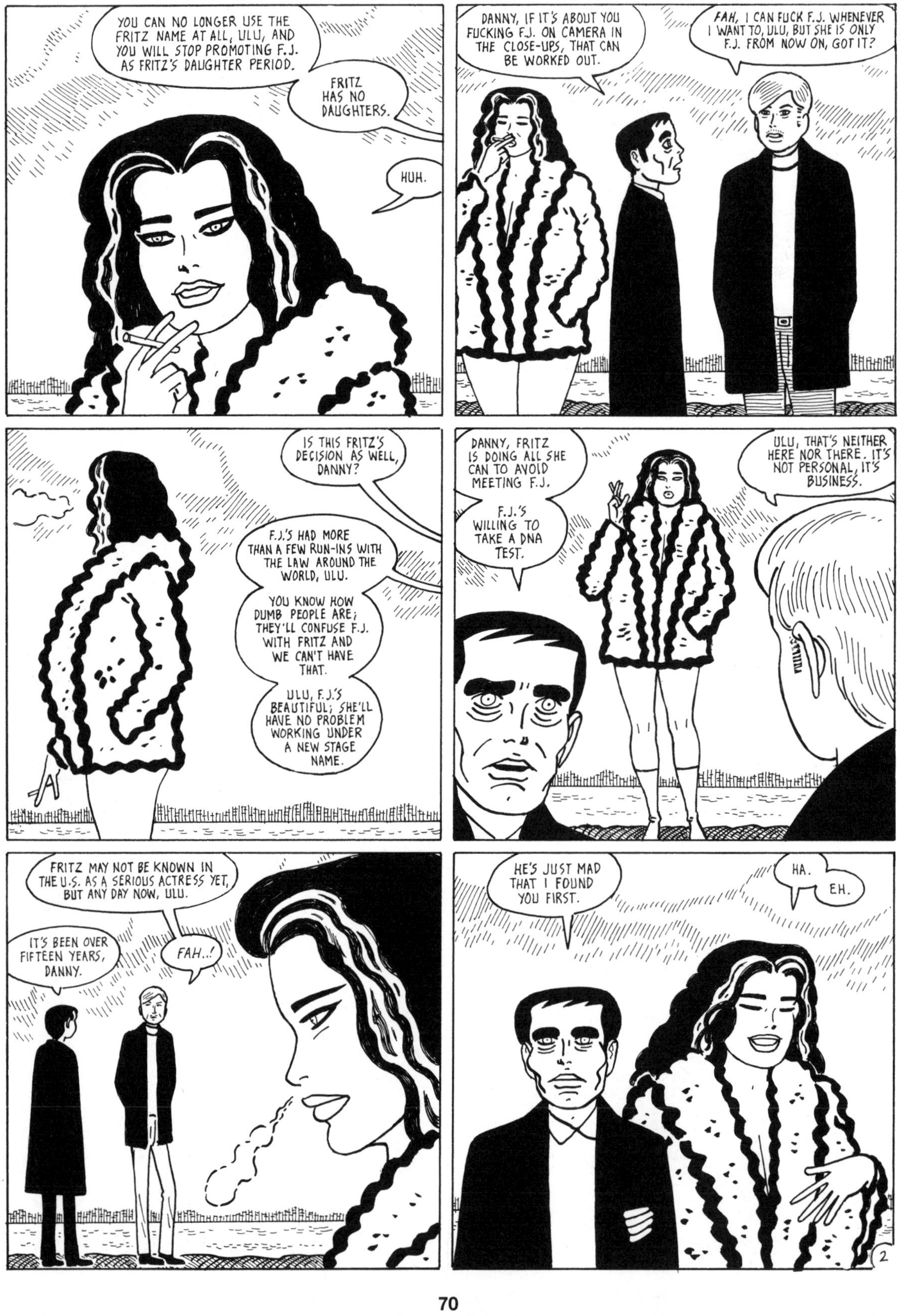
YOU CAN NO LONGER USE THE FRITZ NAME AT ALL, ULU, AND YOU WILL STOP PROMOTING F.J. AS FRITZ'S DAUGHTER PERIOD.
FRITZ HAS NO DAUGHTERS.
HUH.
DANNY, IF IT'S ABOUT YOU FUCKING F.J. ON CAMERA IN THE CLOSE-UPS, THAT CAN BE WORKED OUT.
FAH, I CAN FUCK F.J. WHENEVER I WANT TO, ULU, BUT SHE IS ONLY F.J. FROM NOW ON, GOT IT?
IS THIS FRITZ'S DECISION AS WELL, DANNY?
F.J.'S HAD MORE THAN A FEW RUN-INS WITH THE LAW AROUND THE WORLD, ULU.
YOU KNOW HOW DUMB PEOPLE ARE; THEY'LL CONFUSE F.J. WITH FRITZ AND WE CAN'T HAVE THAT.
ULU, F.J.'S BEAUTIFUL; SHE'LL HAVE NO PROBLEM WORKING UNDER A NEW STAGE NAME.
DANNY, FRITZ IS DOING ALL SHE CAN TO AVOID MEETING F.J.
F.J.'S WILLING TO TAKE A DNA TEST.
ULU, THAT'S NEITHER HERE NOR THERE. IT'S NOT PERSONAL, IT'S BUSINESS.
FRITZ MAY NOT BE KNOWN IN THE U.S. AS A SERIOUS ACTRESS YET, BUT ANY DAY NOW, ULU.
IT'S BEEN OVER FIFTEEN YEARS, DANNY.
FAH..!
HE'S JUST MAD THAT I FOUND YOU FIRST.
HA.
EH.
2

DANNY CHULO!
DON'T GO INSIDE THE CLUB YET.
*RETURN ENGAGEMENT
*ADULT ENTERTAINMENT STAR
PUPUSI.*
SO WHAT ARE YOUR PLANS TO GET THE REAL FRITZ TO COVER FOR ALL THE FRITZ JR. CANCELLATIONS, DANNY?
WELL?
EH, FRITZ DOESN'T DO STRIP CLUBS, GUYS.
DANNY, WE ALSO KNOW THAT YOU'VE BLOCKED ULU FROM RELEASING A FEW PROJECTS THAT HE'S DONE WITH FRITZ.
IT'S REALLY NOTHING YOU GUYS HAVE TO BE CONCERNED ABOUT; IT'S ONLY THE USUAL LEGAL SNAGS AND SHIT.
HEH, C'MON!
WELL, WE'VE INVESTED A LOT OF MONEY IN THOSE BLOCKED PROJECTS.
WE'LL JUST TAKE ENOUGH CASH TO KEEP US FROM GETTING TOO IMPATIENT, DANNY.
H-HEY, MY WALLET!
NOTHING PERSONAL, DANNY.
JUST BUSINESS, LIKE THEY SAY IN THE MOVIES.
HEH!
YOU GUYS!
HEH!
DANNY!
PUPUSI WILL BE FILLING IN FOR FRITZETTE'S CANCELLATION AS WELL AS FRITZ JR.'S.
I WAS LOOKING FORWARD TO MEETING ANOTHER ALLEGED FRITZ OFFSPRING.
NO SUCH PERSON!
UNLESS FRITZ'S ALLEGED SON HAD A SEX CHANGE.
FRITZETTE
CANCELLED
3

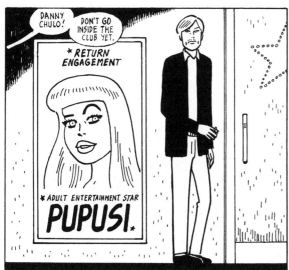

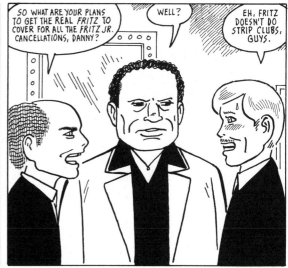

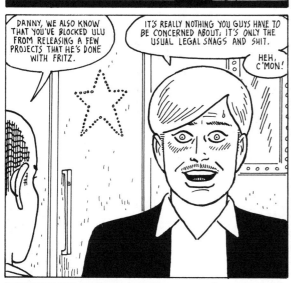

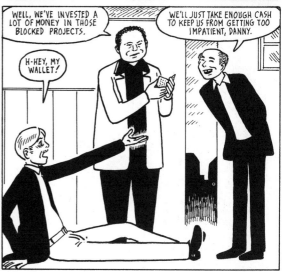

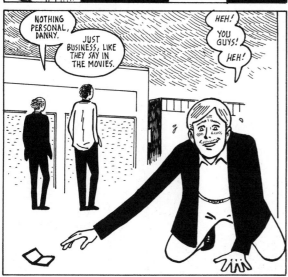

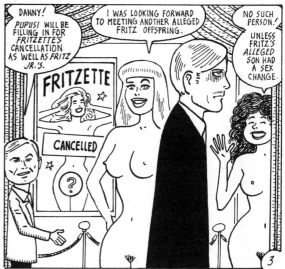

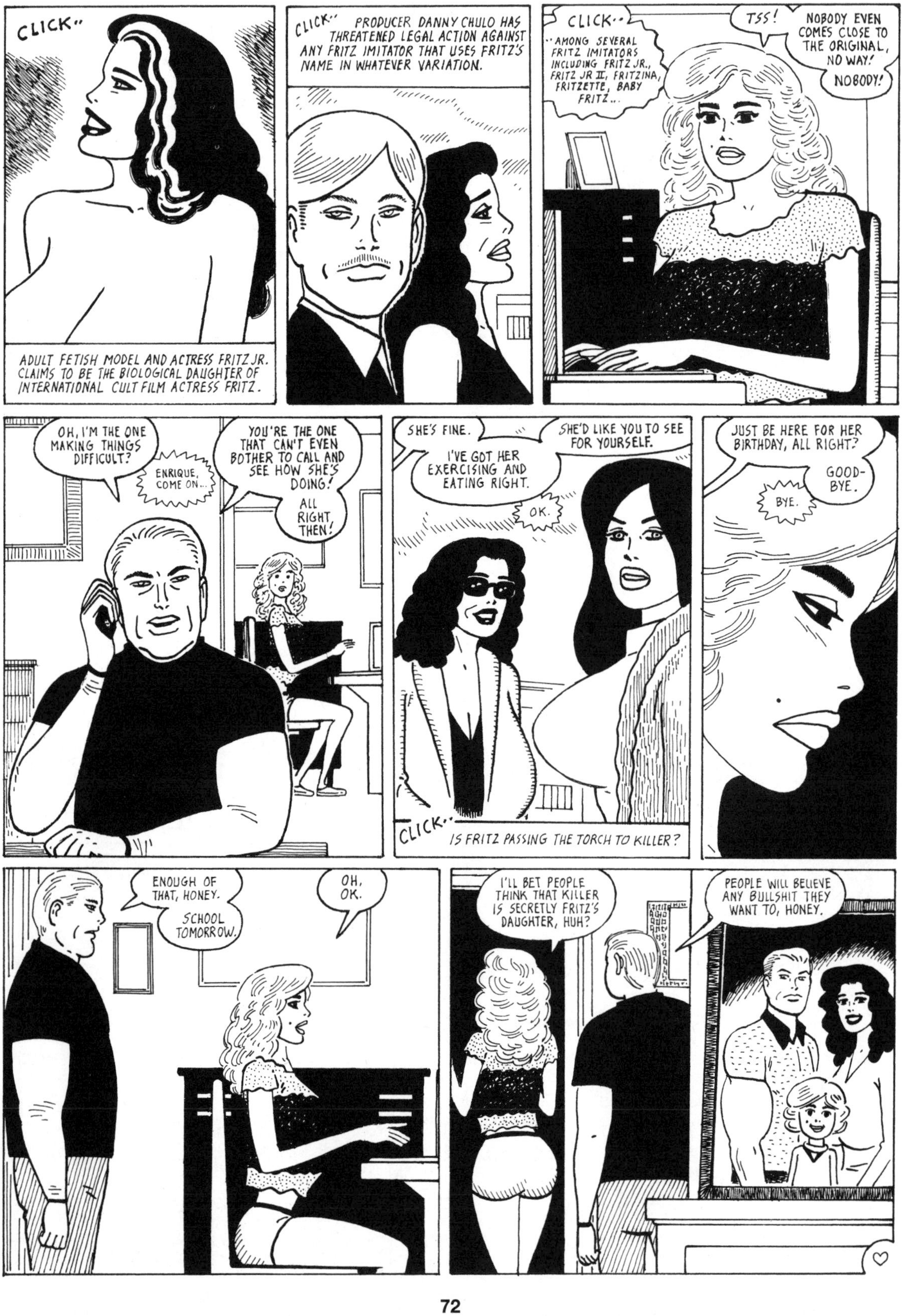
CLICK..
ADULT FETISH MODEL AND ACTRESS FRITZ JR. CLAIMS TO BE THE BIOLOGICAL DAUGHTER OF INTERNATIONAL CULT FILM ACTRESS FRITZ.
CLICK.. PRODUCER DANNY CHULO HAS THREATENED LEGAL ACTION AGAINST ANY FRITZ IMITATOR THAT USES FRITZ'S NAME IN WHATEVER VARIATION.
CLICK..
..AMONG SEVERAL FRITZ IMITATORS INCLUDING FRITZ JR., FRITZ JR II, FRITZINA, FRITZETTE, BABY FRITZ...
TSS!
NOBODY EVEN COMES CLOSE TO THE ORIGINAL, NO WAY!
NOBODY!
OH, I'M THE ONE MAKING THINGS DIFFICULT?
ENRIQUE, COME ON...
YOU'RE THE ONE THAT CAN'T EVEN BOTHER TO CALL AND SEE HOW SHE'S DOING!
ALL RIGHT, THEN!
SHE'S FINE.
I'VE GOT HER EXERCISING AND EATING RIGHT.
SHE'D LIKE YOU TO SEE FOR YOURSELF.
OK.
CLICK..
IS FRITZ PASSING THE TORCH TO KILLER?
JUST BE HERE FOR HER BIRTHDAY, ALL RIGHT?
GOOD-BYE.
BYE.
ENOUGH OF THAT, HONEY.
SCHOOL TOMORROW.
OH, OK.
I'LL BET PEOPLE THINK THAT KILLER IS SECRETLY FRITZ'S DAUGHTER, HUH?
PEOPLE WILL BELIEVE ANY BULLSHIT THEY WANT TO, HONEY.

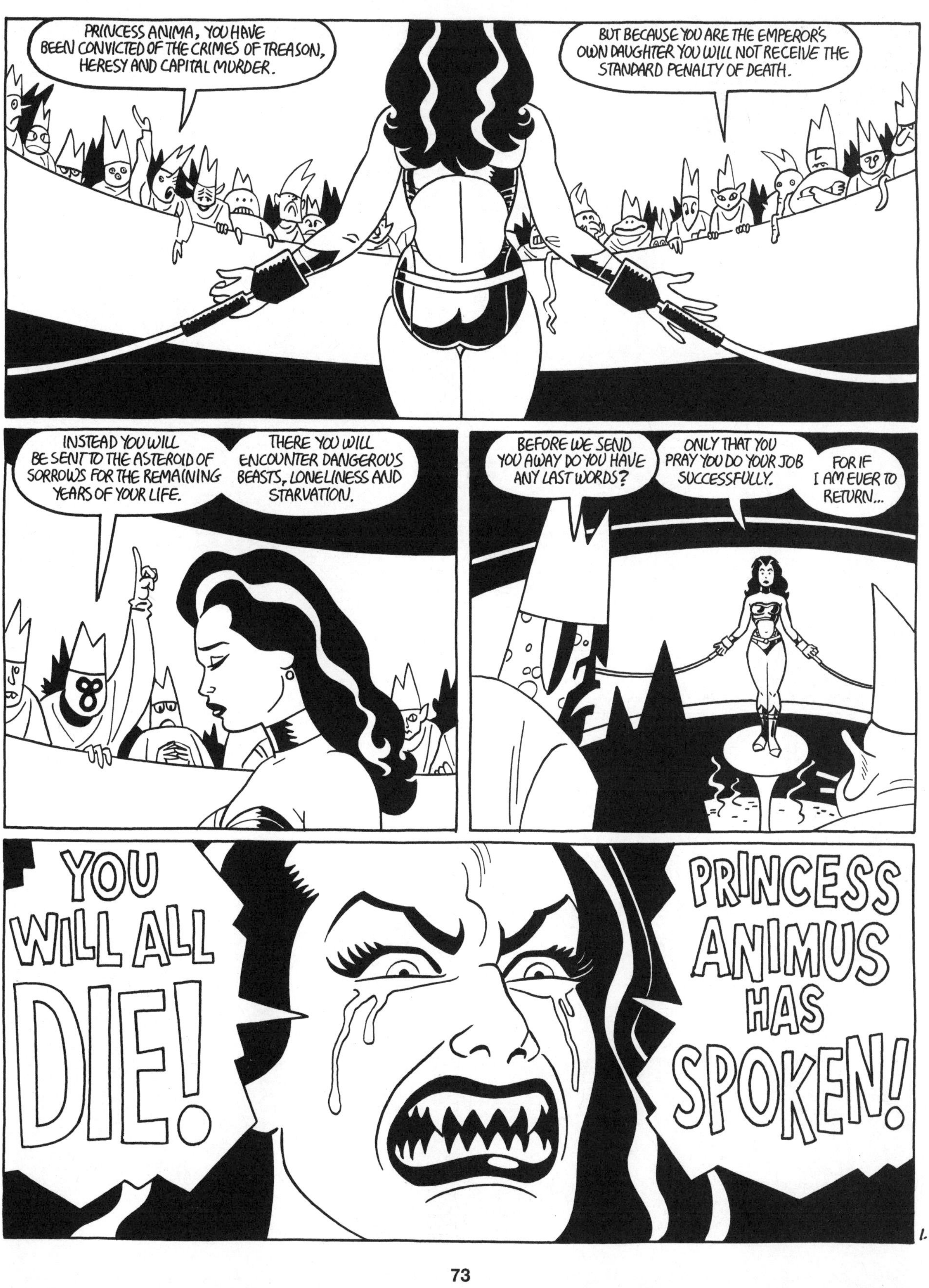
PRINCESS ANIMA, YOU HAVE BEEN CONVICTED OF THE CRIMES OF TREASON, HERESY AND CAPITAL MURDER.
BUT BECAUSE YOU ARE THE EMPEROR'S OWN DAUGHTER YOU WILL NOT RECEIVE THE STANDARD PENALTY OF DEATH.
INSTEAD YOU WILL BE SENT TO THE ASTEROID OF SORROWS FOR THE REMAINING YEARS OF YOUR LIFE.
THERE YOU WILL ENCOUNTER DANGEROUS BEASTS, LONELINESS AND STARVATION.
BEFORE WE SEND YOU AWAY DO YOU HAVE ANY LAST WORDS?
ONLY THAT YOU PRAY YOU DO YOUR JOB SUCCESSFULLY.
FOR IF I AM EVER TO RETURN...
YOU WILL ALL DIE!
PRINCESS ANIMUS HAS SPOKEN!
1.

princess
ANIMASS!

IT IS A SHAME, PRINCESS ANIMA, THAT THIS HAS TO BE.

EAT SHIT AND DIE WITH THE REST OF THOSE CUMFUCKS, THUD.

BY A SHAME I MEAN THIS COULD ALL HAVE BEEN AVOIDED. IF YOU ONLY LET ME STAND UP FOR YOU IN COURT. I COULD HAVE...

YOU MEAN AFTER I HAD TO SUCK THAT USELESS SACK O' SHIT COCK OF YOURS?

2.

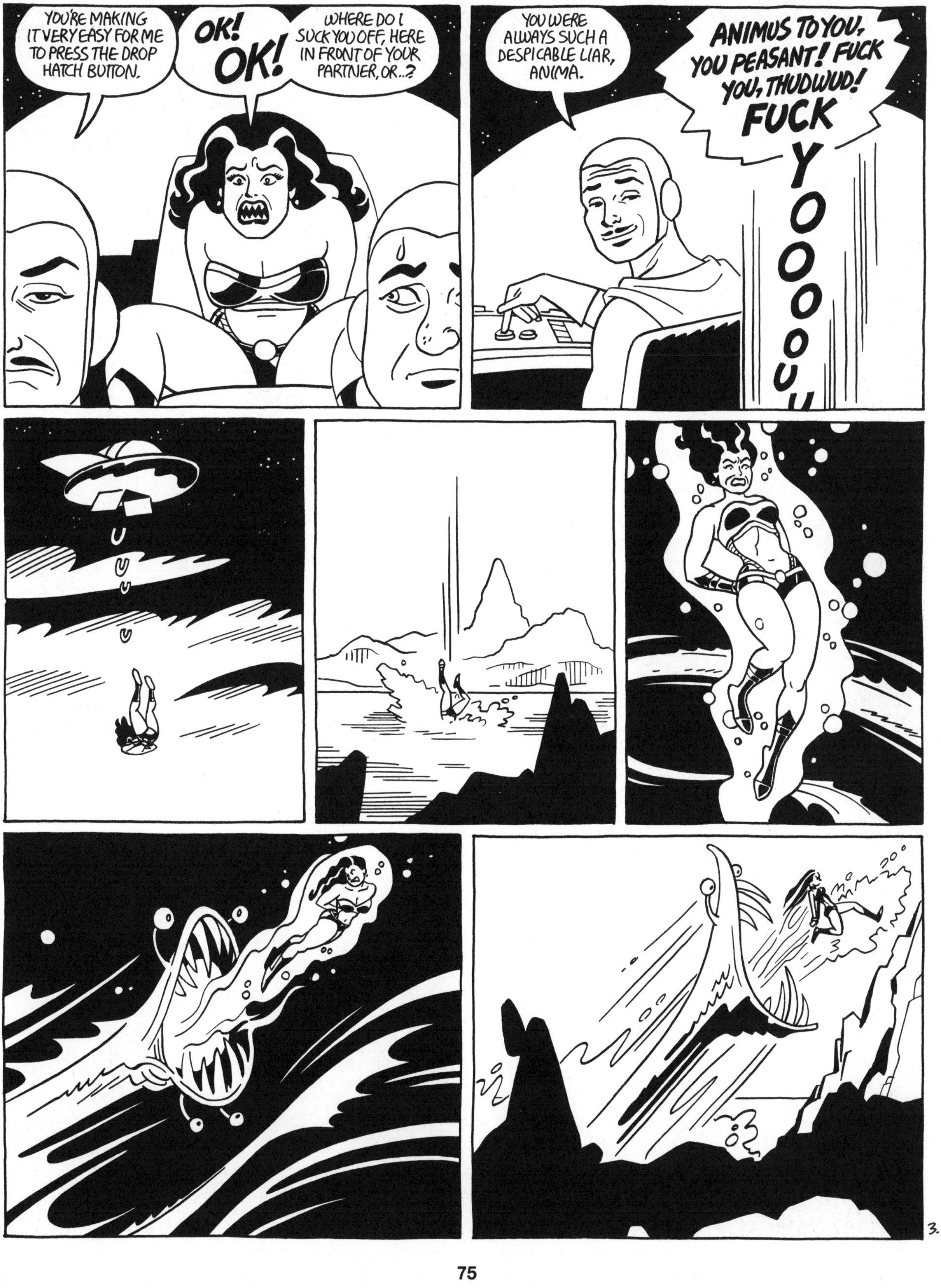
YOU'RE MAKING IT VERY EASY FOR ME TO PRESS THE DROP HATCH BUTTON.
OK! OK!
WHERE DO I SUCK YOU OFF, HERE IN FRONT OF YOUR PARTNER, OR..?
YOU WERE ALWAYS SUCH A DESPICABLE LIAR, ANIMA.
ANIMUS TO YOU, YOU PEASANT! FUCK YOU, THUDWUD! FUCK
YOOOOUU
3.

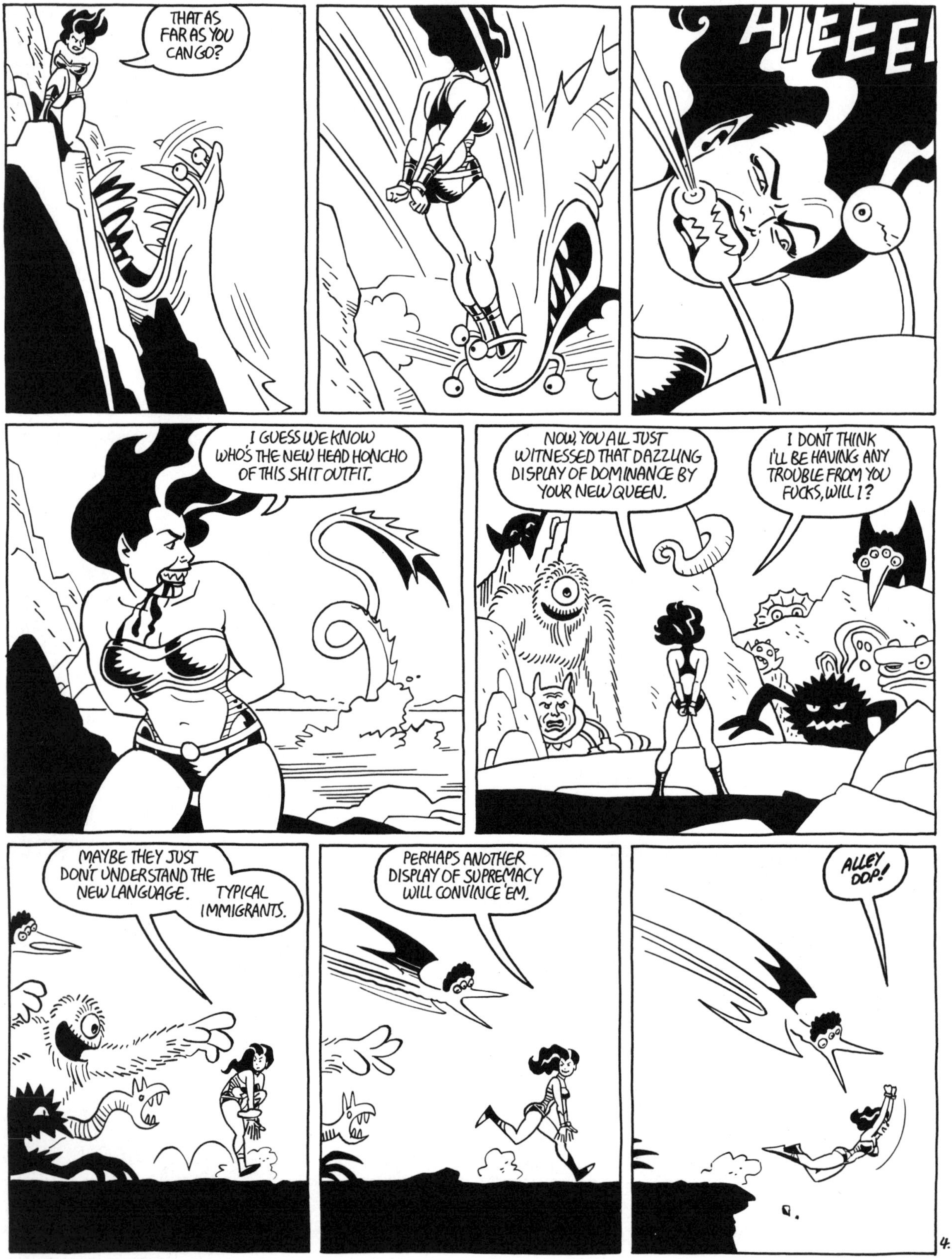
THAT AS FAR AS YOU CAN GO?
AIEEEE
I GUESS WE KNOW WHO'S THE NEW HEAD HONCHO OF THIS SHIT OUTFIT.
NOW, YOU ALL JUST WITNESSED THAT DAZZLING DISPLAY OF DOMINANCE BY YOUR NEW QUEEN.
I DON'T THINK I'LL BE HAVING ANY TROUBLE FROM YOU FUCKS, WILL I?
MAYBE THEY JUST DON'T UNDERSTAND THE NEW LANGUAGE.
TYPICAL IMMIGRANTS.
PERHAPS ANOTHER DISPLAY OF SUPREMACY WILL CONVINCE 'EM.
ALLEY OOP!
4.

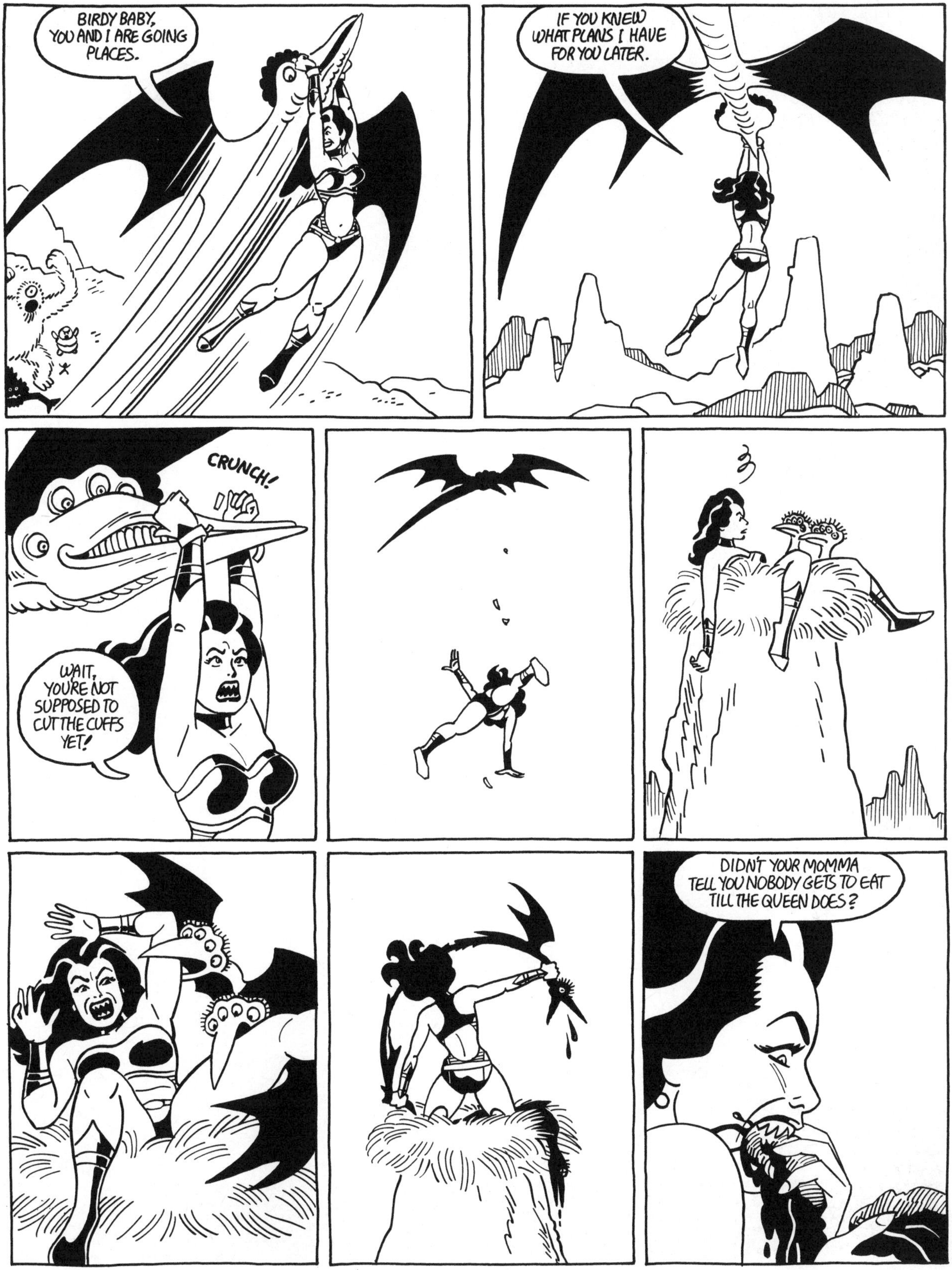
BIRDY BABY, YOU AND I ARE GOING PLACES.
IF YOU KNEW WHAT PLANS I HAVE FOR YOU LATER.
CRUNCH!
WAIT, YOU'RE NOT SUPPOSED TO CUT THE CUFFS YET!
DIDN'T YOUR MOMMA TELL YOU NOBODY GETS TO EAT TILL THE QUEEN DOES?
S.

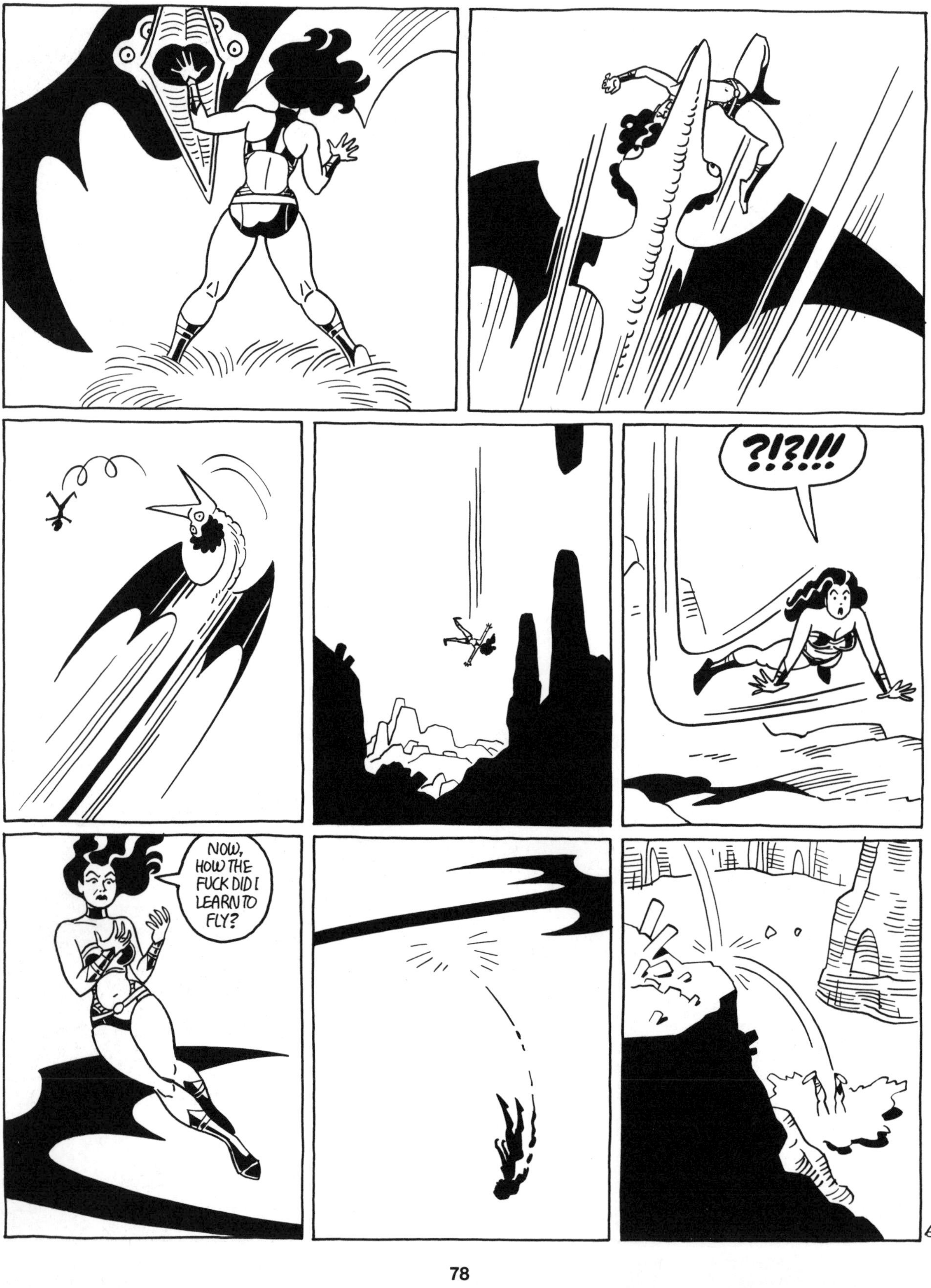
?!?!!!
NOW, HOW THE FUCK DID I LEARN TO FLY?
6.

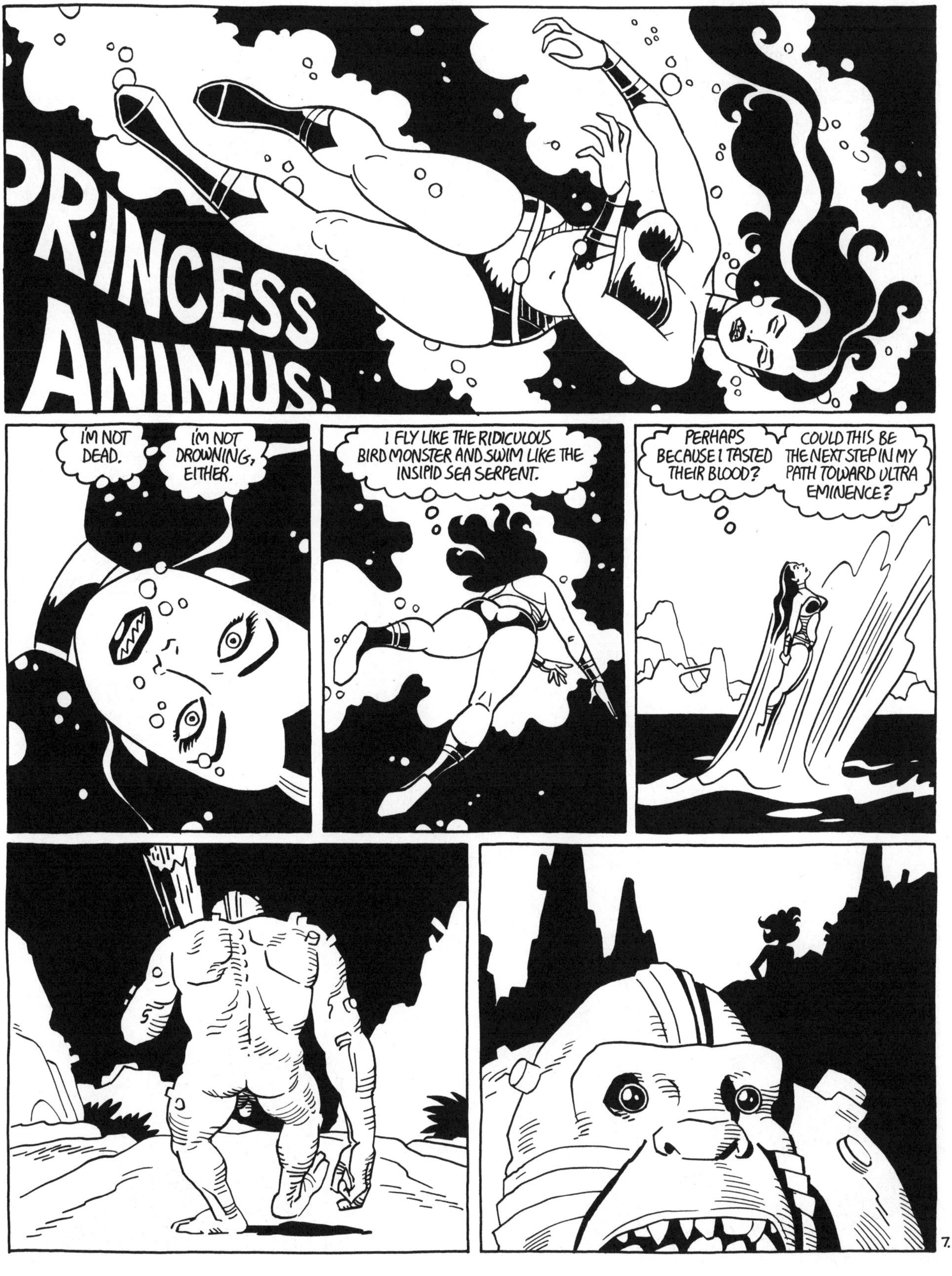
PRINCESS ANIMUS!
I'M NOT DEAD.
I'M NOT DROWNING, EITHER.
I FLY LIKE THE RIDICULOUS BIRD MONSTER AND SWIM LIKE THE INSIPID SEA SERPENT.
PERHAPS BECAUSE I TASTED THEIR BLOOD?
COULD THIS BE THE NEXT STEP IN MY PATH TOWARD ULTRA EMINENCE?
7.

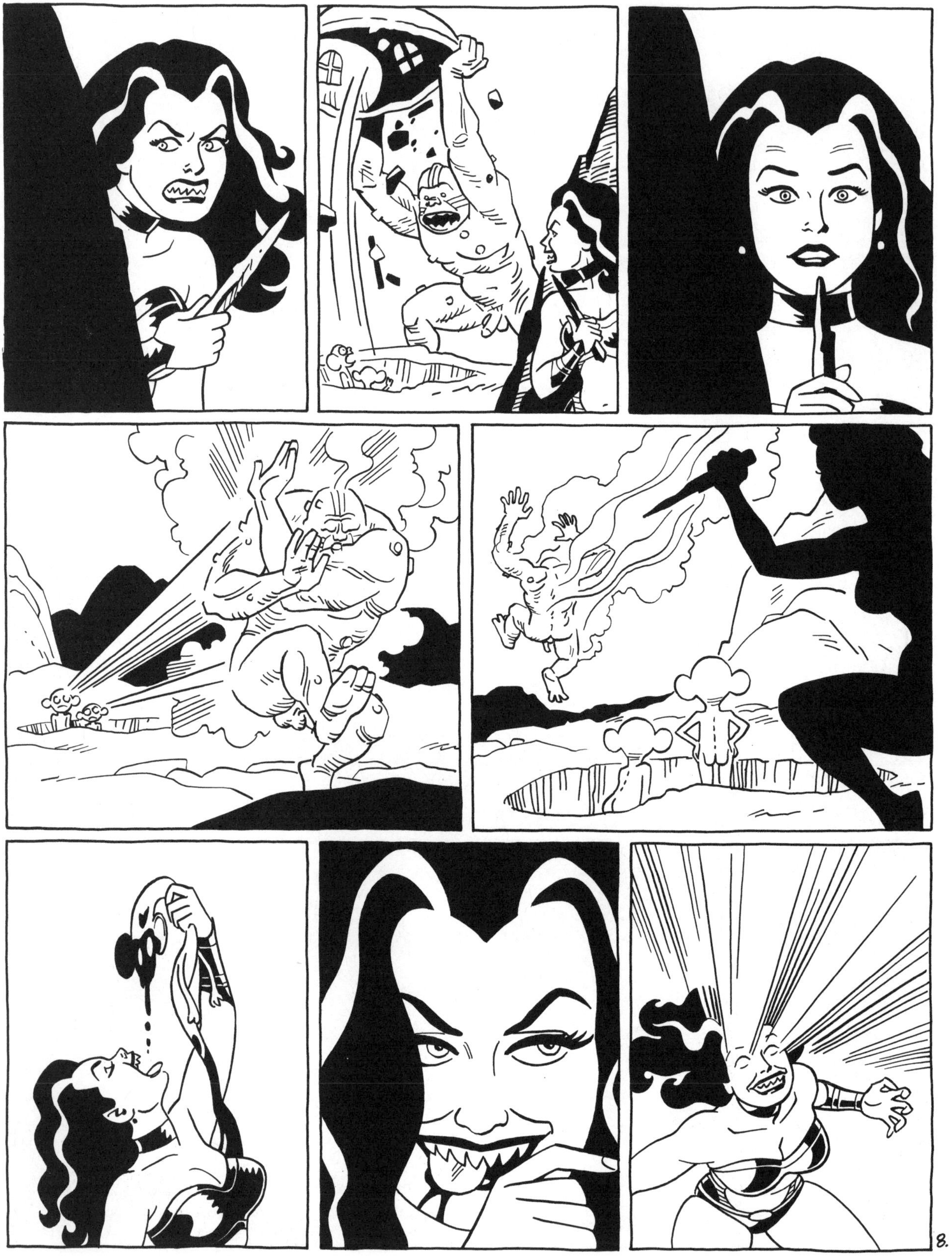
8.

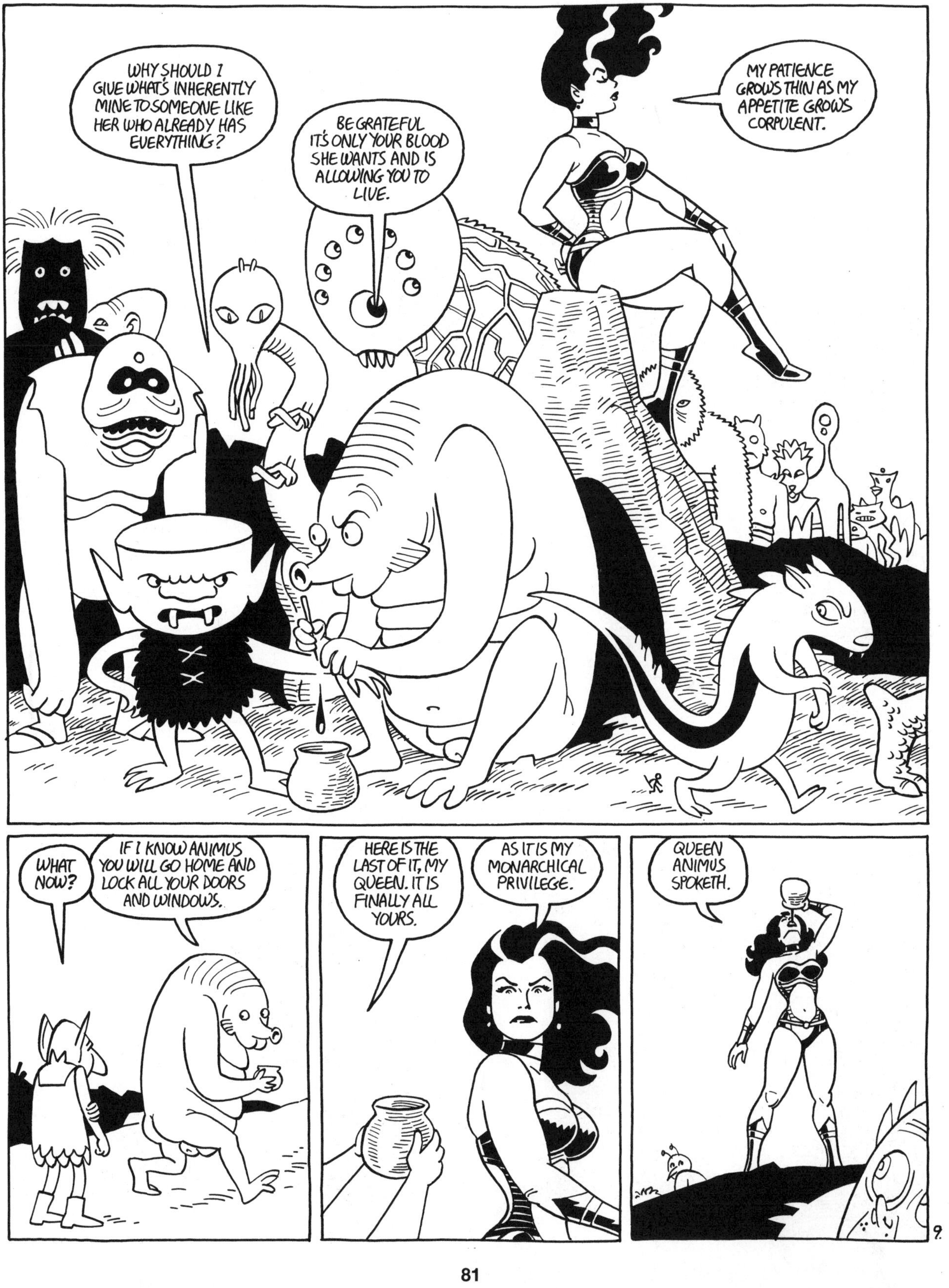
WHY SHOULD I GIVE WHAT'S INHERENTLY MINE TO SOMEONE LIKE HER WHO ALREADY HAS EVERYTHING?
BE GRATEFUL IT'S ONLY YOUR BLOOD SHE WANTS AND IS ALLOWING YOU TO LIVE.
MY PATIENCE GROWS THIN AS MY APPETITE GROWS CORPULENT.
WHAT NOW?
IF I KNOW ANIMUS YOU WILL GO HOME AND LOCK ALL YOUR DOORS AND WINDOWS.
HERE IS THE LAST OF IT, MY QUEEN. IT IS FINALLY ALL YOURS.
AS IT IS MY MONARCHICAL PRIVILEGE.
QUEEN ANIMUS SPOKETH.
9.

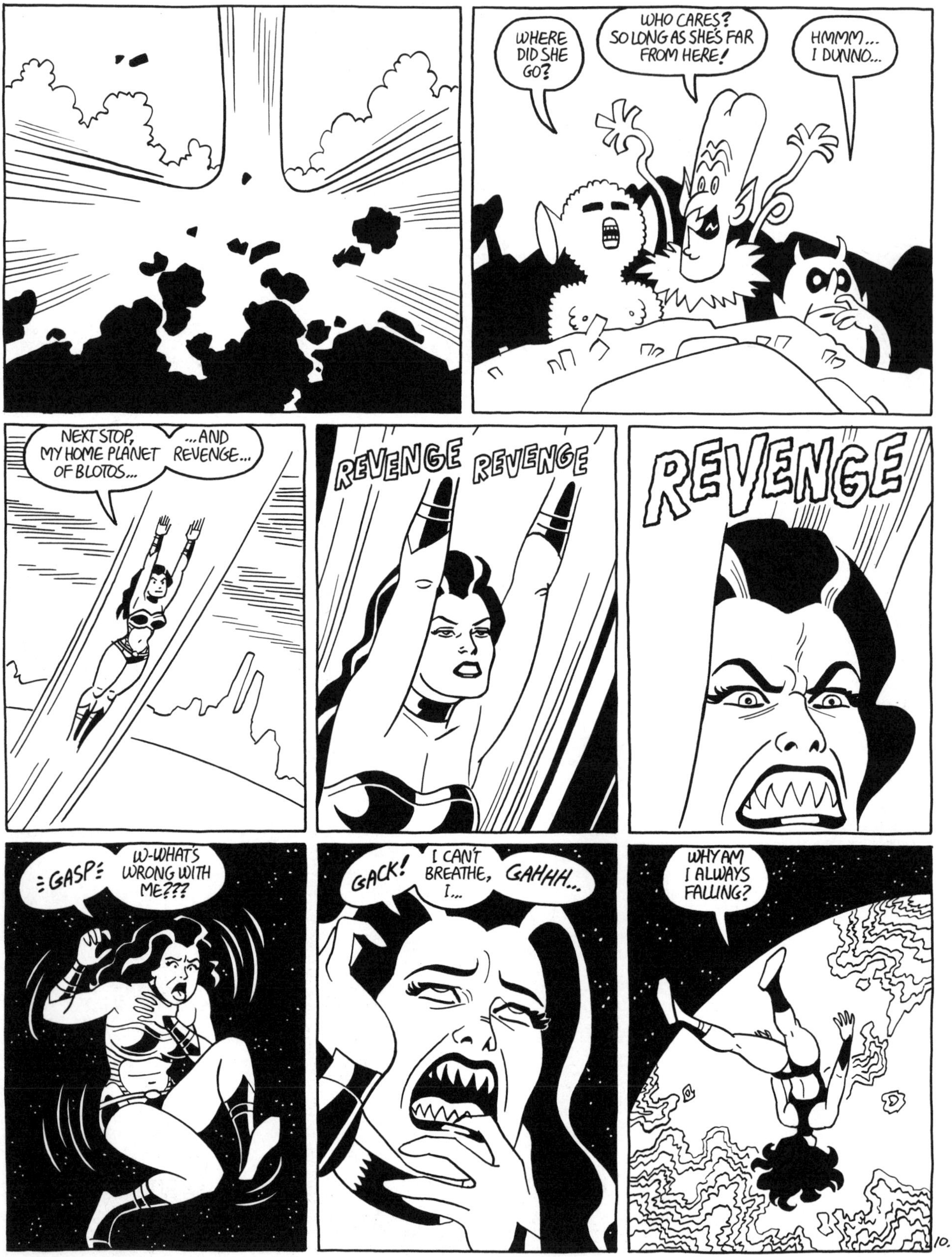
WHERE DID SHE GO?
WHO CARES? SO LONG AS SHE'S FAR FROM HERE!
HMMM... I DUNNO...
NEXT STOP, MY HOME PLANET OF BLOTOS...
...AND REVENGE...
REVENGE REVENGE
REVENGE
GASP
W-WHAT'S WRONG WITH ME???
GACK!
I CAN'T BREATHE, I...
GAHHH...
WHY AM I ALWAYS FALLING?
10.

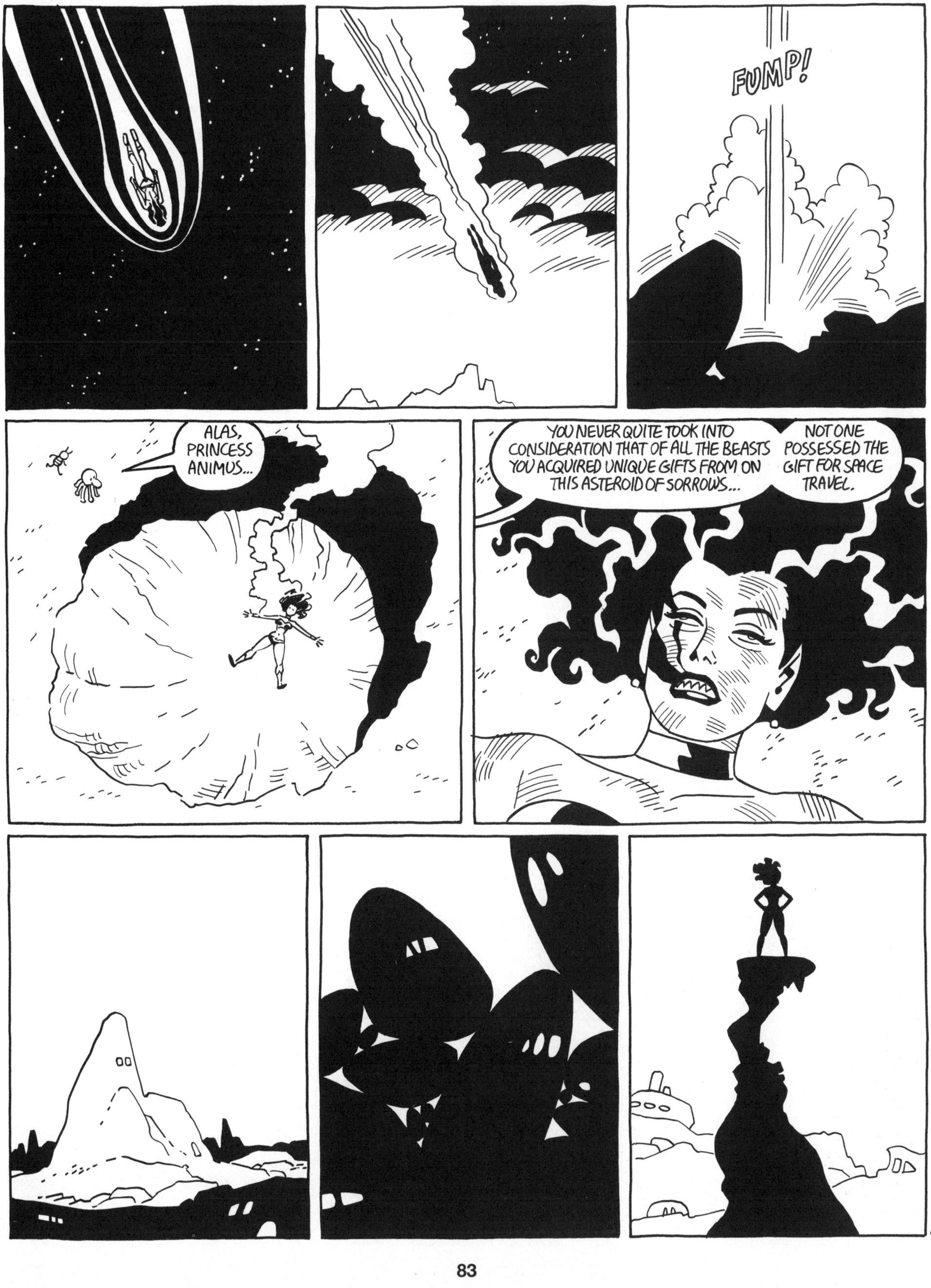
FUMP!
ALAS, PRINCESS ANIMUS...
YOU NEVER QUITE TOOK INTO CONSIDERATION THAT OF ALL THE BEASTS YOU ACQUIRED UNIQUE GIFTS FROM ON THIS ASTEROID OF SORROWS...
NOT ONE POSSESSED THE GIFT FOR SPACE TRAVEL.
11.

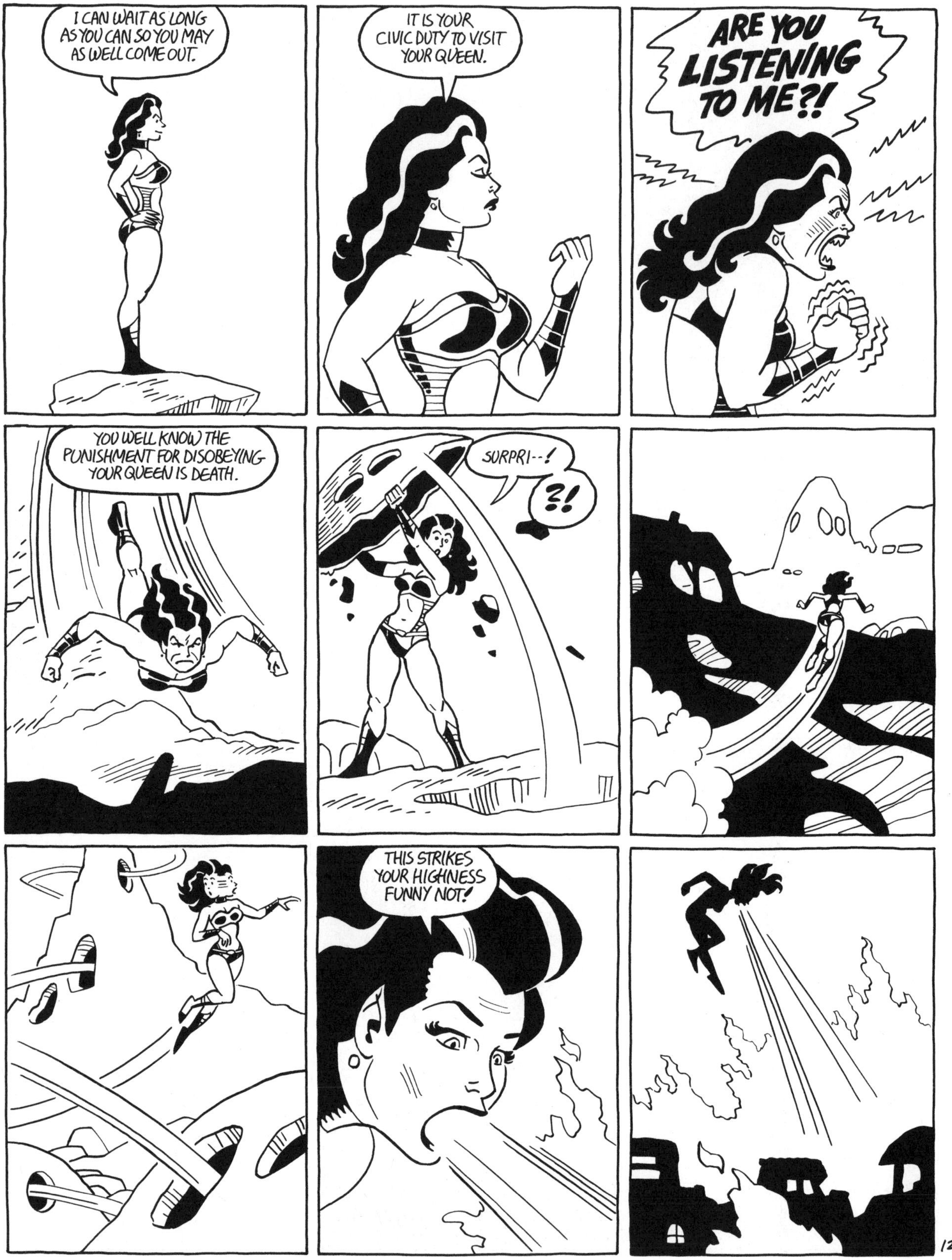
I CAN WAIT AS LONG AS YOU CAN SO YOU MAY AS WELL COME OUT.
IT IS YOUR CIVIC DUTY TO VISIT YOUR QUEEN.
ARE YOU LISTENING TO ME?!
YOU WELL KNOW THE PUNISHMENT FOR DISOBEYING YOUR QUEEN IS DEATH.
SURPRI--!
?!
THIS STRIKES YOUR HIGHNESS FUNNY NOT!
12.

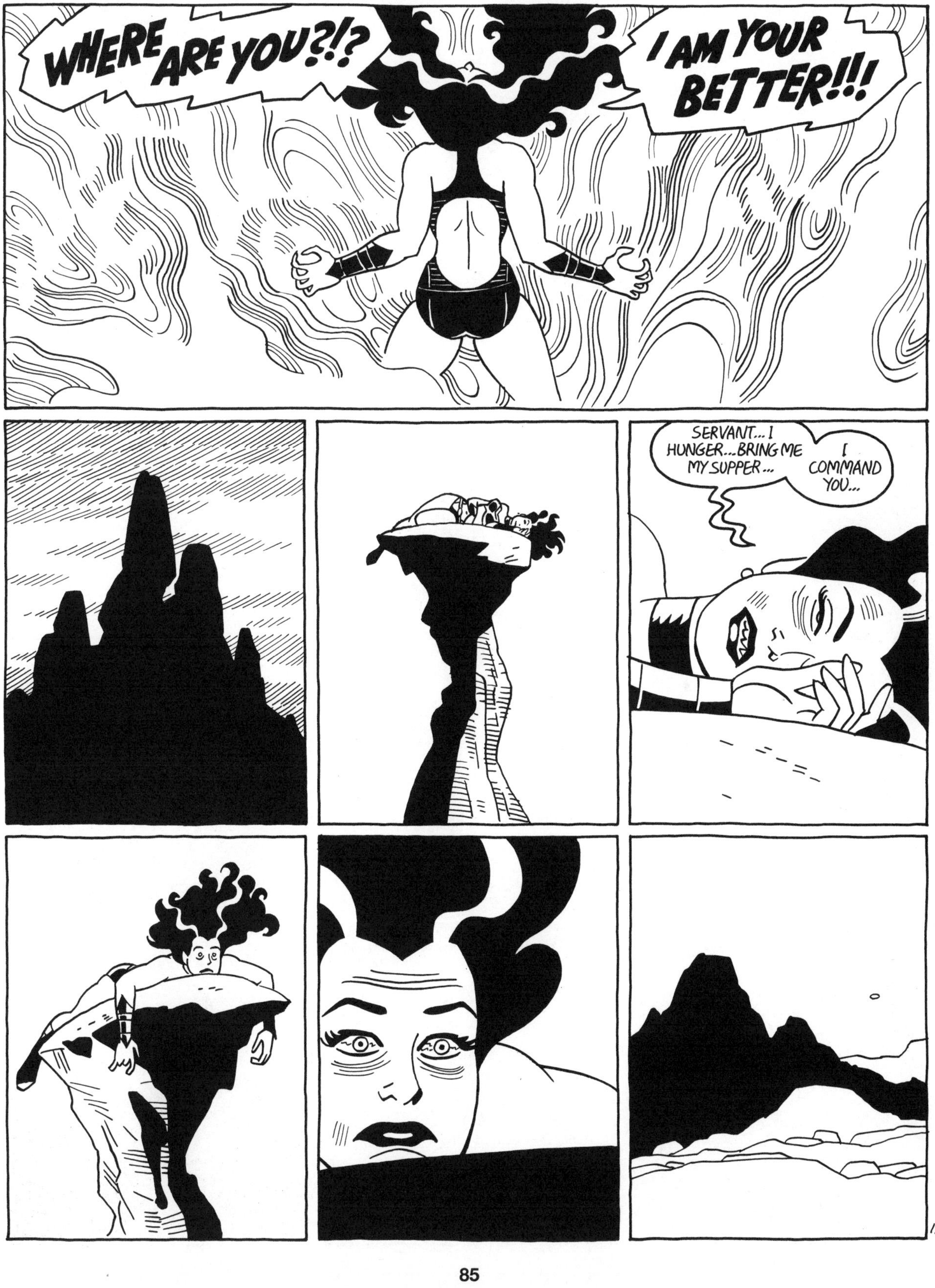
WHERE ARE YOU?!?
I AM YOUR BETTER!!!
SERVANT... I HUNGER... BRING ME MY SUPPER...
I COMMAND YOU...
13.

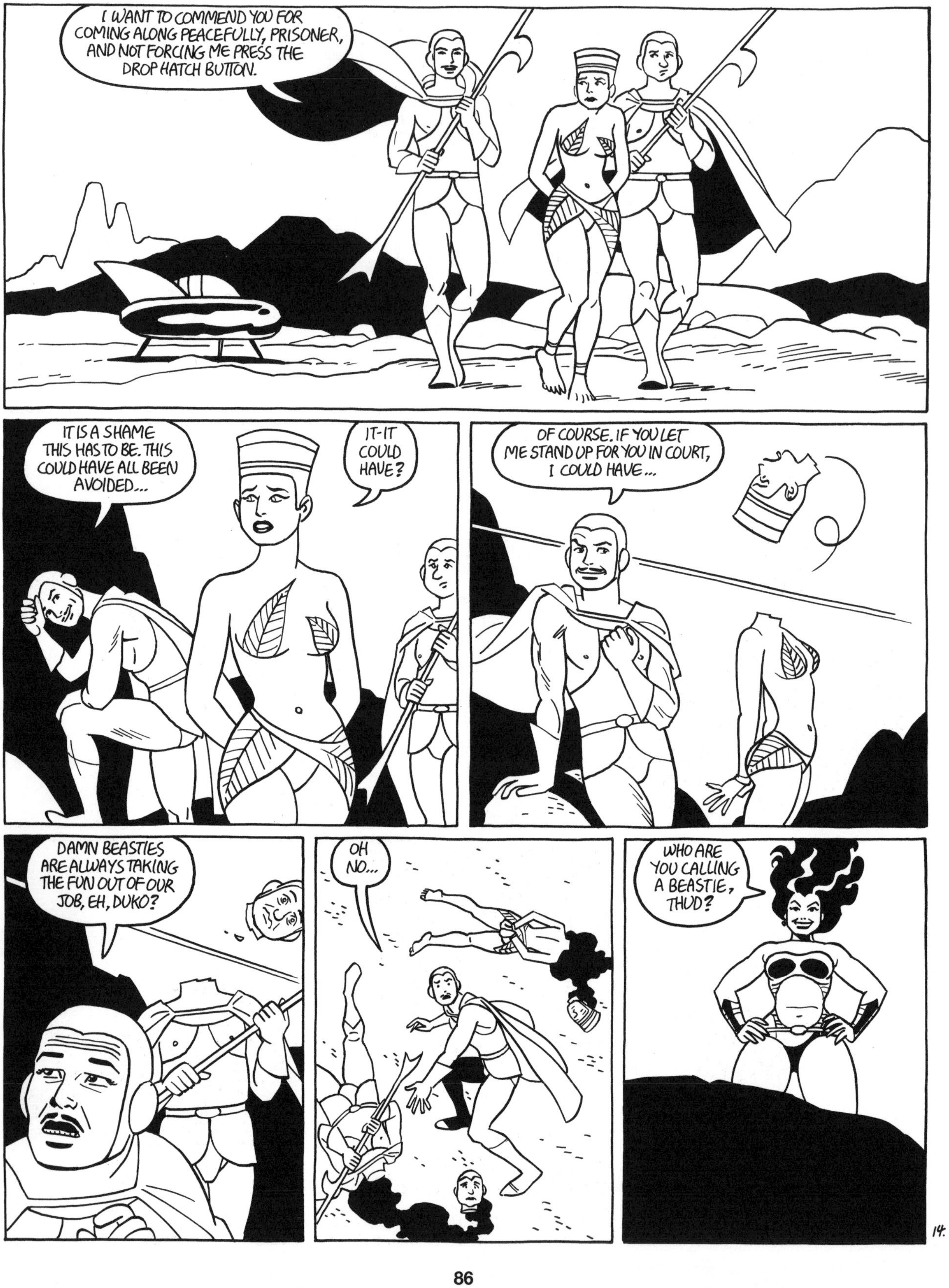
I WANT TO COMMEND YOU FOR COMING ALONG PEACEFULLY, PRISONER, AND NOT FORCING ME PRESS THE DROP HATCH BUTTON.
IT IS A SHAME THIS HAS TO BE. THIS COULD HAVE ALL BEEN AVOIDED...
IT-IT COULD HAVE?
OF COURSE. IF YOU LET ME STAND UP FOR YOU IN COURT, I COULD HAVE...
DAMN BEASTIES ARE ALWAYS TAKING THE FUN OUT OF OUR JOB, EH, DUKO?
OH NO...
WHO ARE YOU CALLING A BEASTIE, THUD?
14.

P-PRINCESS ANIMA! AM I GLAD TO SEE YOU...
I'M RELIEVED THE BEASTS DIDN'T GET YOU.
Y-YOU KNEW I WAS COMING BACK FOR YOU, RIGHT?
WHOA!
HOW DID YOU FLOAT DOWN LIKE THAT? AND THOSE BEAMS...
WHICH BEAMS?
OH, YOU MEAN THESE BEAMS.
I-I SEE THAT YOU CAN KILL ME AT ANY TIME, YET YOU HAVEN'T...
COULD IT BE YOU STILL HAVE SOME FEELINGS LEFT...?
YOU'RE CATCHING ON, THUD...
15.

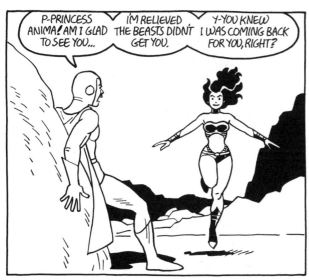

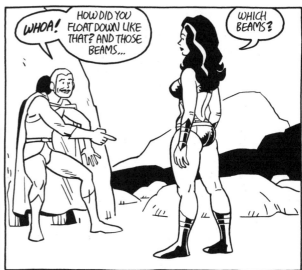

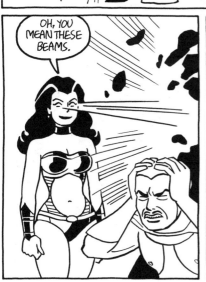

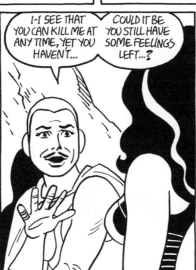

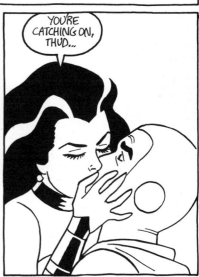

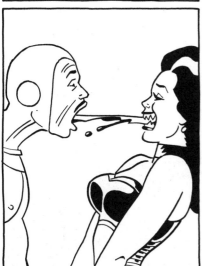

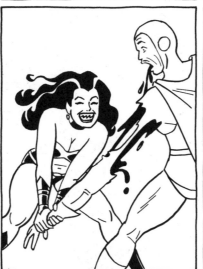

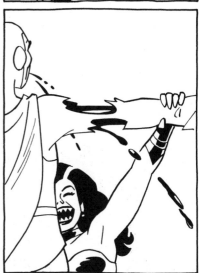

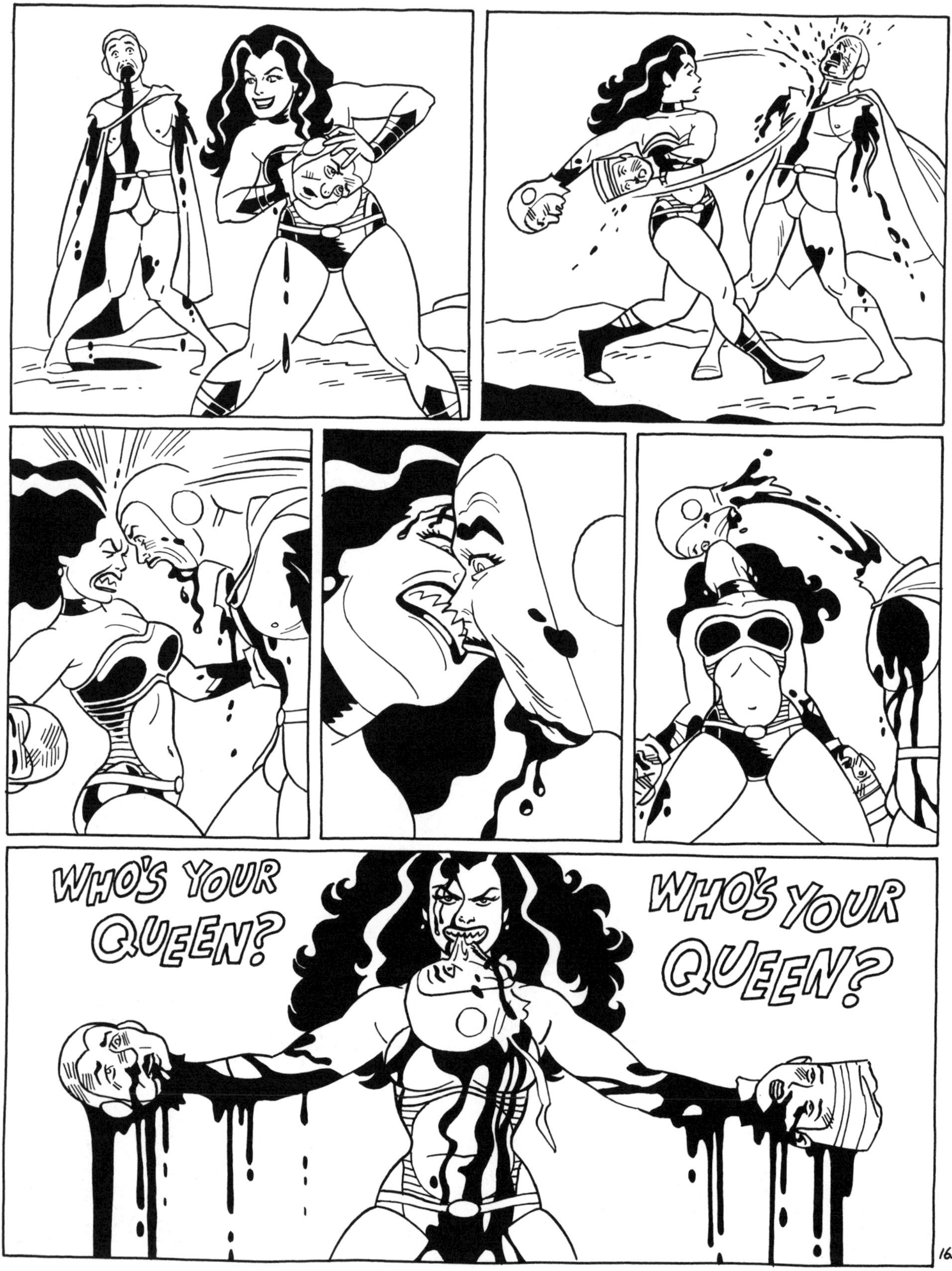
WHO'S YOUR QUEEN?
WHO'S YOUR QUEEN?
16.

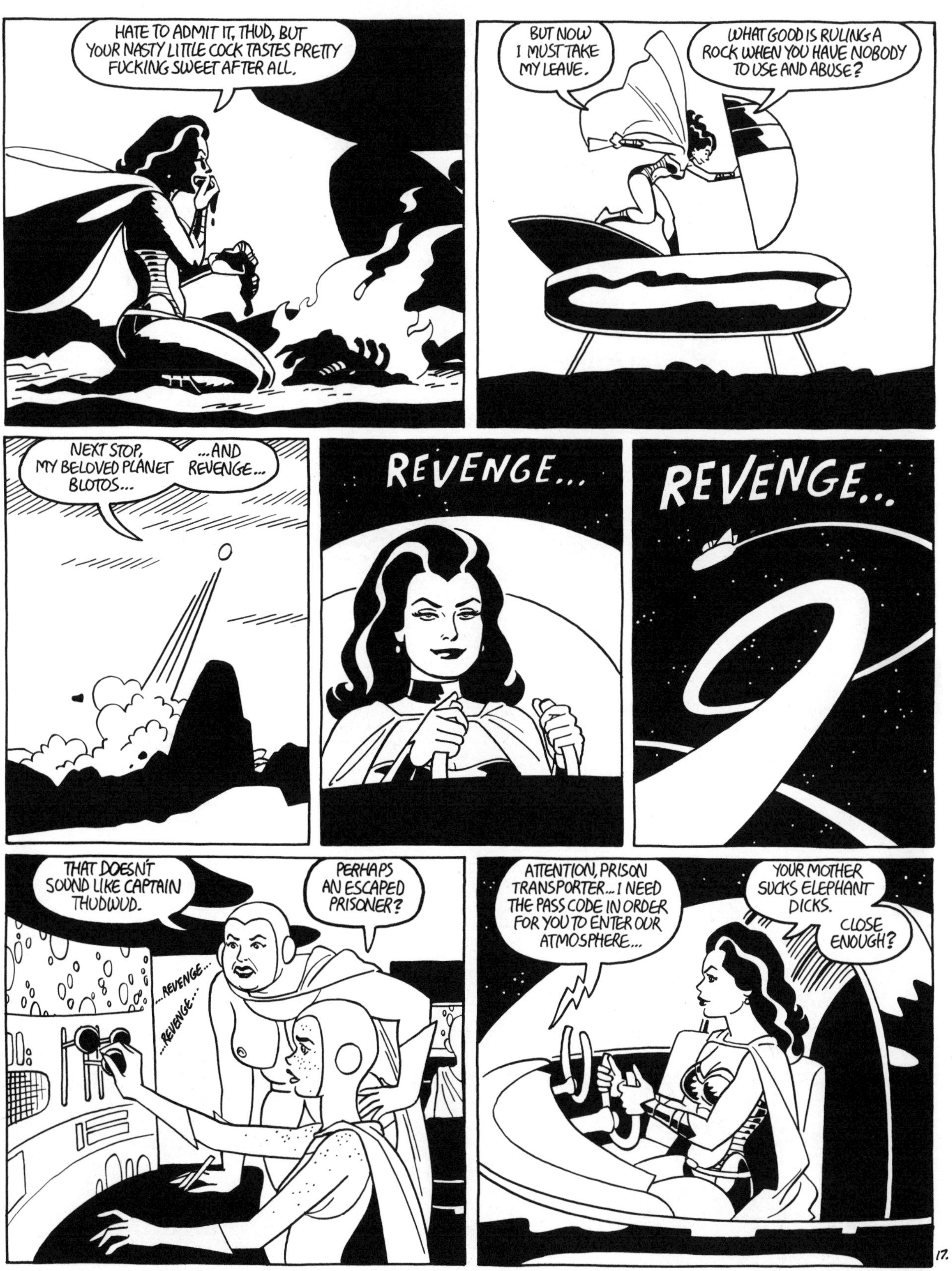
HATE TO ADMIT IT, THUD, BUT YOUR NASTY LITTLE COCK TASTES PRETTY FUCKING SWEET AFTER ALL.
BUT NOW I MUST TAKE MY LEAVE.
WHAT GOOD IS RULING A ROCK WHEN YOU HAVE NOBODY TO USE AND ABUSE?
NEXT STOP, MY BELOVED PLANET BLOTOS...
...AND REVENGE...
REVENGE...
REVENGE...
THAT DOESN'T SOUND LIKE CAPTAIN THUDWUD.
PERHAPS AN ESCAPED PRISONER?
...REVENGE...
...REVENGE...
ATTENTION, PRISON TRANSPORTER... I NEED THE PASS CODE IN ORDER FOR YOU TO ENTER OUR ATMOSPHERE...
YOUR MOTHER SUCKS ELEPHANT DICKS.
CLOSE ENOUGH?
17.

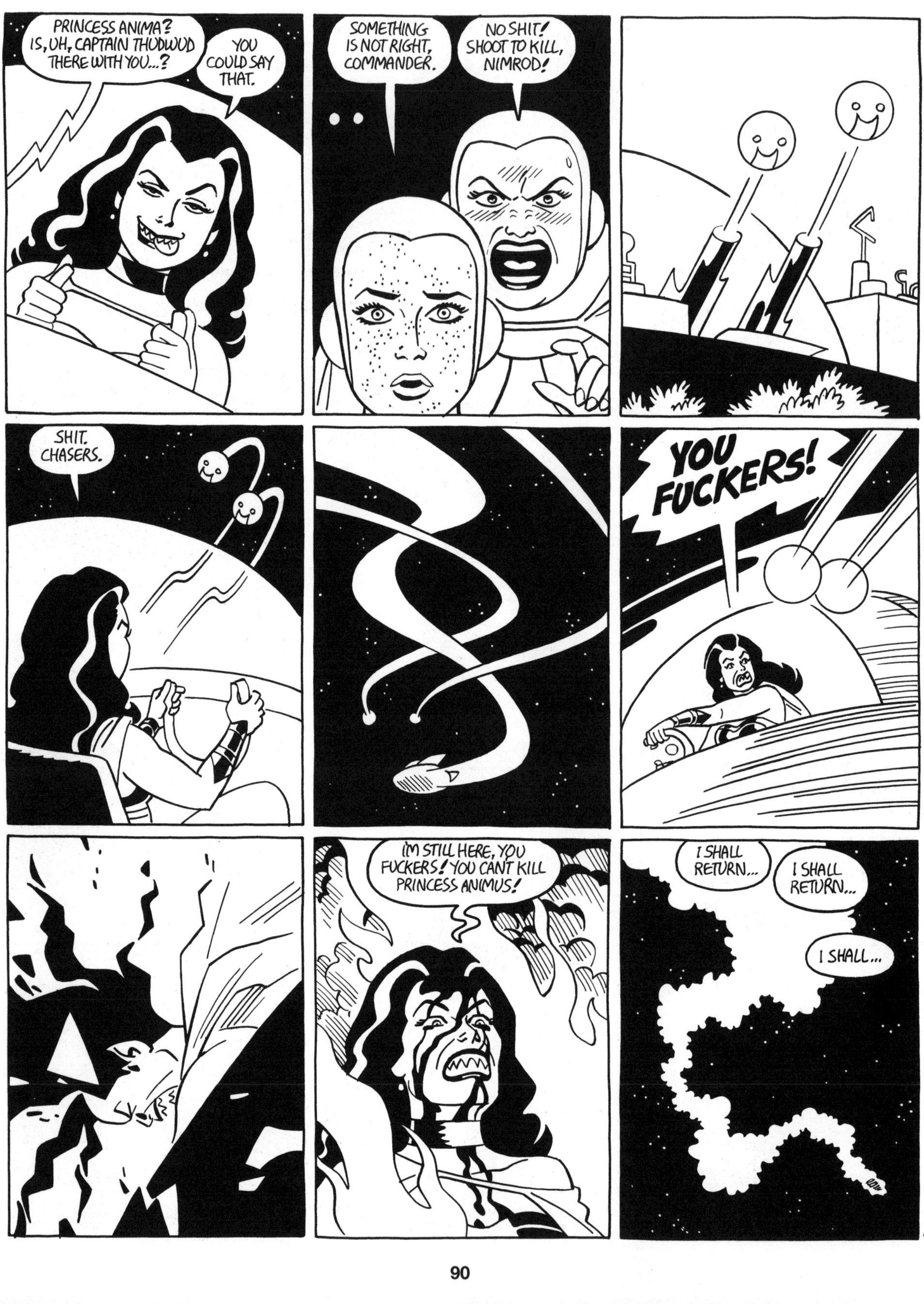
PRINCESS ANIMA? IS, UH, CAPTAIN THUDWUD THERE WITH YOU...?
YOU COULD SAY THAT.
SOMETHING IS NOT RIGHT, COMMANDER.
NO SHIT! SHOOT TO KILL, NIMROD!
SHIT. CHASERS.
YOU FUCKERS!
I'M STILL HERE, YOU FUCKERS! YOU CAN'T KILL PRINCESS ANIMUS!
I SHALL RETURN...
I SHALL RETURN...
I SHALL...

18.

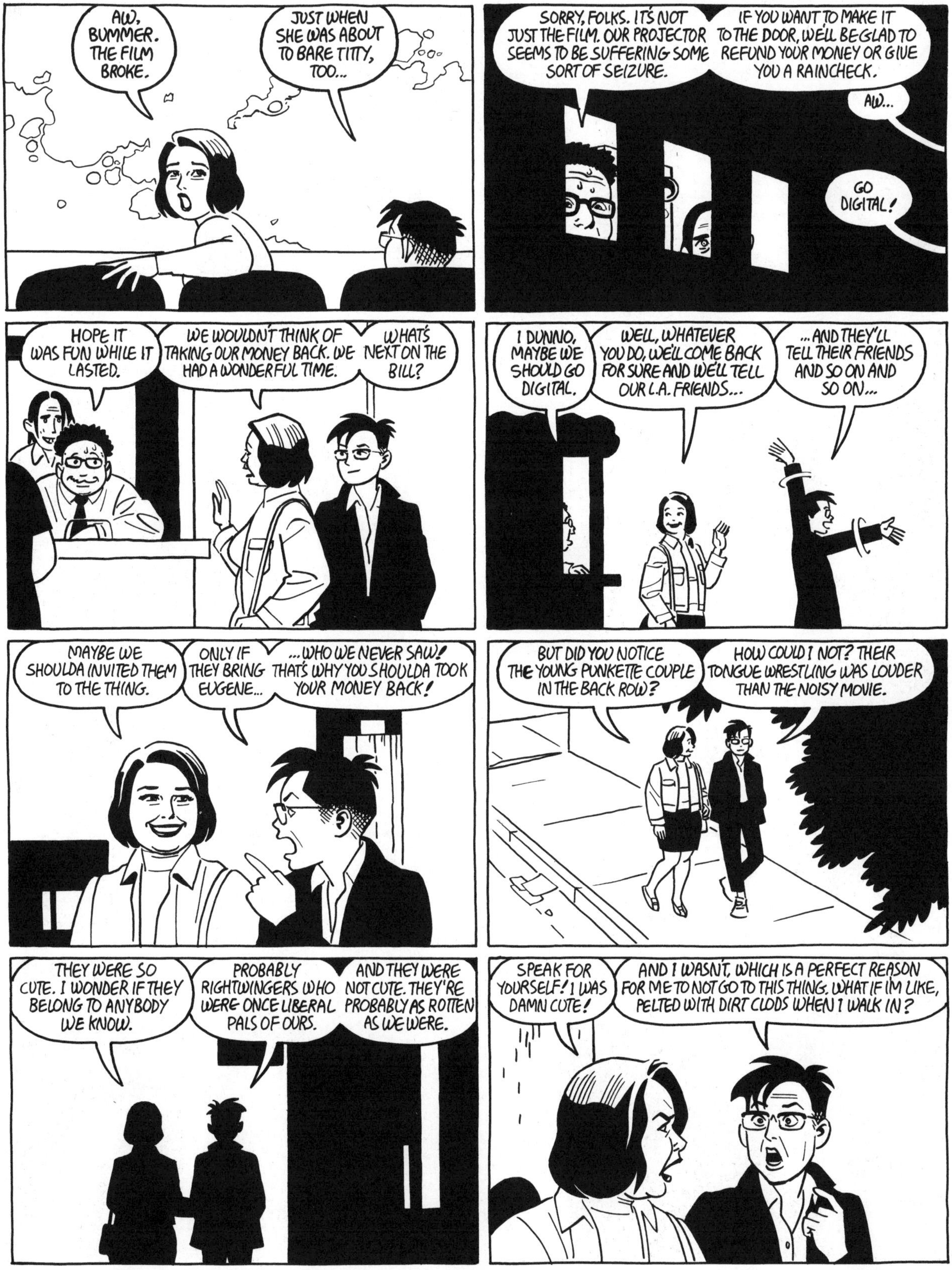
AW, BUMMER. THE FILM BROKE.
JUST WHEN SHE WAS ABOUT TO BARE TITTY, TOO...
SORRY, FOLKS. IT'S NOT JUST THE FILM. OUR PROJECTOR SEEMS TO BE SUFFERING SOME SORT OF SEIZURE.
IF YOU WANT TO MAKE IT TO THE DOOR, WE'LL BE GLAD TO REFUND YOUR MONEY OR GIVE YOU A RAINCHECK.
AW...
GO DIGITAL!
HOPE IT WAS FUN WHILE IT LASTED.
WE WOULDN'T THINK OF TAKING OUR MONEY BACK. WE HAD A WONDERFUL TIME.
WHAT'S NEXT ON THE BILL?
I DUNNO, MAYBE WE SHOULD GO DIGITAL.
WELL, WHATEVER YOU DO, WE'LL COME BACK FOR SURE AND WE'LL TELL OUR L.A. FRIENDS...
...AND THEY'LL TELL THEIR FRIENDS AND SO ON AND SO ON...
MAYBE WE SHOULDA INVITED THEM TO THE THING.
ONLY IF THEY BRING EUGENE...
...WHO WE NEVER SAW! THAT'S WHY YOU SHOULDA TOOK YOUR MONEY BACK!
BUT DID YOU NOTICE THE YOUNG PUNKETTE COUPLE IN THE BACK ROW?
HOW COULD I NOT? THEIR TONGUE WRESTLING WAS LOUDER THAN THE NOISY MOVIE.
THEY WERE SO CUTE. I WONDER IF THEY BELONG TO ANYBODY WE KNOW.
PROBABLY RIGHTWINGERS WHO WERE ONCE LIBERAL PALS OF OURS.
AND THEY WERE NOT CUTE. THEY'RE PROBABLY AS ROTTEN AS WE WERE.
SPEAK FOR YOURSELF! I WAS DAMN CUTE!
AND I WASN'T, WHICH IS A PERFECT REASON FOR ME TO NOT GO TO THIS THING. WHAT IF I'M LIKE, PELTED WITH DIRT CLODS WHEN I WALK IN?

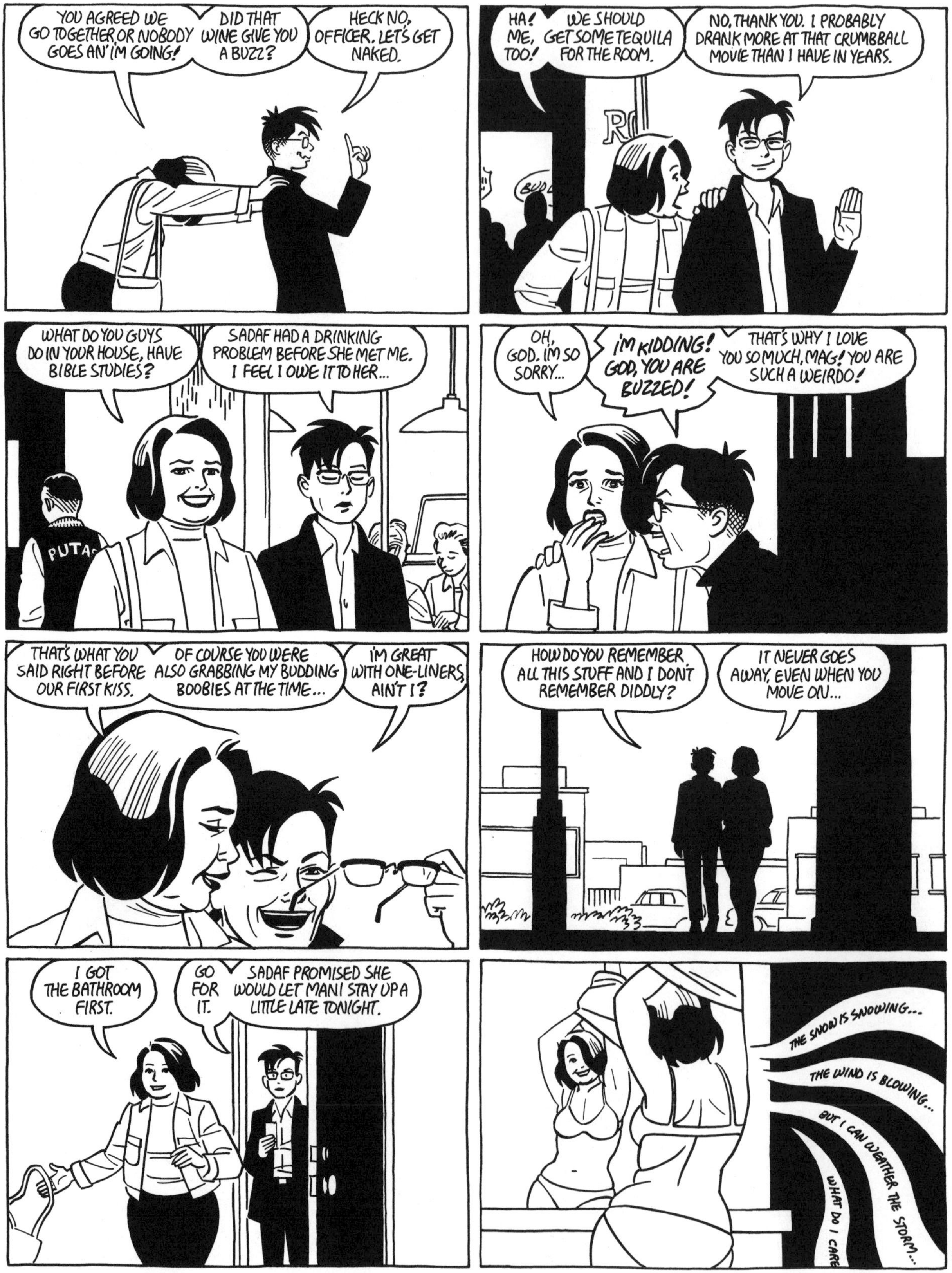

YOU AGREED WE GO TOGETHER, OR NOBODY GOES AN' I'M GOING!
DID THAT WINE GIVE YOU A BUZZ?
HECK NO, OFFICER. LET'S GET NAKED.
HA! ME, TOO!
WE SHOULD GET SOME TEQUILA FOR THE ROOM.
NO, THANK YOU. I PROBABLY DRANK MORE AT THAT CRUMBBALL MOVIE THAN I HAVE IN YEARS.
WHAT DO YOU GUYS DO IN YOUR HOUSE, HAVE BIBLE STUDIES?
SADAF HAD A DRINKING PROBLEM BEFORE SHE MET ME. I FEEL I OWE IT TO HER...
PUTAS
OH, GOD. I'M SO SORRY...
I'M KIDDING! GOD, YOU ARE BUZZED!
THAT'S WHY I LOVE YOU SO MUCH, MAG! YOU ARE SUCH A WEIRDO!
THAT'S WHAT YOU SAID RIGHT BEFORE OUR FIRST KISS.
OF COURSE YOU WERE ALSO GRABBING MY BUDDING BOOBIES AT THE TIME...
I'M GREAT WITH ONE-LINERS, AIN'T I?
HOW DO YOU REMEMBER ALL THIS STUFF AND I DON'T REMEMBER DIDDLY?
IT NEVER GOES AWAY, EVEN WHEN YOU MOVE ON...
I GOT THE BATHROOM FIRST.
GO FOR IT.
SADAF PROMISED SHE WOULD LET MANI STAY UP A LITTLE LATE TONIGHT.
THE SNOW IS SNOWING...
THE WIND IS BLOWING...
BUT I CAN WEATHER THE STORM...
WHAT DO I CARE
2.

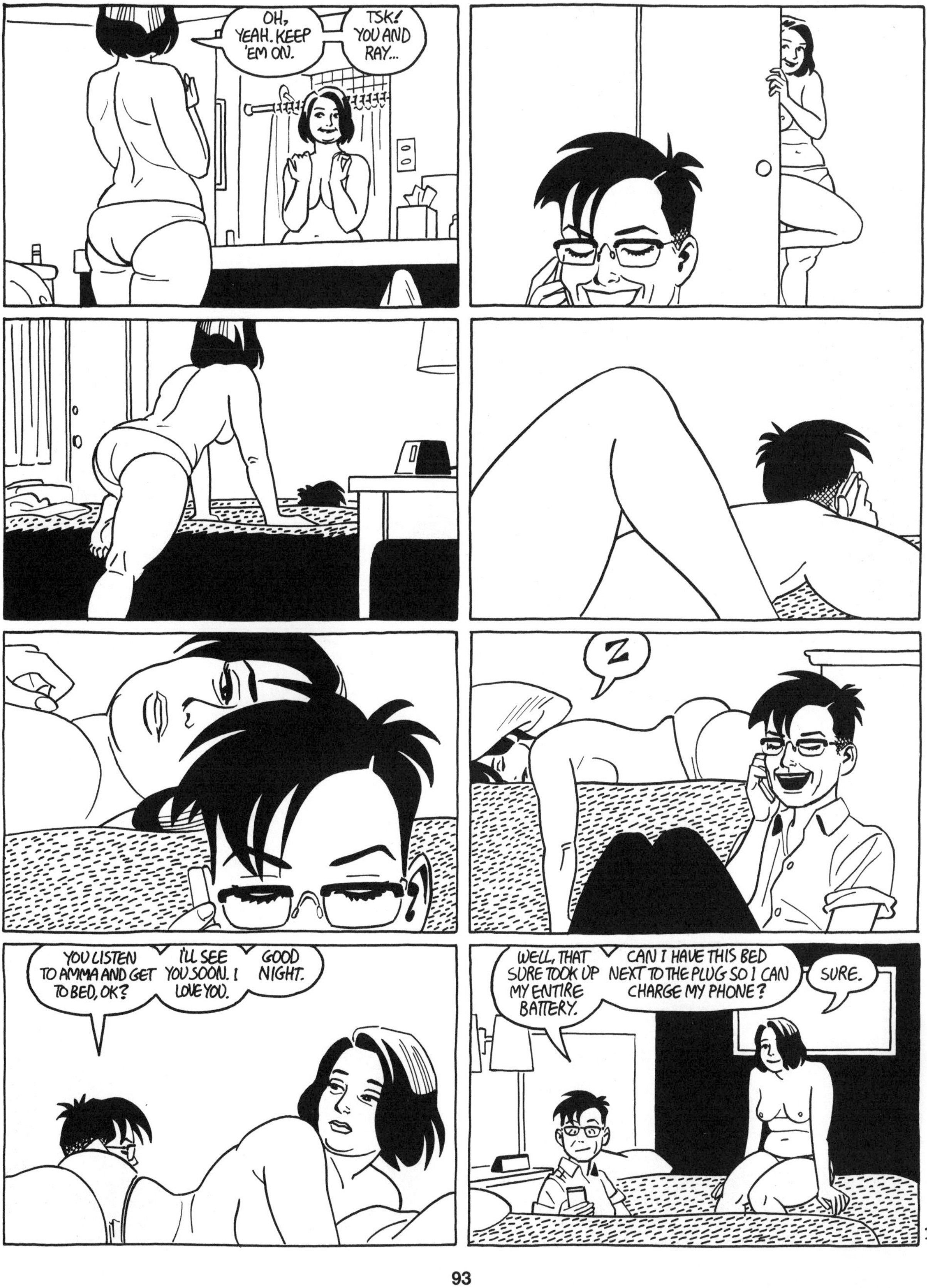
OH, YEAH. KEEP 'EM ON.
TSK! YOU AND RAY...
Z
YOU LISTEN TO AMMA AND GET TO BED, OK?
I'LL SEE YOU SOON. I LOVE YOU.
GOOD NIGHT.
WELL, THAT SURE TOOK UP MY ENTIRE BATTERY.
CAN I HAVE THIS BED NEXT TO THE PLUG SO I CAN CHARGE MY PHONE?
SURE.
3.

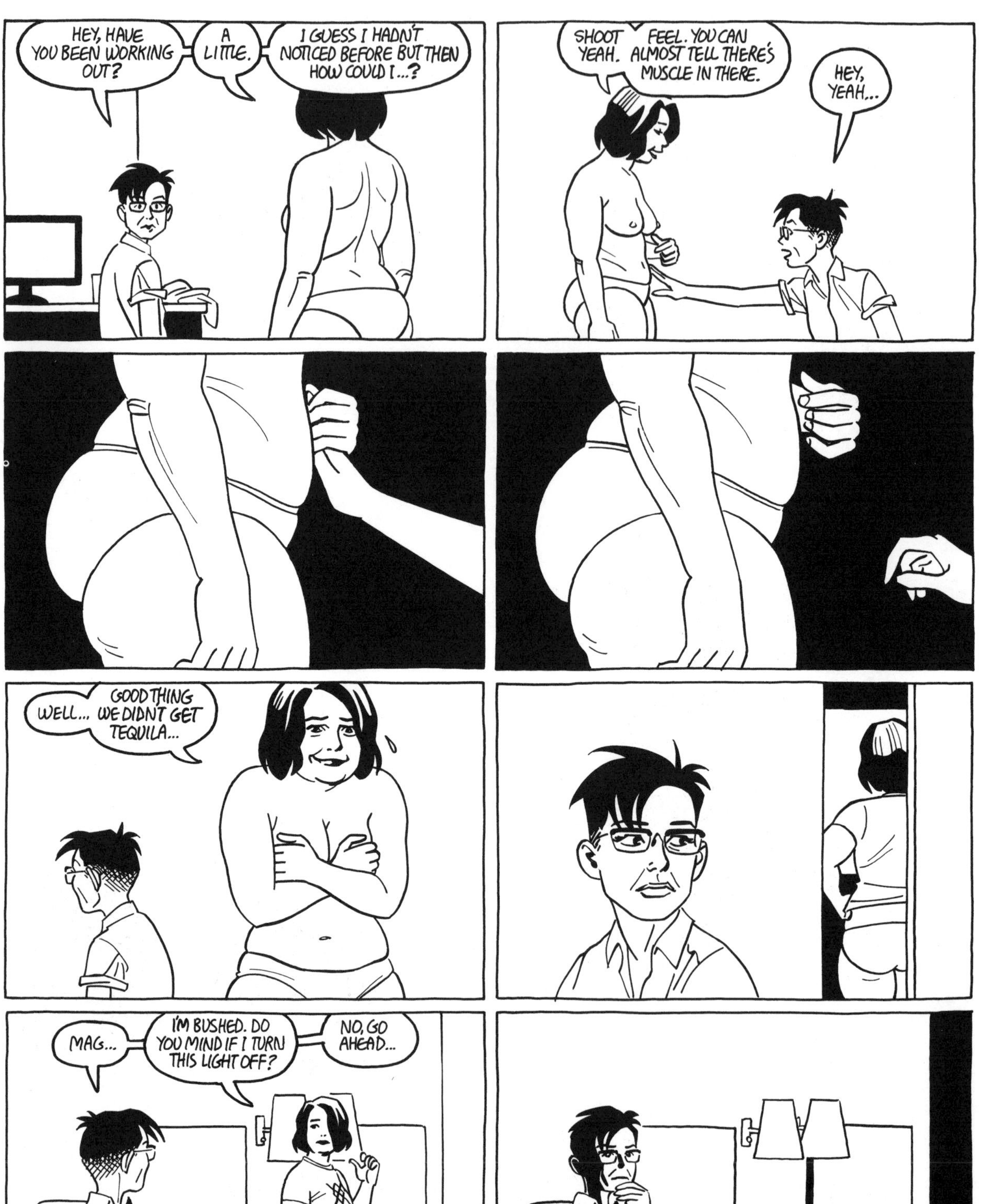

HEY, HAVE YOU BEEN WORKING OUT?
A LITTLE.
I GUESS I HADN'T NOTICED BEFORE BUT THEN HOW COULD I...?
SHOOT YEAH.
FEEL. YOU CAN ALMOST TELL THERE'S MUSCLE IN THERE.
HEY, YEAH...
WELL...
GOOD THING WE DIDNT GET TEQUILA...
MAG...
I'M BUSHED. DO YOU MIND IF I TURN THIS LIGHT OFF?
NO, GO AHEAD...
XAIME 2014
4.

The GOLEM SUIT

starring: *KILLER*

1941

HMM, YOU'RE YOUNGER THAN I EXPECTED. WELL, YOU ARE THE ONLY VOLUNTEER.

LET ME KNOW IF THE TEST SUIT FITS YOU OR NOT. 'S OK.

THINK YOU CAN HANDLE IT? I'LL DO MY BEST, PROFESSOR.

WATCH WHEN I GIVE IT AN ELECTRIC JOLT.

I CALL IT THE *GOLEM SUIT*, GOLEM BEING *HEBREW* FOR MASS OF CLAY.

I BUILT THIS BATTLE ARMOR FOR THE FIGHT AGAINST THE NAZIS.

BUT NO MATTER HOW MUCH POWER I GAVE IT, IT WAS TOO HEAVY TO BE OF ANY USE IN COMBAT.

I WAS READY TO START OVER WHEN THE ANSWER TO MY PROBLEM FELL FROM THE SKY.

THE METEOR SEEMED TO BE MADE OF CLAY, STRANGELY ENOUGH.

JUST THEN, A BOLT OF LIGHTNING CAME DOWN UPON THE CLAY!

ELECTRICITY MADE THE CLAY FLOAT, AND I WAS BACK IN BUSINESS!

I WAS CONVINCED THAT THE CLAY ACTUALLY SEDUCED THE LIGHTNING!

I COVERED THE ENTIRE BATTLE SUIT WITH THE COSMIC CLAY AND THEN RETIRED TO BED DUE TO SLEEP DEPRIVATION.

A PROTECTIVE COAT OF HAIR GREW FROM THE CLAY OVERNIGHT.

I COULDN'T ASK FOR A MORE BEAUTIFUL CLEAR DAY!

I'LL BE MONITORING YOUR EVERY MOVE FROM HERE. OH, BUT I DO ENVY YOU!

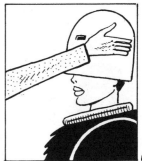

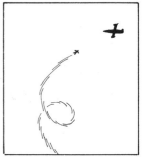

BY THE TIME THE AMERICANS REALIZE THAT HOLLYWOOD WAS DESTROYED BY A SECRET NAZI ATTACK PLANE, IT'LL BE TOO LATE.

DEAR GOD, WHAT HAVE I DONE...

I LOST CONTROL, I-I..

THE IMPORTANT THING IS THAT YOU'RE UNHURT.

I-I DESTROYED THAT AIRPLANE. DIDN'T I...?

I ACCEPT FULL RESPONSIBILITY.

OH, GOD.

THE BATTLE SUIT.

GONE.

I'LL GET DRESSED AND REPORT MYSELF TO THE AUTHORITIES.

WE'LL FIND A WAY TO DEFEAT THE NAZIS.

WE WILL.

MY SECRET NAZI ATTACK PLANE WAS OBLITERATED ABOVE AMERICAN SKIES!

BUT HOW?

HOW?

EWW, DID YOU WATCH IT AGAIN TO BE REMINDED HOW BAD I WAS?

AW, YOU WERE FINE, HONEY. REALLY.

DING DONG!

DOOR!

IT'S AMY!

WE'RE GOING TO THE CONCERT NOW, DAD!

OH MY GOD, AMY, YOU LOOK JUST LIKE PINK!

AND YOU LOOK JUST LIKE KATY PERRY, KILLER!

EEEYAY!!

SLAM!

BTO

BETO 2014

96

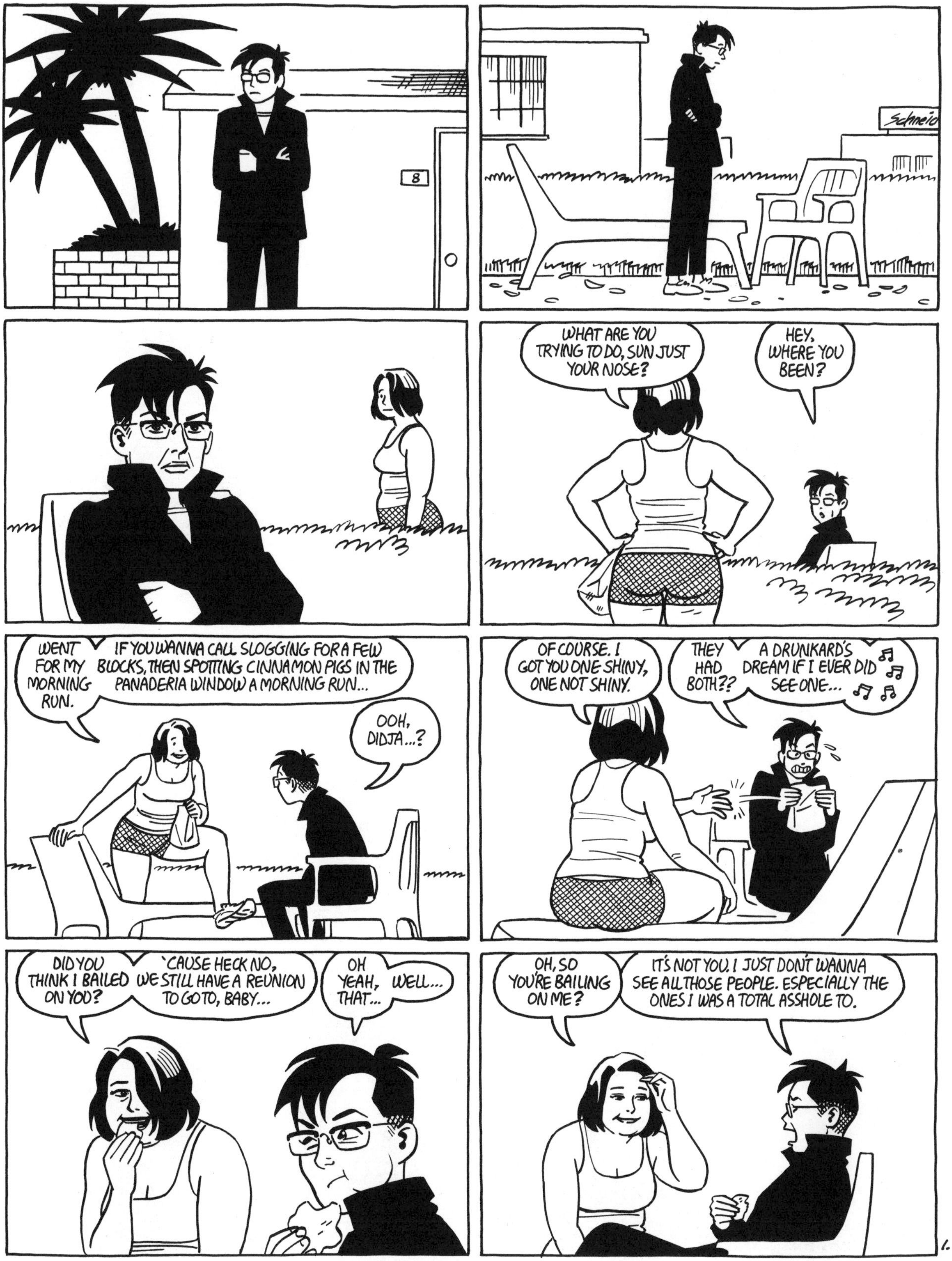
WHAT ARE YOU TRYING TO DO, SUN JUST YOUR NOSE?
HEY, WHERE YOU BEEN?
WENT FOR MY MORNING RUN.
IF YOU WANNA CALL SLOGGING FOR A FEW BLOCKS, THEN SPOTTING CINNAMON PIGS IN THE PANADERIA WINDOW A MORNING RUN...
OOH, DIDJA...?
OF COURSE. I GOT YOU ONE SHINY, ONE NOT SHINY.
THEY HAD BOTH??
A DRUNKARD'S DREAM IF I EVER DID SEE ONE...
DID YOU THINK I BAILED ON YOU?
`CAUSE HECK NO, WE STILL HAVE A REUNION TO GO TO, BABY...
OH YEAH, THAT...
WELL...
OH, SO YOU'RE BAILING ON ME?
IT'S NOT YOU. I JUST DON'T WANNA SEE ALL THOSE PEOPLE. ESPECIALLY THE ONES I WAS A TOTAL ASSHOLE TO.
1.

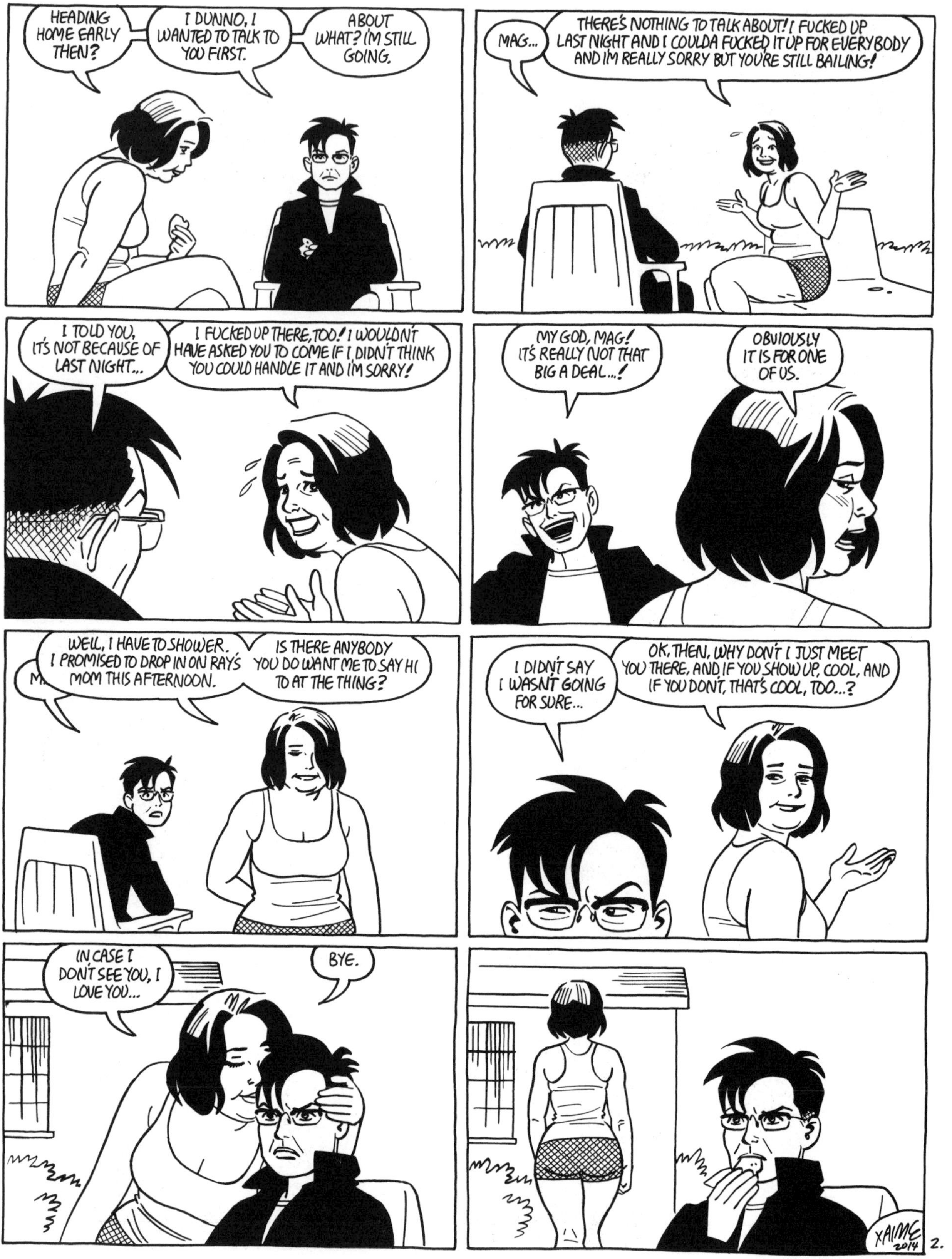
HEADING HOME EARLY THEN?
I DUNNO, I WANTED TO TALK TO YOU FIRST.
ABOUT WHAT? I'M STILL GOING.
MAG...
THERE'S NOTHING TO TALK ABOUT! I FUCKED UP LAST NIGHT AND I COULDA FUCKED IT UP FOR EVERYBODY AND I'M REALLY SORRY BUT YOU'RE STILL BAILING!
I TOLD YOU, IT'S NOT BECAUSE OF LAST NIGHT...
I FUCKED UP THERE, TOO! I WOULDN'T HAVE ASKED YOU TO COME IF I DIDN'T THINK YOU COULD HANDLE IT AND I'M SORRY!
MY GOD, MAG! IT'S REALLY NOT THAT BIG A DEAL...!
OBVIOUSLY IT IS FOR ONE OF US.
WELL, I HAVE TO SHOWER. I PROMISED TO DROP IN ON RAY'S MOM THIS AFTERNOON.
IS THERE ANYBODY YOU DO WANT ME TO SAY HI TO AT THE THING?
I DIDN'T SAY I WASN'T GOING FOR SURE...
OK, THEN, WHY DON'T I JUST MEET YOU THERE, AND IF YOU SHOW UP, COOL, AND IF YOU DON'T, THAT'S COOL, TOO...?
IN CASE I DON'T SEE YOU, I LOVE YOU...
BYE.
XAIME 2014
2.

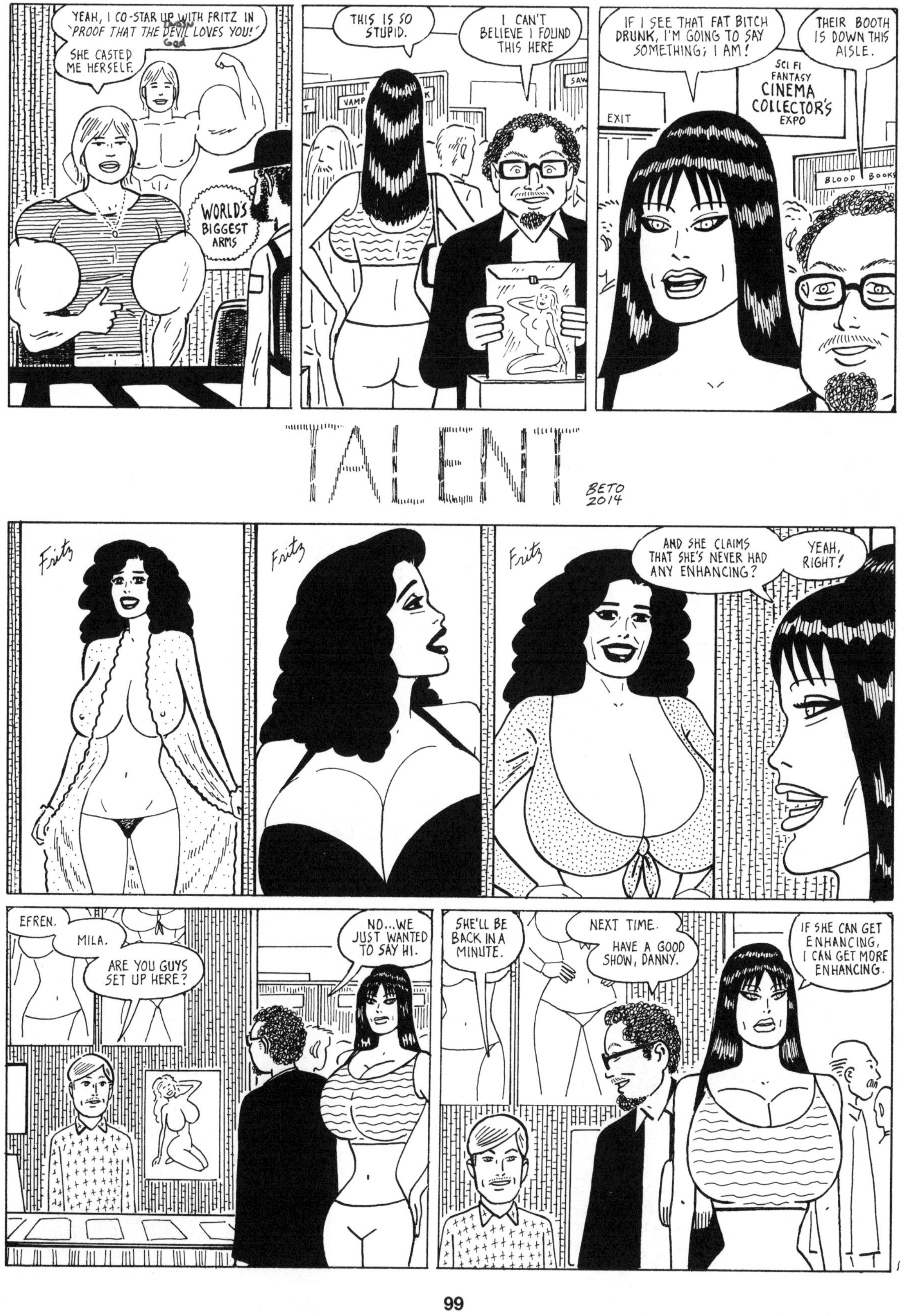
YEAH, I CO-STAR UP WITH FRITZ IN 'PROOF THAT THE DEVIL LOVES YOU!'
SHE CASTED ME HERSELF.
WORLD'S BIGGEST ARMS
THIS IS SO STUPID.
I CAN'T BELIEVE I FOUND THIS HERE
VAMP
SAW
IF I SEE THAT FAT BITCH DRUNK, I'M GOING TO SAY SOMETHING; I AM!
THEIR BOOTH IS DOWN THIS AISLE.
SCI FI FANTASY CINEMA COLLECTOR'S EXPO
EXIT
BLOOD BOOKS
TALENT
BETO 2014
Fritz
Fritz
Fritz
AND SHE CLAIMS THAT SHE'S NEVER HAD ANY ENHANCING?
YEAH, RIGHT!
EFREN.
MILA.
ARE YOU GUYS SET UP HERE?
NO...WE JUST WANTED TO SAY HI.
SHE'LL BE BACK IN A MINUTE.
NEXT TIME.
HAVE A GOOD SHOW, DANNY.
IF SHE CAN GET ENHANCING, I CAN GET MORE ENHANCING.

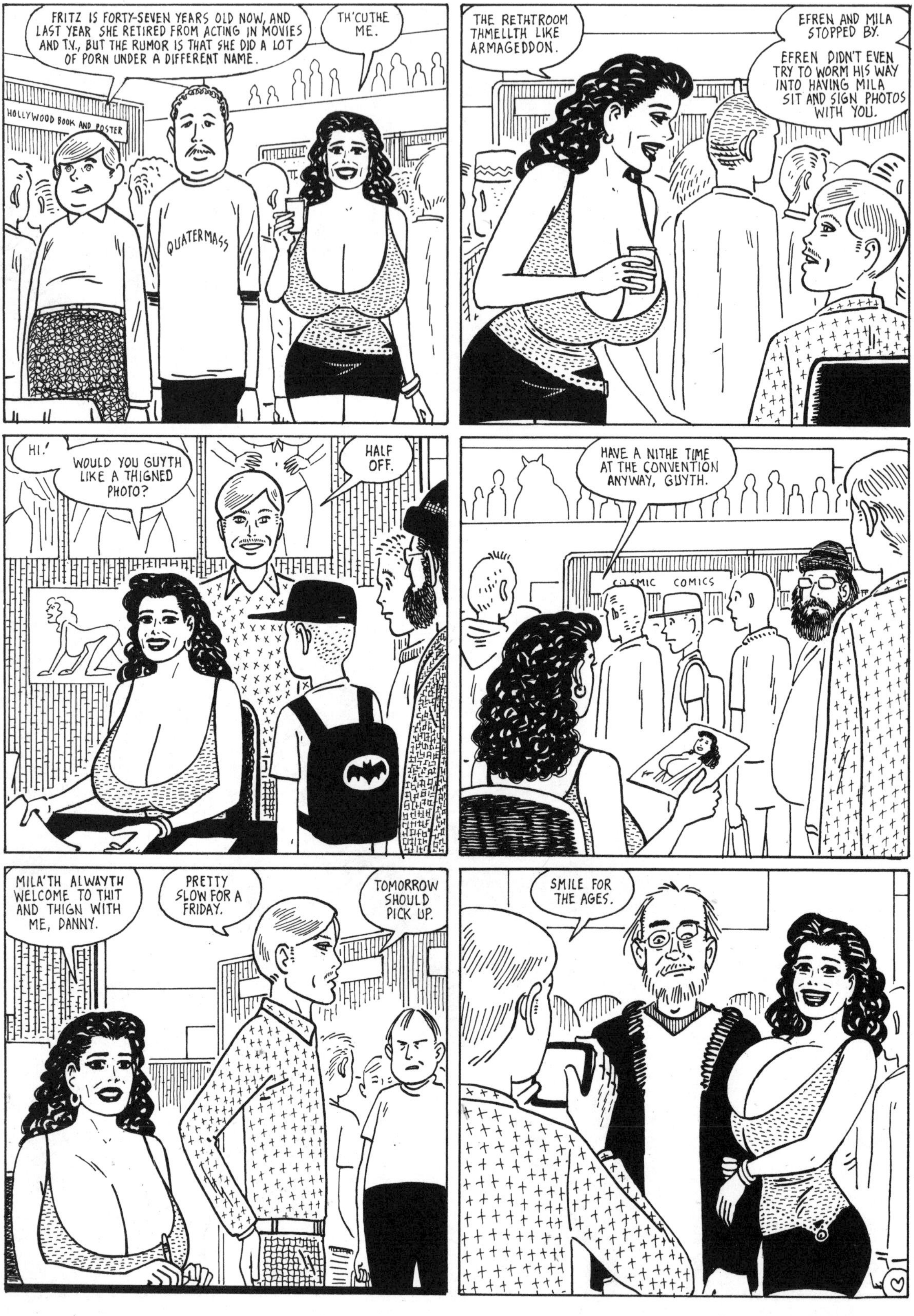
FRITZ IS FORTY-SEVEN YEARS OLD NOW, AND LAST YEAR SHE RETIRED FROM ACTING IN MOVIES AND T.V., BUT THE RUMOR IS THAT SHE DID A LOT OF PORN UNDER A DIFFERENT NAME.
TH'CUTHE ME.
HOLLYWOOD BOOK AND POSTER
QUATERMASS
THE RETHTROOM THMELLTH LIKE ARMAGEDDON.
EFREN AND MILA STOPPED BY.
EFREN DIDN'T EVEN TRY TO WORM HIS WAY INTO HAVING MILA SIT AND SIGN PHOTOS WITH YOU.
HI.'
WOULD YOU GUYTH LIKE A THIGNED PHOTO?
HALF OFF.
HAVE A NITHE TIME AT THE CONVENTION ANYWAY, GUYTH.
COSMIC COMICS
MILA'TH ALWAYTH WELCOME TO THIT AND THIGN WITH ME, DANNY.
PRETTY SLOW FOR A FRIDAY.
TOMORROW SHOULD PICK UP.
SMILE FOR THE AGES.